You're gonna miss me someday

You're gonna miss me someday

a memoir

KEN GAGNE

This memoir is a work of creative nonfiction comprising stories inspired by true events. Some names and locations have been changed.

*To families whose stories are hidden or lost,
to Caleb and Lucy whose story starts here,
but mostly, and always, to Jackie*

"The greatest way to live with honor in this world is to be what we pretend to be."

—Socrates

"All lives, once lived, are fiction."

—Anonymous

CONTENTS

PROLOGUE

IMAGINE MY MOTHER and father are still alive. Her cancer and his failed liver remain villains lurking somewhere in the future. We have many more years left together.

We sit in my boyhood church. I'd said goodbye to them here at their funerals, but in my mind, they're with me again. The pews are empty, just us and the hymnals. My parents look like they always do when I remember them: Dad's not yet bald, not yet gray, but concedes to a middle-age paunch. His wide smile introduces yellowing teeth that never met a dentist. A mischievous glint behind a wire-framed tint suggests he has something else to say. Mom's short brown hair blurs the line between classic and trendy. Her delicate facial features fight back the wrinkles of time. Her quiet manner boasts an attitude all its own.

The sanctuary smells like redemption and furniture polish. Thin rays of light strain through a stained-glass window, warming the back of my neck. A stillness invites me to open up to my folks. I tell them they're the backbone of my life, say that without them it'd be hard for me to stand up straight. I thank them for being my foundation, for loving me and letting me dream, for sacrificing and staying strong for me and my sisters. I tell them how grateful we are as their children; how lucky we are to still have them. *I love you both so much*, I say. The words sound natural and routine, as if I've said them often, or ever before.

The scene changes, and we're relaxing by the ocean, on the New England coast. Once, when I was a child, I'd lost my parents here, but now they've found me again. The beach is empty, just us and the gulls. The summer sun hangs high above the horizon, and we're surrounded by time. The air's full of salt, wistfulness, and the rumble of waves. I take the opportunity to ask Mom and Dad about the past. There's so much I want to know; it's strange I never asked. *Why did your grandparents immigrate to this country? What were your childhoods like? How about first loves? Where did you two meet?*

My mother and father answer every question, talk openly, like they never could, and I finally understand them. I know who they are, who they were, who they wanted to be. I know the truth—even if none of it's real. Then the beach, and the truth, disappear.

I imagine the three of us standing by a grave in the back corner of a cemetery, where my older twin brothers are buried. I'd put Mom and Dad in the ground here too, but now we're together again. The place is empty, just us and the ghosts. Next to a headstone, my mother lays flowers, lilies perhaps. My father bows his head. Elms loom, their tired branches casting off unwanted leaves. Muddy clouds thicken as dusk covers us in shadows. The air grows cold. Darkness is on its way; time is running out. I seize the chance to ask my parents the one question I never could: *What really happened with Robert and David?*

They shoot looks at each other, stammer and stall and scuff the grass until Mom gives in. *It's difficult to talk about*, she says, *but it's something you should know.* She returns to that horrific day in September of '63, conveys the sadness and pain of sending their sixteen-month-old sons to live in a state-run institution. She puts a hand to her mouth. Dad steps in and acknowledges the agony and confusion of the previous year, confesses his faults, regrets not providing more emotional support for his wife. They stand there, listening to each other, allowing space for reflection, recalling an experience they've spent years trying to forget.

She describes how she cared for the twins at home that final morning, how she dressed them and fed them, these boys she was put on Earth to mother. She details how she pressed her warm skin against theirs and tried to hold herself together. She talks of paying extra-close attention to their faces, imprinting them on her memory, knowing her boys would never again be with her in that house. My father clears his throat and speaks of how conflicted he was about the decision, how it all felt so surreal. My mother says she feared it'd tear their marriage apart but knew that regardless of the choice they made, it'd take a brutal toll. More than ever before, I sympathize with both of them and tell them I understand. *I'm so sorry*, I say. It's something I can only dream of saying.

I imagine the cemetery grows colder and darker. Dad puts his jacket around Mom's shoulders and tells me that committing Robert and David to Monson Developmental Center was not the only option, but it made the most sense. *Everyone thought keeping two disabled children at home would be too much for us to handle*, he says. *Their needs were too great, and we wanted more kids.*

Mom nods in agreement. *The doctors sat us down and told us the twins would never be normal*, she says, *predicted they'd die young.*

When I heard that, my father adds, *I lived every day waiting for the end.* Dad tells me he's convinced giving the boys up was the right thing to do, says he backed my mother's feelings, wishes he could've shared his, still hasn't forgiven himself for not being more sensitive to her needs, more evolved. *It just wasn't something I could do*, he explains. *To my generation, talking about feelings is a sign of weakness.*

My mother laments how her husband retreated into himself,

how he found closer companionship with a bottle than with his own wife. My father says he tried to recover the bond he and Mom once shared, but there was always something pulling him away from her.

He describes driving his wife and sons to the institution that dreadful day, recollects the crisp afternoon, the twisting roads, the silent boys, the radio playing softly.

I sat between your brothers in the back seat, my mother says, *held their tiny hands the whole way*. She stares at the clouds watching over us in the graveyard. Dad puts his arm around her. He doesn't say a word, doesn't have to. He's there, and that's all she needs. All she ever needed. She rests her head on his shoulder. She's tired, still torn deep down, still in search of peace. Her eyes say so.

I ask about Robert and David's condition, curious to know what erased their futures. My father says that maybe the twins had Tay-Sachs disease, maybe not. Maybe he passed down the gene, maybe he didn't. Mom adds that the doctors never gave them a definite answer.

How did you feel when you left the developmental center that day? I ask.

I had to talk myself into staying strong, my mother says. Then she tries to explain how it feels to lose part of yourself, to know it's there somewhere but to have no way to get it back. She reminds me that she was two months pregnant with her third child at the time, my older sister Cheryl. She says the thought of bringing another baby into the world after giving two away ripped at her soul, says she tried to hold on to hope, but the feelings of inadequacy and resentment and failure formed a darkness, a heaviness she couldn't get out from under. *I knew there was a light somewhere*, she tells me. *There was hope, but finding it seemed impossible*.

My father says he tried to capture that light for her by focusing only on the positive, the future, the children yet to come. He realizes now this approach made it seem like he didn't care about the twins. He asks my mother to accept his apology, tells her he always cared but thought forgetting the past was the right thing to do, the only way to move on. *Most of the time*, he says, *I was able to forget, but there were days I felt dead inside.*

It must've been strange at home without Robert and David, I say.

Setting his eyes on the lilies, my dad describes the empty house, the awkwardness, the nursery they kept for the new baby; a fresh coat of pink on the walls could cover up the blue but couldn't erase the memory of it. It's at this moment when my mother begins to cry. It's the emptiness that still wets her eyes, the six months of nothingness between her sons leaving and her first daughter arriving.

That was the hardest part, Mom says. *It was the in-between that hurt the most. The guilt of starting a new family without my sons. And the frustration of so many people not understanding our decision or what we were going through.* My father takes her hand and gives it a squeeze. It's dark now, time to go. We turn from the grave and walk away.

I imagine all of this so I might understand some of it. In real life, my parents didn't share their feelings or stories with me, and I didn't share mine with them. And the longer we held it all inside, the harder it was for any of us to ask. I knew precious little of their ancestors, or their childhoods, or how they got together, to say nothing of what lay in their hearts or how they navigated the pain of giving up my older brothers.

I know one thing: I'm here now because Robert and David aren't. And I admit, I'm glad Mom and Dad sent my brothers away. Because they did, I got to live. But with that gift came an implicit responsibility to be worthy of the sacrifice my parents made, to never disappoint. I needed to be a good son, even if it meant pretending to be someone else, even if it meant losing myself.

INTRODUCTION

Summer, 2015

*W*ELL, *I* PERSONALLY *think there was some darkness in their childhood.*

The Facebook message from my cousin Karen piqued my curiosity. She was talking about my dad and his siblings.

I'd reached out to my cousin, whom I hadn't spoken to in twenty years, to get in touch with her mother, whom I hadn't spoken to in thirty years. Strike that—I did chat with Auntie Connie for five minutes at Dad's wake back in 2007, and for another five at Memere's a few years before that, but we didn't do a whole lot of catching up in those collective six hundred seconds. Now that I was investigating my family's past, I subpoenaed Connie Fleury, my father's last living sibling, to serve as an expert witness. She'd give up the goods, I thought, and tell me all about growing up with my dad, her little brother.

Every day since Mom died in 2005, I considered writing a book about my parents, and I appreciated the opportunity to finally put pen to paper. My job as a TV producer for the National Basketball Association, an occupational fantasy, allowed me the time I needed when the league instituted an eight-week sabbatical program for anyone with more than twenty years of service.

As soon as the program was announced, I pounced, filling out the paperwork requesting July and August off and punching my ticket for a literary trip down memory lane. My wife, Jackie, and teenaged kids, Caleb and Lucy, looked forward to having me around the house for the summer. In so many ways, a homecoming awaited us all.

As part of my research, I'd arranged to spend a couple of days in Western Massachusetts to meet with Connie and her husband, my Uncle Ronnie. Then I'd visit with my mother's sister, my Auntie Elaine. And lastly, with family friends Susan and Jimmy Cassidy. After my interrogations, I'd surely find out where all the bodies were buried. (Not literally, I hoped.) I called them all, briefly explained my intentions, and made plans to travel north from New Jersey the following week. *Tick-tock* said the clock.

At forty-eight, my life had been split down the middle; twenty-four years growing up in Massachusetts; twenty-four on my own in New Jersey. Suffering from a literal mid-life crisis, I grieved over my soon-to-be outnumbered boyhood days and, with every passing moment, sensed the scales of my life tipping toward manhood. I swayed in that reality, unprepared to deal with the imbalance.

My Volkswagen Jetta transformed into a time machine during the 175-mile trip from Maplewood, New Jersey, to Chicopee, Massachusetts, east of the Berkshires, ninety miles west of Boston. In those three hours, waves of childhood memories flooded the meshwork of my mind. I flashed back to lunch boxes, skinned knees, kickball, puppy love, cold feet, roller-skating, Nerf hoops, and dungarees. My head somewhere in 1982, I cruised alongside the smug waters of the Connecticut River. On the surface, the sun's reflection shimmered like opportunity, pulsing through the tree line, persuading me into believing I was fifteen again. In the corner of my eye, a fleeting glimpse of the

Grattan Street exit sign snapped me back to the present. I yanked on the steering wheel, swerved across two lanes, and veered off the highway, tires squealing. Coming home to Chicopee always took the edge off.

Before heading to Auntie Connie's, I got reacquainted with the section of my hometown called Willimansett, where my father grew up. Teenage glory days flickered in my memory as I passed Rivers Park, home field for my high school baseball and soccer games. I pictured my father there, on a spring morning long ago, standing where he always stood—separate from the other parents, hands in pockets, peacock proud—watching me field a nasty grounder at short. On a faraway fall afternoon, I saw Yvette Beaulieu, dark eyes in a blue-and-gold cheerleader's sweater, waiting for me after a soccer game, asking if I'd save her a dance at the school gym later that night. (Of course I would.) I felt a familiar fever in my cheeks, blushed more from a girl's interest than the exhaustion of heated competition.

Beeeeeeeeeep!

The impatient occupant of a tailgating Toyota leaned on his horn, and a dull brick block of buildings wiped away my nostalgia, their boarded-up storefronts, bandages on an injured local economy. My head on a swivel, I rolled along in my car, squinting to determine the name of an unfamiliar bodega. I slalomed around a pack of potholes, hungry for rubber, and lost sight of a never-before-seen Dollar Store. Five minutes into my visit, I recognized only one thing about this place: I didn't know it anymore.

I coasted past "The Y," a skinny plot of real estate at the split of Chicopee Street and Meadow, the condensed location of Dad's childhood home and his elementary school and his used car lot/service station (formerly Gagne & Sons, now renamed Chicopee Tire & Auto Repair). From what little I knew of my father's lonely boyhood, his slacking academics, and his unlucky business career, these three structures within a hundred feet of each other formed his very own Bermuda Triangle.

I slowed in front of The Y Café, which my Pepe Rheo Gagne established eighty years earlier. Above the entrance, a faded metal sign featuring a frothy beer stein announced, *You Are a Stranger Here but Once!* On the sidewalk, a twenty-something Hispanic girl propped an infant on her hip and threw a glare my way, her nameless face confirming that I was, indeed, for once, a "stranger here."

I pulled a uey at the Nativity of the Blessed Virgin Mary, my dad's one and only childhood sanctuary. Sails set for my aunt's house on Empire Street, I passed historic French-Canadian landmarks: Brunelle's Funeral Home, Perrault's Market, Aubuchon Paint, and Lacroix's Luncheonette. Along with Gagne & Sons, these iconic businesses once thrived here in Willimansett, known a century before as "Little Quebec." In those days, the Gagne family (pronounced GONE-*yay* then, GAG-*nee* now) filled an entire chapter of this city's colorful history. But somewhere in the night, during the narcissism of my youth, my father gagged our origin stories, and when I awoke, they were gone.

I parked in front of the Fleury residence unnoticed. Hunched with his back to me, Uncle Ronnie weeded the flower bed along the walkway. I took a sharp look at the house and the flowers and the weeds, flipping through a million mental pictures vaulted away for too long. The wood shingles on the mid-century ranch, still the color of burnt toast; the craggy hedges below the bay window, still a wiry green matrix of mini lightning bolts. My uncle wiped his forehead with a gardening glove, ambled out of the flowers and into the lawn. I saw myself there, on that same grass forty summers ago, tossing a water-logged softball with that man's youngest daughter, Rhonda, while our parents "shot the breeze" in the kitchen.

I grinned and turned to the other side of the street where

a cluster of tumbledown, low-income duplexes pleaded with me to call a maintenance man. The U.S. government built the development, called Chicomansett Village, as military housing during World War II, when my grandfather served as director of Chicopee's Housing Authority. The irony of a ramshackle seventy-five-year-old housing project residing on Empire Street struck me as funny. The Romans would *not* have approved.

I got out of the car and closed the door. At the sound, my uncle wheeled around. "Holy shit! Kenny?"

We shook hands and walked into the house, demystifying what it felt like to warp into another dimension. I sat at the kitchen table with my aunt and broke the ice. "Should we make some coffee?"

"I don't settle on coffee," cackled Connie, offended by the notion. "I'm a Gagne."

In addition to rhyming first names, Connie and Ronnie had matching personalities: loud, brash, and brutally honest. She was eighty-five, he was eighty-seven, but both looked ten years younger. Was the secret to anti-aging in their French-Canadian blood? Were those bottles in their liquor cabinet refilled at the fountain of youth?

Uncle Ronnie resembled Johnny Cash on two hours sleep. Auntie Connie always reminded me of Bea Arthur with a mean streak, tough and gruff and able to hold a grudge tighter than G.I. Joe with Kung Fu Grip. I knew how to handle characters like them because my dad was cut from the same cloth. I measured the vibe in the room, tailored my body language to fit theirs, and blended in with the curtains, hemming an air of suspicion with a spool of jokes.

"Jesus Christ! You are just like your father," Ronnie blurted, admiring a fridge bursting with beer. "Prolly gonna be a pain in the ass like him too. Wanna drink? I'd give you the hard stuff, but you couldn't handle it."

He was right, at eleven in the morning, I probably couldn't handle it. But I reminded him I was a Gagne too, and we agreed on a couple of Yuengling lagers while Connie poured herself the first of three voluminous tumblers of Southern Comfort, neat.

"Cheers!" I said. "It's really good to see you guys. You both look great."

"It's the booze," squawked Connie, and we raised our drinks high.

Ronnie guzzled half his beer and shook his head. "God, you are just like your old man," he repeated. "I don't believe it. Whataya doing here anyway?"

After getting past the fear I wanted to talk them into joining a religious cult, Connie and Ronnie shared enlightening tales about my parents, grandparents, and great-grandparents. Over the ensuing three hours—and two more lagers—we caught up on each other's lives while I mined cavernous shafts of Gagne family history.

Whenever a sensitive subject arose, the "darkness" my cousin had forewarned poked out its head, but Connie and Ronnie watered down each toxic topic like cheapskate bartenders. Talk of my grandfather's alcohol abuse, and consequent death from cirrhosis of the liver at fifty-three, had Ronnie recalling how his father-in-law "could really hold his liquor" and asking, "How do ya tell a guy to stop having fun?" Later, allusions to my grandmother's iron-fisted maternal instincts and cold-heartedness blended with Connie's remarking how her mother was "a two-face who didn't like anyone" and that the family labeled Annette Gagne "The Admiral."

And that was that. Until—

"It was a shame what happened to your brothers, those beautiful babies."

Connie's comment came from nowhere and rattled me. I clammed up and waited for her to continue. What else might she say? If she were like my father, this discussion would be brief and uncomfortable, true feelings ignored like debutantes in a monastery. My dad didn't just guard his emotions, he had them under twenty-four-hour surveillance. And in the compassion department, Bob Gagne displayed the empathetic depth of a bird bath. Of course, I didn't know Auntie Connie on the same level but assumed she was similar. Eyes on me, she took a never-ending sip of SoCo. I swallowed hard and followed up. "How tough of a time was that for my father?"

"All I know is it was a goddamn shame. How old are your kids now, Kenny? They must be gettin' big. Jesus, I don't even know if I'd recognize them."

I slouched in my chair, a fool. I'd braced for shocking, tragic family secrets, for an army of jangly skeletons to ramble out of a closet, but I wasn't even thrown a bone. And as we carried on, I was the naïve boy my aunt and uncle used to know, their innocent nephew, "Little Kenny Gagne," wandering down forbidden pathways, needing protection from the dangerous truth.

They were hiding something, but I wasn't one to pry and didn't press, forgave their reticence. Did I expect them to be *totally* honest and rake long-gone family members over the embers, drag them through the metaphorical mud? Should they divulge their innermost psychological traumas and real-life nightmares to an estranged relative who'd teleported onto their doorstep from someplace called Maplewood? No, their darkness wasn't mine to illuminate.

The sliver of light Connie did shine on my father's life only mucked up the conundrum she still called "Bobby," who morphed from the easygoing child, friendly with everyone, to the smart-aleck student, kicked out of two high schools, to the soldier in France, honorably discharged with a bad back, to the functioning alcoholic, in love with an angel, to the poor soul who went through hell and back with his family and his business.

Over-seasoned by the whiskey and the past, my aunt leaned back and set a wary gaze on the outdated pewter chandelier hanging above her head like a guillotine. "I loved your father," she sighed with a dash of melodrama. "He never got mad or argued with anyone. He was just like my father. And you? You are the exact same." Then she paused for effect before peppering in one final sigh, and I took her compliment with a grain of salt.

Connie and Ronnie escorted me to the door. I thanked them both and said goodbye with a promise to come back soon. Next time I'd bring the whole family, I assured them. We exchanged drawn-out hugs on the front steps and, as I turned away, I doubted I'd ever see them again.

∽

Sharp-minded with a girlish laugh—and much too spunky to reside in an assisted-living complex—Elaine Rideout had difficulty admitting that, like the elderly surrounding her in this unadorned compound of weathered brick and splintered wood, she needed help these days. After several surgeries in the past fifteen years, my mom's sister had slowed a bit and downsized to a one-bedroom efficiency in South Hadley, just over the bridge from her childhood home in Holyoke.

To me, the neighboring towns of Holyoke, South Hadley, and Chicopee were like siblings. Nestled near a nourishing river, in the shadow of a distant mountain, they were loving rivals, earnest and flawed, with distinct, endearing qualities. Holyoke, the eldest and most independent child—stubborn yet reliable—supported the river and stood up to the intimidating mountain. South Hadley, the predictable middle child—peaceful and unassuming—mimicked the river's beauty and forgave the mountain's detachment. Lastly, Chicopee, the scrappy and outgoing youngster—fighting for attention and respect—appreciated both the river and the mountain, the nourishment and the shadows.

Of my mother's eight siblings, I was closest with Auntie Elaine, probably because she and my mom had been so close themselves. Growing up in the middle of a bountiful brood, Cynthia and Elaine Colthart shared bedrooms, sisterly secrets, and the task of tending to the munchkins in the family. Together, they celebrated and commiserated the ups and downs of adulthood, and their bond strengthened. As a kid, when my parents hit the town, I'd sleep at Elaine's house, where my teen cousin Alison drew lipstick hearts on my cheeks as I snoozed; then at daybreak, her older brother Ethan walked me to a nearby creek, overgrown with brush, to fish for trout.

Three years younger than Cindy, Elaine wore her seventy-six years like a favorite sweater. Sitting close to me in her cluttered, comfortable living room, she spoke with an easy manner, belying how hard life had been on her recently. "I miss your mother every day," she admitted. "Sometimes I feel like I can give her a buzz just because, but then I catch myself. You know?" (Oh, I knew. Just a few words from Cindy and the world seemed to soften.)

Six years after Mom passed, the torture of losing someone and the difficulty of letting go reintroduced themselves to Elaine when Ethan died of cancer at forty-nine. "For the longest time, I went to his grave every day. I just wanted to talk to him." As she spoke, her eyes drifted further away, searching somewhere for her son. "I finally had to ask my doctor if there was something wrong with me. I only visit a couple times a week now." She forced a smile and shuddered. A chill swept through the room, and we sat quiet for a moment.

Back in 2007, with both parents gone, our house in Chicopee sat empty, somber as a shipwreck. My sisters and I welcomed Ethan and his family to stay there when he was too sick for steady work and payments on their own home became unaffordable. Resuscitating a heartbeat within those walls, while aiding

Ethan and his loving wife, Teresa, held at bay the day we'd have to sell.

They spruced up the place, gave it new life, while their children found stability through their high school days. Those were good days, some of the best days. But four breathless winters after they moved in, Ethan's health faded until one evening—in the same tiny bedroom where I dreamed ten thousand dreams—my cousin fell into an endless sleep.

After reopening an unhealable wound, I wanted to give my aunt time to compose herself, but my words spilled out. "Do you remember what was wrong with my brothers?"

Elaine lowered her eyes. "You know, Kenny, I don't think anyone ever figured it out. Even the doctors couldn't agree. I think maybe the twins just cut off each other's oxygen in the womb." She looked up at me. I waited. Her silence apologized, sorry to disappoint.

She wanted to tell me more, but the details had always been foggy. She wasn't exactly sure what happened, and I believed her. Why, after all this time, would she obscure the story? The Coltharts, proud Scots through and through, wore brave faces, gushed reluctantly, and held their tongues, but not in private prisons like my father's family. The Gagnes kept the pesky truth bottled up, honest spirits flowing free-and-easy only when poured into thirsty mouths.

Elaine did know, for certain, that my mother loved her family with uncommon zeal. And that love flashed like a beacon in anecdotes about the sacrifices Mom made for her parents; the care she gave her siblings; the patience she showed her husband; the strength with which she raised her children. Every story, an exquisite quilt threaded with themes of family and devotion.

With broad brushstrokes, my aunt outlined the mystery behind her sister: how Cynthia traced an indelible spirit over childhood; shaded in adolescence with grace, personality, and kindness; then, after marriage and motherhood, colored in the rest with loyalty and faith. Till her journey's end, my mother painted life's road with willful purpose, always putting the needs of others before her own.

⌁

"That business kicked the shit out of him, that oil spill. It went on forever."

Jimmy Cassidy, a slender man in baggy jeans, leaned forward in his easy chair and adjusted his faded Red Sox cap. I sat across from him in his Holyoke home, admiring the sympathy he still felt for his dead friend.

"If the EPA didn't get involved, the fire department would've just buried it," Jimmy said. "They destroyed your father, took everything he had."

His wife, Susan, handed me a glass of water and sat beside me on the couch. "I know there were times when they barely ate, and your mom would buy as little as she could at the store. She felt so bad because they couldn't give you anything." Like a medium, Susan channeled my mother and relayed a psychic apology from beyond the grave.

Dear friends for more than thirty years, no one knew the late-life struggles of Bob and Cindy Gagne better than Jimmy and Susan Cassidy. As the couple spun their yarn, they stunned me with details of my family's apparent destitution and how my parents lessened the effects. I took an extra-long gulp of water, scratched a make-believe itch on my face, and cleared my empty throat. Hadn't I lived under the same roof? Wouldn't I have known if we were penniless as pocketless paupers?

I had *some* knowledge of the Environmental Protection Agency's relentless lawsuit against my dad, hoovering his bank account in the late eighties. I was aware that, as he was about to retire, they forced him to pay for the cleanup of contaminated soil found on his business property. But he locked away the details of the case, shielded me from the truth, and I never learned the ugly facts (just like I never *really* saw my father drunk or my parents fight). It all happened in front of my nose, but my folks pinched my nostrils shut, blocking out the odor of grown-up matters. Was Dad to blame for the leaky underground tank? Did he take accountability? Exactly how much money did he lose? Jimmy didn't know any of this; that made two of us.

Members of our church, Jimmy and Susan remained loyal acolytes when my parents needed them most—after giving away my brothers *and* their life's savings—as if God had fronted my folks the retainer fee. An affable couple with three kittenish children, the Cassidys were true friends when the kind was hard to find, and harder to keep. Jimmy rivaled my father with his quick wit and joking insults, while Susan was a carbon copy of my mother: smart, pleasant, and caring, with an infectious laugh.

Over the phone, a week prior to my visit, Susan agreed to field whatever questions I had about my parents but warned she wouldn't tell me everything. She was one of the few who knew the extent of my mother's agony over her lost sons and wayward marriage, but because Susan cherished and honored their relationship, she made it clear certain confidentialities would stay classified.

"She went through a lot with your father." The quiet in her voice told me this wasn't easy to talk about. "But she always loved him, even with the way he was, and the drinking, and the stuff we won't get into. She may have fallen out of that wonderful love, but he was still her husband, and she would never jeopardize their marriage."

Without giving me the whole story, Jimmy and Susan described the pride my parents had for my sisters and me; expressed how my mother lived and died with dignity; and mused that people at church still speak fondly of my father and his reputation for cracking wise. Listening to the Cassidys reflect, I was struck by how Mom and Dad stuck together while everything around them fell apart. Bonded by holy acrimony, they set aside grating hostilities and united when it mattered most. And as life dealt one body blow after another, they fought to keep their priorities straight and their family protected. To us kids, they confirmed we needed only the basics to survive, reinforcing that happiness didn't hinge on "things."

"Even when they had money, they never flaunted it," said Jimmy. "It just wasn't important to them."

"They didn't care," said Susan, "which was fortunate, because when all that serious stuff happened, they could deal with it. It never brought them to their knees. They would say as long as you kids were happy and healthy, they were okay."

❧

Daylight slunk away, looking for a place to hide.

Back in my four-wheeled time machine, I negotiated the streets of Holyoke with my mind cemented in the past, keeping an eye out for mileposts of my mother's childhood. I rode by former Colthart residences on Oak Street, Maple Street, Pleasant Street, and Jackson Parkway. I spotted their house of worship, the First Presbyterian Church, on the corner of Cabot and Chestnut, across the way from Mom's elementary school. While roving High Street's historic district, I envisioned her as a girl, floating on innocence down the busy sidewalks of a safe and supportive community.

Without knowing exactly how to get there, I made my way to the river. Along the lifeless banks, mortared to the outline of the city, a chain of abandoned paper mills and textile factories cast titanic silhouettes against the shrunken sky. Rolling along the Water Street canal, I admired the mammoth structures, engineering marvels of their day, formidable symbols of the Industrial Revolution. In the late nineteenth century, more than twenty-five paper mills lined this narrow strip of Holyoke. In those days, the "Paper City" manufactured more pads, notebooks, and newsprint than any place in the world. These crumbling mills once formed the castle walls of a perfectly planned metropolis, protecting and providing for its citizens. Now, only an eerie ghost town remained, an ancient fortress barely standing, orphaned by progress.

I pulled off the road and walked to the water's edge. As the sun eavesdropped over my shoulder, I sucked in the stench of dead fish and neglect. Decades ago, demolition's scythe had reaped these mills, leaving behind few survivors, skeletons of the past, vacant reminders of an American Eden teeming with vitality. I imagined throngs of immigrant workers, including three generations of my dad's family, filling those bustling buildings a century earlier, eager to earn an honest wage, clutching at a chance to recreate their lives. I imagined, as they had, hope and promise for the future, in a place where they were wanted and needed. But Hope and Promise are mere shadows of a former age, of a city in its infancy. And over time, like paper and people, cities turn brittle. Everything, and everyone, disintegrates.

I got back into the car. With dusk hot on my trail, I drove over the iconic Willimansett Bridge, from Holyoke into Chicopee, and parked at an auto body shop. What better place to stretch my legs, and extend my visit? I strode toward the bridge, stepped onto its grated walkway, placed a damp hand on the steel rail, and started across.

My parents grew up two miles apart—my mother in Holyoke, my father in Chicopee—but between them raged a river and a religion and a culture. The bridge under my feet connected them to each other, to their homes, to their past. I regretted wasting the chance to make a stronger connection with my mom and dad. When I was a kid, I was oblivious to their past *and* their present, mostly because I didn't care. Their troubles and concerns weren't served at the dinner table each night, and I never bothered to ask. Back then, all I needed from my parents was a clean baseball uniform, plenty of cereal in the cupboard, and $7.50 to take Kelly Glanville to see *Beverly Hills Cop*.

I paced the walkway, noting a fresh coat of sea-foam green paint covering four span trusses above. As traffic passed, to and from both cities, I felt disoriented, alone and out of place. Halfway across, I paused and peered over the rail. Dark and beautiful rapids rumbled below. I reflected on the deep waters my parents treaded, the deadly currents they fought, the bridges they built, and the one they destroyed.

Time for one last stop.

The warmth of a strung-out summer's day hung in the Chicopee air as I stood in front of my childhood home. Hanging from a tar-black lamppost abutting the driveway, a rectangular wrought iron sign, with *The Gagnes'* etched on its face, falsely advertised the dwelling's inhabitants. I grew up in a house perfectly situated halfway down Langevin Street, a quarter-mile-long asphalt funfair shaped like a giant horseshoe. In my mind, I was the luckiest kid in town. Our modest, one-story ranch called little attention to itself but quietly fulfilled our suburban dreams. The egg yolk–yellow aluminum siding meshed with the rainbow palette of the neighborhood, complementing pale green patches of crab grass in our front yard that yielded barely enough space for a claustrophobic game of freeze tag or limited round of red rover.

I walked down the driveway to the side of the house, where a rusty basketball hoop clung for dear life on the garage wall. Its nylon net had plummeted to its death during my middle school days, less the result of a thousand swishes than my incorrectly looping the twine through the rim's metal eyelets. At the end of the driveway, a lofty elm rooted itself at the crest of a slight hill that rolled into the backyard. Nailed to the trunk, a wooden birdfeeder I built for a Cub Scout project during the Ford administration—with help from a neighborhood dad— still held strong.

Our house offered more than met the eye. To the casual observer, the front of our place, like our family, appeared to have only one story. But the flip side disclosed a hidden "second" story and, as with my college mullet, there was a lot more happening in the back. Behind the house, from an exposed foundational wall, our basement door led to a concrete patio, aproning an in-ground swimming pool. Above the door, a floor-to-ceiling, wall-length picture window revealed the soul of our home and bore witness to the wide world outside.

I evoked my father, who always said the panorama in our backyard was the most amazing in all Chicopee. Back then, I never appreciated the spectacle, never saw his point of view. But in the yard that day, with the landscape stretching out farther than the limits of my sight, I sensed an intimate awe. Prominent in the vista's backdrop, the steep green slopes of Holyoke's Mount Tom snooped behind the unsuspecting Connecticut River. Over the South Hadley Falls Dam, growling water tumbled out of sight while church steeples peeked through treetops, like flummoxed detectives, trying to crack the case of the disappearing river. I looked over my shoulder at the picture window and smiled. The ghosts of my parents smiled back.

To my left, the pool sparkled, cool and inviting. To my right, a wall of mature oaks bordered the yard, signaling a whopping drop into a wooded valley we called "the dingle." All around, voices clamored from the past, echoes from an alternate dimension bouncing off the trees, reams of relatives from another realm gathering for our annual Colthart family reunion.

Look, over there, my mom's gangly and kind-hearted Uncle Sammie, with his wife, Grace, by his side, dumping a barrel of little necks (imported from Rhode Island) into a copper tub gurgling on a pit of coals. And there, my mother's father, the patriarchal Pop-Pop, royalty on a woven nylon throne, reciting the entirety of Ernest Thayer's "Casey at the Bat" to a batch of enthralled minions at his feet. Oh, and there, my hippie-like cousin, Bruce, a talented teenage cartoonist, teaching me how to sketch a caricature of a man with oversized shoes and a balloon nose under bubble letters reading, *Keep on Truckin'*. "When you draw someone, Kenny," my phantom cousin says, "start with the eyes. Life is in the eyes." And yes, there, Bruce's mother, my Auntie Dottie, on the patio under my open bedroom window, laughing her piercing hyena laugh that ricochets for hours around the yard, keeping me awake late into the stuffy summer night.

I chuckled at these jigsaw pieces of memory and strolled near the yard's end. Where our vegetable garden used to be, I came across a makeshift fire pit assembled with cracked alabaster cinder blocks; it was like stumbling upon an archaeological dig. It dawned on me the blocks were from our built-in living room planter once overwrought with plastic fronds and flowers, a ten-foot-long dinosaur from the Groovy-assic period. When Ethan and Teresa moved into our house, they made a handful of home improvements. Big-banging that Tacky-o-saurus into extinction was a wise decorating choice. Change hurts, but it's usually for the best.

Where the grass of the lawn meets the hay of the field, I stepped over wild blueberry bushes that, in my formative years, marked the edge of civilization. Ages ago, beyond this point, adventure and exploration awaited. Out there, roaming endless acres, I was free. I belonged. I was loved. This place built my confidence, courage, and sense of curiosity. My mother's call from the house, my security. My father's presence in the garden, my protection. I learned to be brave and independent, but I was never alone. My childhood was golden.

My mom and dad believed in me. And I flourished. They expected me to be polite and respectful. And I obliged. They trusted me and allowed me to fail. And I failed. They forgave me when I was wrong so long as I tried to be right. They encouraged me to imagine, to consider wonderful possibilities, and to empathize with others. Protective but not obsessive, they let me be me. They thought I was special. I'm not sure if I agreed, but I didn't want to do anything to prove them wrong.

The mountain consumed the last morsel of sun.

Recalling a lifetime of yesterdays, I sat on a familiar bed of moss and picked up a speckled stone that had surely seen me play as a child. I strained my eyes to make out the river through a screen of trees, their branches waving hello and goodbye to me. I missed this place and what used to be; I missed my parents and their love for me. And it hit me then that I'd never know the truth about my mother and father, what their lives were really like, or who they really were. They were gone, the people and the stories. And none of them were ever coming back. I had my chance, had all the time I could've wished for, and I threw every second away. Now the only piece of them I had to hold, the single story they left behind, was in me.

I surveyed the hills and listened to a sparrow sing the day's final song. And there in the dying light, I cried.

ONE

"Ah-Tu Mu-Tu Hi-Ya"

Fall, 1981

MY FATHER'S POEM demanded attention.

Displayed in mock grandeur on the laminate kitchen counter, his half-hearted apology was scrawled in blue ink on a page ripped from one of my drawing pads. He'd broken off this clever olive branch—barely legible but shockingly without misspellings or grammatical errors—as a peace offering, with intentions of returning to his wife's good graces, following a typical night of unknowable foolishness. Peeking through the window, the Sunday morning sun flashed a beam of notoriety onto his latest masterpiece.

Cyn,

I know I'm not Prince Charming; I'm sure that you'd agree.

And there might be someone else who'd
make a better mate than me.

I like my beer, and like my wine, and love to socialize.

Those are habits I possess but things that you despise.

I agree I'm very fortunate to have a girl like you.

So if you kind of hang in there, I'll see what I can do.

"Big Bad Bob"

Satisfied with his witty words, my dad sank into the living room couch, his back to the cinder-block planter, its ten wooden dowels sprouting up, connecting to the popcorn ceiling. Serving as a partition between the living room and kitchen, the planter's blocks and bars formed a partial jail cell, redefining the term "house arrest." Church wasn't for two more hours, but he'd been ready for three.

Decked out in a gin-tinted short-sleeved dress shirt, with one too many buttons unbuttoned, and time-worn trousers the color of Baileys Irish Cream, my father rested a crooked forearm atop his bald head, stubby fingers dangling aside his cheek like bells on a floppy court jester's cap. In his mitt, on the edge of the armrest, he clutched a glass of Tabasco-infused V8 doused with vodka. A copy of his personal Bible, Dale Carnegie's *How to Win Friends & Influence People*, lay brazen on the brass coffee table.

The Magnavox in the corner amplified the booming, Godlike voice of televangelist Dr. Robert Schuller sermonizing from California's Chrystal Cathedral during his weekly *Hour of Power*. That program, heavy on repentance and forgiveness, was my father's favorite Sunday morning show, a fitting hangover elixir considering his favorite Saturday night activities.

Dad called himself "Big Bad Bob," a flagrant misnomer since there was nothing big about him, except his beer belly, and nothing terribly bad, save for his two-pack-a-day smoking habit.

True, his name *was* Bob, though his mother always called him "a little shit." As a boy, he'd owned a kind heart but pretended to be tough to withstand harsh surroundings. A teddy bear stuffed with teardrops, brandishing a foam sword, he cowered from the bigness and badness all around, incapable of slaying the giants trampling his childhood.

"Let your hopes, not your hurts, shape your future," said Pastor Schuller.

Our dad wore his lot in life like a badge of honor, claiming he graduated from the University of Hard Knocks, his way of normalizing the adversity he'd faced and a nod to the pride he took in prevailing. From his bully pulpit, he espoused dozens of daily idioms to us kids, sacred commandments and philosophies, unsolicited advice to help us navigate the twists and turns of life. I lampooned these fortune-cookie credos as nothing but fatherly drivel, the dogmatic rantings of a middle-aged loon. My sisters found our father's ideological doctrines far less humorous. They didn't want to hear any of it. Ever.

A self-proclaimed know-it-all, Dad observed the world from a watchtower of omniscience. Spying my older sister Cheryl sneaking a phone call to a boyfriend, he'd announce, "I don't miss too much." If the neighborhood girls picked on my middle sister, Linda, he'd say, "It takes all kinds to make a world." And the more our father declared, "You're gonna miss me someday," the more my sisters were convinced they wouldn't. Who was he to tell them about life? The guy was just a used-car salesman, for crying out loud.

Draped in a teal terry-cloth bathrobe, our mother entered the kitchen, her slipper steps slow and groggy, her permed hair a matted mess. She grabbed a canister of Nescafé from the cupboard and placed it on the counter next to my father's poem. She filled a mug with water, heated it up in the microwave, and stirred in a teaspoon of coffee grounds. She adjusted the eyeglasses on her tired, pretty face and stared blankly at the words written for her. She slid the paper aside and blew steady into her mug. Ripples of scalding liquid splashed over the rim, and a skosh of droplets splattered onto her husband's act of contrition. A wry smile crossed her lips.

She put the poem on a pile of junk mail at the end of the counter and weighed down the stack with her latest Danielle Steele romance, *To Love Again*. She remembered a time when silence wasn't the preferred method of communication in the house, a time when the twins were healthy and the future bright, when their family was perfect, and her husband lavished her with words so sweet they could've been embroidered on a pillow. But then everything changed, including him. And as time worked its way under her skin, she got used to it all. She took a sip of coffee. It was already cold.

Through the smudgy picture window, my father looked out at the backyard and into the gut of his ghosts. Haunted by his youth and tortured by manhood, he lived in purgatory—trapped between what was and what never would be, surrounded by apparitions of regret and bitterness and hopelessness. Paralyzed by the tandem sting of past and present, my dad could move only one arm and lifted the Bloody Mary to his mouth.

On the other side of the blocks and bars, like a resentful wife visiting her imprisoned husband, my mother sat rigid as a hammer toe at the kitchen table. She flipped through her Methodist handbook of daily affirmations and found that morning's reading from Corinthians: *I am not who I once was; I am forgiven. Therefore if anyone is in Christ, he is a new creature; the old things passed away; behold, new things have come.* Her hands wrapped around the tepid mug, she looked out the window at the front yard and braced herself for the day. Soon, her children would be awake. Soon, the whole family would be at church. Soon, her prayers would go unanswered.

If I'd taken the time when I was a kid to see my parents as individuals, if I'd understood the reasons *why* they were who they were, then I would've appreciated their contrasting qualities. If I knew then what I know now, I would've described them, and our lives together, differently.

It'd be like this...

My mother and father are counterparts, two sides of the same wooden nickel, compatibly incompatible and perfectly imperfect. But it'd be wrong to say their marriage is a fatal car wreck; it's more like an aggravating fender bender that happens every single day for forty-four years.

Bob insults and embarrasses family, friends, and strangers alike. Cindy praises and compliments them all. Bob "hits the sack" each evening by nine and rises before the birds hit Snooze. Cindy conks out on the couch around midnight—lulled by a Johnny Carson monologue—and slumbers till midmorning.

Bob's a teasing prankster. Cindy's a sensitive caregiver. Bob sucks on three dozen Marlboros per day and washes down the nicotine with a conveyor belt of alcoholic beverages. Cindy puffs on lite cigarettes, now and then, while sipping chardonnay with girlfriends.

Cindy's a dreamer longing for adventure. Bob's a creature of habit longing for an afternoon nap. Cindy reacts to us misbehaving children with a bowed head, closed eyes, and a deep, decompressing breather. Bob reacts to our malfeasance by yanking open the utensil drawer with a terrifying rattle, snatching a foot-long plastic soup spoon, and threatening to emulsify three tiny fannies into puree.

When demanding our attention, our father barks a nonsensical phrase: "Ah-Tu-Mu-Tu-Hi-Ya!" Concocted out of thin air (we assume), the jibber-jabber is undefinable, yet effective. Dad sometimes breaks up the six syllables into thirds. No matter the variation, we take notice.

"Ah-Tu-Mu-Tu!"

"Yes?"

The gruff syllables sound serious, but something facetious in my father's annunciation—a good cop/bad cop vibe—signifies firmness and fun in the same beat. My sisters and I resist apathetic shrugs and respond at once to Dad's demand.

"Ah-Tu!"

"Yes?"

Before we can play with our friends, my sisters and I complete chores: empty the trash, clean our rooms, wash and dry and put away the dishes, feed the animals—rabbits, guinea pigs, hamsters, and a dog always—vacuum the carpets, sweep the driveway, weed the garden, fill the birdfeeders, clean the pool, and mow the lawn. For all this, Dad pays us two quarters each per week. Complain about any of it and the following week begets twice the work and zero quarters.

Our parents disapprove of video games. To play Space Invaders, we travel elsewhere in the galaxy. Until we turn thirteen, we aren't allowed to eat anywhere in the house except at the kitchen table. Enjoying my first bowl of ice cream in front of the living room TV is like an invitation to take batting practice at Fenway Park.

My father communicates with me in pseudo-intellectual, repetitive bursts. In the only way he knows how, he teaches me the ways of the world, a world that's knocked him down and put a boot on his neck. I learn to infer meaning from him, to fill in the blanks, to pay attention to the message, not the delivery. I understand him when he warns me to "keep off the grass" or explains that "your wealth is your family."

When my mother drifts, lost in her marriage, on a ship to wherever, I see the longing on her face and understand her as well. Her eyes show deep significance behind every look, hidden emotion in every glance. Strength in silence. Loyalty in suffering.

My parents teach me without teaching. I watch and listen and learn, training my ears for changes in the tones of their voices. Reading between the lines on their furrowed brows, I glean valuable knowledge about empathy and apathy, devotion and demise.

Bob and Cindy invest in people, offer help whenever they can. The fun-loving duo (more fun than loving) revel in life's delights, always ready with a smile, always up for a spontaneous drink with friends. To the outside world, they are free and easy. But inside the walls of 166 Langevin, they govern with unrestrained authority, strict as parochial school lunch ladies. Our parents don't always agree with each other, but they agree on the rules of the house and keep a unified front against their offspring.

Downright deprived compared to the other neighborhood children, we Gagne kids don't enjoy candy dishes filled with M&M's or stockpile cans of 7UP in the fridge. We snack on stalks of rhubarb from the garden and wet our whistles with tap water. We Gagne kids don't gawk at R-rated movies on HBO or litter our sentences with curse words. The most salacious TV show we watch is *The Love Boat*, and the only expletives we're allowed to yell are "Golly!" and "Rats!" and "Doggonit!"

To our parents, disrespect and negativity are high crimes, derogatory language a major offense. They outlaw profanity and forbid name-calling. They tabulate an unlimited list of inappropriate words we mustn't utter, and stuff a bar of Dial soap in our mouths if we do. "Hey! We don't say that word in our house," our father roars when his radar-equipped ears pick up any of the following: hate, jerk, ugly, shut up, idiot, lie, dumb, stink, stupid, gay, queer, moron, loser, suck, lame, dunce, butt, dope, dork, nerd, etcetera, etcetera.

Few Chicopeans could construct a participle phrase without those words; we hear worse from our Sunday school teachers.

Topping the taboo chart, the most vulgar obscenity of all—the one we dare not think, never mind say—is the R-word, which carries a punishment unlike the others, for unspoken but understood reasons.

Retard.

❧

I glanced at my father's poem buried beneath the Danielle Steel novel and turned to my mother. "Do I have to go to church today?" I whined.

"Yes," she replied without a tinge of sympathy. Mom was ready to go, and my complaining was a hurdle she hadn't planned to clear.

"But I have soccer practice at eleven. I'm gonna be so late." This was not the way I wanted to kick off my high school athletic career.

"That's the way life goes." My father's verdict from the couch came down like a judge's gavel pounding a period onto the end of the conversation. I arched an eyebrow and looked to my mother for a response. She shook her head, her hazel peepers imploring me, for both our sakes, to keep my trap zipped.

I leafed through the white pages for my JV coach's number, rolled my finger around the dial of our rotary phone, and left an answering machine message preemptively apologizing for my tardiness.

Dad moseyed outside for a smoke while Mom wrote a five-dollar check for the collection plate. My sisters hogged the bathroom, touching up their hair and makeup, making it impossible to weasel my way to the sink without getting maced by Aqua Net. In lieu of brushing my teeth, I popped in a stick of Fruit Stripe gum. Ten minutes till service. Not to worry.

Driving to Faith United Methodist Church, at the end of our street, took two minutes. In fact, from our house, I could almost hear choir director, Roger LaCross, tuning up the pipe organ. I bounded out the door on that chilly autumn morn—the kind that put our abrupt New England summers way out of sight—and knew instantly my skimpy pink Izod wouldn't be warm enough, even with the collar turned up. Too lazy to throw on a sweater, I ignored the discomfort.

Two steps ahead, my father had already warmed up the car, a beige Coupe DeVille with a rusted back bumper and tattered landau roof, yet another jalopy off his used-car lot. There was always a different something-or-other in our driveway, and though the neighborhood kids figured we were loaded, we never owned a car. When life gave my dad lemons, he sold them, but finding a buyer for the DeVille would take some time due to its shredded rooftop, courtesy of an agitated troop of baboons bushwhacking us during our drive-through tour of Catskill Game Farm. Anyone would tell you Bob Gagne was no stranger to monkey business.

Out of the cassette deck Nat King Cole crooned "As Time Goes By" while I doubled over in the back seat, blowing warm air into my hands, rubbing my exposed arms, using friction to fry gooseflesh. Dad checked on me in the rear-view mirror. "Want the heat up some more?"

"No, it's okay," I fibbed. He adjusted the control knob anyway.

"You know, you and I can leave church early, and I can take you to soccer," he offered. "Then I'll swing back to grab Mom and the girls."

"Are you sure? I can be a little late."

"Nah. We'll take off right after the sermon. You can change at home, then I'll get you to the park. No sweat, KG." He got a kick out of calling me by my initials like my buddies did.

"Thank you," I said.

In the mirror I caught a glimpse of a happier man. But then

he was gone, and his eyes reflected the subtle look a father gives his son after years of not telling him all he wants to say. He turned away and sang along with Mr. King Cole, both men urging me to remember that "a kiss is just a kiss, a sigh is just a sigh."

The rear doors opened in unison. My sisters scrambled inside and crushed me with a perfectly executed "Malachi Crunch," forcing me onto the back seat's lumpy middle hump. Busting out of the breezeway, Mom pushed the storm glass door off its hinges and rummaged through her macramé pocketbook for a tube of lipstick. As she scurried down the steps, my father tooted the car horn, playfully advising her to get a move on. She didn't like being late for church. She liked his tomfoolery even less.

"Let's go, Cindy. Ah-Tu!" Perky puffs of cigarette smoke whooshed out his open window, joining in the mockery.

She strode in front of the car, and Dad laid hard on the horn. My mother jumped, the levels on her annoyance meter pinned. I squirmed.

"Don't get nervous, Cindy," he yelled.

She froze in her tracks and shot him a glare that melted the windshield glass. She hustled to the passenger side and lunged for the door handle. My father shifted the car into reverse, jerking it backward, and stopped a few feet from the end of the driveway.

"C'mon, Cindy. We're gonna be late."

Mom stomped to the side of the car again, snatched the latch and jumped in.

Slam!

Beside herself, she stewed like a declawed house cat drooling over a showy cardinal through a window, denied her God-given instinct to kill. My dad tickled the back of his wife's ear. She swatted his hand away and shook her head, irritated by the nuisance she married.

"Just go," she said.

TWO

"Take What You Want, but Eat What You Take"

Winter, 1977

FOUR EMPTY KITCHEN chairs judged me as I nudged three boiled brussels sprouts across my plate with an indignant fork.

My stomach turned at the sight of the horrible orbs, slimy and mushy on the outside, bitter and hard at their core. The stink crumpled my facial muscles. Why the heck did I take these darn things anyway? Because I knew Mom wanted me to eat my veggies? Because it took her a long time to cook dinner, and I wanted to show some appreciation? Whatever the reason, I needed to stay at the table till I cleaned my plate; that was the rule. And getting dessert now was totally out of the question; my bread, butter, and sugar would have to wait till another night.

In a pickle, I hacked each of the sprouts in half, hoping their decreased size would increase their palatability. They *were* dinkier, but now there were six. The judging chairs derided my efforts. No way I'd skate scot-free after this pitiful parole hearing. I slumped, a chump, and removed the paper napkin from my lap, ready to surrender.

I detested brussels sprouts even more than raw onions, which my sneaky sisters sometimes chopped up and, when I wasn't looking, folded into my mashed potatoes. (When the revolting crunch ambushed my molars, and I ejected a mouthful of mush, Cheryl and Linda would die laughing. *Yeah, yeah, real funny.*) My dislike for the sickening sprouts tempted me to' use the H-word. No other term matched my level of disgust, aversion, and revulsion. No other feeling compared to my distaste, repugnance, and loathing. I snarled at the plate, my rage boiling.

I hate these! I silently screamed.

In the living room—steps away from my suffering—pine logs crackled in the fireplace as my parents and siblings watched a lioness tear a hunk of flesh from an out-of-luck antelope on Mutual of Omaha's *Wild Kingdom.* On the couch, my mother snuggled with her daughters under a patchwork quilt, while my father reclined in his easy chair, sipped Kahlúa, and dragged the tar out of a cigarette.

Nearby on the floor, a crusty dog bowl spoke to me, like a demonic voice in the head of an asylum patient, persuading me to coax our faithful pup into eating my sprouts. I doubted she'd haul in my Hail Mary but prayed she'd at least take a leap. Madness poisoned my brain. "Where's Bambi?" I asked no one.

The lioness yawned under a Serengeti sausage tree as Mom threw her voice toward the kitchen. "I haven't seen her since this afternoon," she said. "Cheryl, did you feed her earlier, like I asked?"

Already peeved, Cheryl replied, "Yes, I fed her and let her outside to go to the bathroom right before we—"

"Call her in, please," our father said, uninterested in the rest of Cheryl's story. "You wouldn't want to be out there right now, would you? Ah-Tu!"

Claiming it was merely "cold" outside would've insulted Mother Nature, in general, and Snow Miser, in particular. The intolerable air on frigid Chicopee nights like this stiffened nose hairs, frosted cheeks, and sent the brawniest of kids crying for their mommies. An afternoon of steady sleet had pierced fifteen inches of snowfall leftover from the day before, and a whipping wind crystalized the entire town in an icy crust that glistened in the moonlight like twenty-four square miles of lacquered diamonds.

Cheryl called for our dog, holding open the breezeway door just wide enough for her voice to fit through. "Bambi." Her lame effort blew back, slapping her in the face, and she yelled again. "Bambi!"

My big sister returned to the living room and settled under the quilt. "She's not coming."

Linda jumped off the couch. "How can you just not care?" Then she raced to the door and sang out, "Bambi! Come on in, girl!" The bitter air rifled down her throat and punctured her lungs. "Baaaaammmmmbiiiii!"

Linda's voice echoed through the neighborhood, and a pit grew in my stomach. Normally in conditions like this, Bambi would scratch impatiently at the door, begging to come in. She didn't have a thick enough coat, or tough enough demeanor, to brave this kind of weather. A mongrel mix of collie and dingo and hound (and who-knows-what-else), she rarely exhibited enough courage to mess with a squirrel. Part of our family for ten years—same as me—Bambi was lively and spry, contradicting her human age of fifty-six. Factoring a temperature of five degrees into the equation, I calculated our dog's chances of surviving the night, and the answer was irrefutable: zippo.

"Where could she be?" I surprised myself with a modicum of worry, shifting my focus from my sprouts' disappearance to my dog's reappearance.

My whole life I'd treated Bambi like a furry piece of furniture. I bounded over her and sidestepped her, hustling through my daily routine on automatic pilot, mindlessly filling her food and water bowls, letting her in and out of the house. To me, she was an inanimate fixture, a pet based on muscle memory alone. I couldn't even remember the last time I played with her. But on that arctic January evening, as each extended second linked with the next, lengthening an excruciating chain of minutes, I agonized at the thought of never seeing her again.

My father rose from his chair like a Kodiak sniffing wildflowers on a breeze. "Quiet." His voice jabbed the air. "Listen." The rest of us sat in silence, still as stars, waiting for a sound, any sound. Dad sloughed across the room and turned down the volume on the TV. "Hear that?" he said. "It's her."

From somewhere far behind the house, a faint yelp carved through the cold. My sisters and I sprang like jack-in-the-boxes and sprinted to the door. There it was again, barely audible, but clearly Bambi's bark, coming from the dingle.

"Let's go!"

We scrambled to the breezeway closet, flung open the slatted double doors, and dove headfirst into the storage bin overstuffed with winter clothing. We plucked out crocheted mittens, wool hats, ski gloves, and knitted scarves. We littered the shag carpet with panicky haste, dusting up Bambi's shed hair. The weightless strands sailed in the moonlight shining through the window before falling for the siren song of Cheryl's sweater's static cling.

"Mom! Do you know where our snow pants are?" Linda shouted.

Already halfway down the cellar stairs, our mother called back, "I'll find them."

Like a magician swiping a linen cloth from a table setting, I yanked my Baltimore Colts NFL jacket out of the closet leaving the wire hanger spinning on the dowel. I pushed my arms through the white leather sleeves and popped in the snaps up to the blue-and-white striped collar. I rubbed the horseshoe logo emblazoned on my chest, hoping my jacket—like a superhero's costume—would provide some bravery. Or at least a little luck.

I'd worn that coat every day since I unwrapped it on Christmas morning two weeks earlier. My obsession began in the fall when I noticed the athletes from Chicopee Comprehensive High School wearing their blue-and-gold letterman jackets around town, *Colts* boldly stitched across their backs. An impressionable fourth grader, I put those cocky jocks, with their acne-scarred faces and greasy mops of hair, on an unreachable pedestal.

At the kitchen table one night in late October, while I flipped through the pages of a Sears, Roebuck & Company catalog, crafting my list for Santa, Mom sat beside me with the patience of a monk stuck in traffic at a tortoise crossing. Facing me: the impossible task of choosing an NFL jacket with the same *colors* as my hometown high school, or the same *nickname*. The St. Louis Rams wore blue and gold too but, deep in my soul, I wanted to be a Colt. (Mom insisted on also ordering the matching hat with poufy white pom-pom.)

Armored in layers of thermal shirts, long johns, sweaters, and coats, my sisters and I attacked the deep freeze, lurching toward the dingle atop the hardened snow like mini-Frankenstein's monsters in astronaut suits. The wicked wind slid through the sockets of my ski mask, frosting my face. I leaned over the gully's lip and listened for Bambi's cries in the skeletal darkness. I panned from Cheryl to Linda, hoping one of them had a plan. "How are we going to do this?"

We'd rushed out of the house with valiant intentions, but none of us realized the danger in store. Our parents hadn't held us back or warned us about the hazards of our daring deed. They likely figured—should we find ourselves in *actual* jeopardy—the experience would only toughen us up, teach us what sacrifice really means. We had no choice anyway. Bambi had pinballed down a wooded slope the length of a football field on a nasty winter's night. She was certainly injured, definitely terrified. We had to save her. No turning back.

"All we have to do is get down there and carry her back up," Linda screamed into the wind tunnel. Her solution was simple but naive. None of us weighed enough to thump through the snow's icy top layer and descend the hill without careening to our deaths. There wasn't one platelet of heroism in my blood, and I was never more afraid. I looked to Cheryl.

For her third birthday, she got the best gift ever: a baby brother. Cheryl and I shared a cake each March and, with her candles on one side and mine on the other, we made wishes and blew out dancing flames together. Many times, I'm sure, we wished for the same thing, but only she had the guts to demand it come true.

"Follow me," Cheryl said, scooting over the precipice in her puffy nylon pants. She picked up speed and slid down ten feet, aboard an invisible runaway sled, before reaching out and clutching a dead tree branch locked in the snow. Hanging on with a mitten, our leader shouted orders through the bluster. "Come down the same way and do the same thing as me."

Then, flat on her back, Cheryl lifted a leg and drove the heel of her boot through the ice like a sledgehammer through Styrofoam. Fastened into the foothold, she jackknifed into a sitting position, inched her way forward a few feet, lifted her other boot, and crunched through again. For twenty minutes, down the face of the frozen gorge, Cheryl grabbed onto every twisted twig and scraggy shrub within reach, forging a boot-busting track for Linda and me to follow.

At the bottom, Bambi lay whimpering under a thorn bush. There was blood on her snout and paws, but she wasn't badly hurt. Linda stroked our pooch's wet coat, choking back tears while calmly reassuring her. "It's going to be okay, girl. We've got you now."

Hands on hips, Cheryl stood to the side, enclosed in the wintry plumes of her breath, and considered the trouble ahead.

Cheryl

If I'd paid closer attention to my older sister when we were teenagers, if I'd taken one second to consider her feelings, then I'd know when and how she pushed away from our parents in her search for independence. If only we'd talked to each other more, I wouldn't have to imagine her anxiety at the time.

It's a day like any other...

Seventeen-year-old Cheryl stampedes through the kitchen and breaks the stillness of the morning. "Where are my clogs? I left them right here last night," she barks from the breezeway, demanding an answer from anyone listening. Our dirty-blonde mutt raises her head from a nap, the only one close to caring about Cheryl's distress.

"All you have to do is look," Dad announces from the living room. Cheryl huffs, barely containing her rage, seething and hissing like a wet log on a fire. Terrified plates shake in the sink as she thunders back through the kitchen and down the hall in pursuit of a suitable replacement pair of shoes to match her outfit. In the char of scorched earth, she leaves her father in the dust.

Mom and Dad have their hands full with their eldest daughter. A senior in high school, Cheryl's short-fused blowups are a common occurrence. But away from our house, she converts from brassy brute to unassuming wallflower, rarely speaking up in school or with friends. Feathered-back cinnamon hair, frictionless features and a petite frame accentuate her façade, fooling the outside world into thinking she's a softy.

Only on the soccer field does the public get a glimpse of

Cheryl's "Ms. Hyde," a tenacious monster who alarms opponents and teammates alike with ferocious speed and competitive fire. With those attributes, she mutates into one of the best players in the state. Cheryl shies from the limelight, turns from attention of any kind. But deep down, she's a fighter.

At home, Dad pushes her buttons like a frenzied switchboard operator, crossing wires purposefully, sabotaging frayed lines of communication. Scarcely able to exist on the same planet with him, Cheryl holds nothing but contempt for our father, resents his behavior and his being. She has zero patience for his drinking or his immaturity or the way he embarrasses her in front of her friends. At the core, she deplores the way he treats his wife.

His condescending slights hurt our mom, and every comment, no matter how subtle, infuriates my big sister. What our dad considers harmless teasing, Cheryl considers an unforgivable affront.

During private moments, she questions Mom. "Why do you stay with him? He doesn't respect you, or any of us."

"It's more complicated than that, Cheryl," our mother says, wrapped again in a discussion she knows won't help.

Her head-strong daughter has a point. But Mom understands the rawness of teenage emotions and hopes someday, when the doors stop slamming and weekly threats to run away end, Cheryl will appreciate her father for his decent qualities. Though neither would admit it, the combatants are more alike than different.

"I just want to live long enough to see how you handle your kids," he remarks after one of their squabbles.

"I'm never having kids." She's dead serious.

It wasn't always like this.

In another lifetime—when he was still our hero—Dad whisked us kids away on snappy Saturdays for marathon hikes throughout the Pioneer Valley. Hauling sacks of ham sandwiches and Little Debbie Oatmeal Creme Pies, we explored the echo caverns of the Mohawk Trail, the pebbly shores of Quabbin Reservoir, and the rock formations of Shelburne Falls. We picked out perfect walking sticks for treks deep into forests and high over mountains, keeping our voices down to avoid scaring away any wildlife. Cheryl loved those expeditions: the freedom, the excitement, the stimulation of the outdoors. On those unbroken days, she shared an intense appreciation for the wonders of nature with our father.

"Remember, Cher, the best things in life are free," he'd tell her. And she'd listen. With no demands or judgments on them, and no one to answer to, they sucked pure air into their lungs and released their tensions. They walked together, yet alone, the wilderness sweeping them away from the untamable world.

Back home, Dad would sit Cheryl on his knee by the picture window, hand her his prized field binoculars, then help her identify black-capped chickadees and downy woodpeckers and tufted titmice alighting in the shade trees. Linda and I played on the floor while the fine-feathered friends flipped through their bird-watching handbook, Cheryl quizzing our father on how the nuthatch got its name or begging the difference between a starling and a grackle.

On serene mornings, they'd march in step through the backyard, across a sheen of dew, pointing out deer tracks and spreading cracked corn for the pheasant. Together, they filled the feeders and devised ways to keep the squirrels from raiding the seed.

Once upon a time, they had admiration and respect for each other. They were the starling and the grackle—same class of animal, separate species of bird—sharing the same branches and flying the same skies. But as Cheryl got older and wiser, she spread her wings, and Dad pushed her out of the nest.

Linda

If I'd taken one step in my middle sister's shoes when we were kids, if I'd uncovered why she felt the need to be so nice, then I would've cut her a little slack. If only I'd admitted how much I admired her, maybe she would've revealed more of herself, and I wouldn't have to invent this memory.

It's a random weekend morning...

Sixteen-year-old Linda pours herself a heaping bowl of Cookie Crisp cereal, a rare treat in our house, where standard breakfast fare is Grape-Nuts or, if we're lucky, Bran Chex. The sugary wafers, in all their tooth-rotting glory, cascade from the box like coins from a winning slot machine.

"Take what you want, but eat what you take," our father bellows from the couch. (He really doesn't miss too much.) Linda rolls her eyes and dumps in a torrent of milk. A dozen miniature discs catch the creamy wave, surf over the bowl's edge, and pitter-patter onto the plastic pastel place mat. "Take your time, Linda," the all-knowing voice booms again. She grimaces and cleans up the mess.

Fifty-one weeks younger than her big sister, Linda wants to keep the peace. Kind, caring, and sensitive to a fault, she worries about the fighting in our family. Unlike Cheryl, Linda behaves herself at home and doesn't argue much with our dad. He frustrates her as well, for all the same reasons, but instead of lashing out or internalizing brewing emotions, Linda deflects his negativity—or absorbs it—and keeps smiling. Years of observing our mother practice the same patience has paid off. They choose a similar course of non-action when dealing with Big Bad Bob, and their passive attitude further fuels Cheryl's ire. Mom avoids Dad's thorniness and carves a conciliatory path through the thicket, blazing a trail for Linda to follow. Together, they iron out my father's dark edges, fold him up, and compartmentalize him on the bottom shelf of their shared psyche.

Directly out of central casting, Linda claims all the qualities of a typical middle child: agreeable, loyal, and social. (Technically, if we count our older brothers, Robert and David, then Cheryl is the middle child. But our brothers never lived with us, had never been part of our family, so we don't count them.) As the eldest, Cheryl should be our de facto chief, but she defers, loath to take the title due to her distaste for attention and her mutinous attitude toward our father. Linda is comfortable in front of a crowd, consistent and reliable, and gladly fills the role of spokesperson. Cheryl seconds the motion.

With change on the horizon, the familial dynamics in our house shift like tectonic plates. Soon, Cheryl will flee Chicopee to pursue a secretarial degree at Bay Path Junior College in nearby Longmeadow. Neither of our parents made it past high school and expect all us kids to further our educations. Cheryl can't get out of the house quick enough, but Linda drags her feet. The stress at home is palpable, corrosive. Everyone's on edge.

With decent grades and enough athletic talent to participate in Division III sports, Linda's prospects beyond Langevin Street are promising. But shaky self-confidence and a distinct disdain for school hold her back. Our mother tries to pry open Linda's mind, to sell her on the opportunity college affords. She wants her daughters to be independent women—not beholden to a man—and views Linda's hesitation as a future roadblock.

At the kitchen table one night, I scuffle with an essay on the Enlightenment for Mr. Clancy's European history class. In the living room, my mother and Linda, two of the sweetest people I know, fight like rabid possums.

"You don't know what you're saying. You at least need to give college a try." Mom's voice constricts. Her hands tremble.

Linda cries, "I don't want to. You can't make me. How many times do I have to tell you?" She's cut by the conflict, frustrated by her mother's incoherence. "Why don't you understand?" She turns her back, on the brink of tears.

"You're right, I don't understand. Why in the world wouldn't you want to be the best you can be?" Mom's yelling now, crushed by an avalanche of disappointment. "Why limit yourself?"

Linda shouts back. "I'm fine with who I am. That's okay with me. Just because you're unhappy doesn't mean I have to be unhappy."

The arguments die down, eventually, and attrition wins the day.

After a slew of brutal battles, mother and daughter surrender, grappled in a knotty stalemate. Both regret saying some things, blaming the heat of the moment, but neither relinquishes her stance. In the end, they both get a piece of their wish: Linda enrolls at Holyoke Community College, plays soccer for the Lady Cougars in the fall of her freshman year, and drops out after one semester.

Reconciliation hangs in the balance, but all is not lost. Mom is proud of Linda's conviction and passion, the trueness of her heart. She will pray for her happiness but insists she accept responsibility for her decisions. And she hopes—somewhere along the way—her daughter will find contentment. The feeling, for Linda, is mutual.

≈

The wind picked up, swinging like a sword.

Bambi's whimpering was more frantic, more human somehow. We needed to get her up the hill and into the house, pronto. Reaching the bottom of the dingle, down a slanted skating rink, had been nearly impossible. How would we climb back up hauling sixty skittish pounds of frozen fur?

We decided that Linda—the biggest and strongest of us—would carry Bambi, with Cheryl following close behind to help her keep balance. My role? Go up first and reinforce the holes we'd punctured in the snow, ensuring they were deep and wide enough for my sisters to remain steady. If Linda slipped or tripped, Bambi likely wouldn't survive another treacherous slide. We had one shot.

My older sisters followed my footsteps, and I led the way, praying they wouldn't tumble in my tracks. For a half hour, we climbed in blackness, battling the Winter Gods of Chicopee, our fingers and toes hard as iron, our lungs rupturing. At the top, Linda set Bambi down and we collapsed.

Back inside, huddled like penned sheep on the couch, we thawed under blankets, sipped scalding Swiss Miss, and dazzled our parents with an inflated rehash of our accomplishment.

"I knew the three of you would figure it out," our father said. "Never a doubt in my great mind. And you went up first, Kenny, huh? What a natural leader you are. You got my genes, you know."

A leader? Who was he kidding? Sure, when deciding what kind of sandwich to make myself or whether to watch *Star Blazers* or *The Brady Bunch*, I made snap judgments. But in groups, I was a follower, acquiescing to the wishes of the crowd, seldom offering an opinion to avoid steering anyone wrong.

The youngest in my family, I never called the shots and hardly cared. I was an introvert, happiest when alone without anyone relying on me. A focused listener and rule-follower, I did what my parents and sisters and teachers and coaches and friends asked—as long as I didn't have to lead. I never criticized choices made on my behalf, no matter the results, having willingly shirked the decision process, waiving my right to complain.

By myself in my tiny bedroom, however, I ruled over all the land. In my ten-by-ten-foot kingdom, a twin bed ate up the far wall, leaving barely enough space to open my mouse hole of a closet. Above the bed, a teensy window squinted into the backyard. My trampled carpet was blue or black, depending on the time of day and cloud cover. On a nightstand, my dinky clock radio sang songs and counted paneled numbers flicking and clicking like lagging castanets to the beat of each minute.

I placed everything in my shrunken room tightly along the walls to allow a three-step takeoff toward the Nerf hoop clipped onto my bedroom door. I stood only hip-high to my metallic KISS wastebasket and couldn't dunk from under the hoop (unless guitarist Ace Frehley lent me his eight-inch Spaceman boots). But from the opposite corner, I built up steam and flew down the lane for crushing, one-handed jams, my shoulder slamming into the door, agitating the whole house, sending Mom barreling down the hall to check if I (or the door) required first aid.

The low ceiling forced me to shoot line-drive jump shots that clashed against the flimsy plastic rim with warbling *boings* straight out of a *Tom and Jerry* episode. For hours, I tossed that linty, tangerine sponge ball off the side walls, peeled around imaginary high-post picks, and received perfect passes in the lane for easy layups. I threw underhand lobs that ricocheted off my *Six Million Dollar Man* poster and floated in front of the hoop, where I snatched them up like a Hungry Hungry Hippo and hammered down alley-oops, my fictional teammates mobbing me after every improbable game-winning play.

On rainy summer afternoons, in my fantastic domain, I'd lie on my stomach and fill drawing pads with vast civilizations of outlandish cartoon characters. On cold winter mornings, I'd divide my action figures into teams—Green Arrow and Black Falcon always the captains—then throw my blankets and pillows onto the floor to form rugged mountains and caves where I'd stage epic superhero battles. In the background, my clock radio played the AM Gold *Hits of the Week* while flipping away the minutes and hours and days. The cheesy soundtrack to my Nerf highlights might include Alan O'Day's "Undercover Angel" or Glen Campbell's "Southern Nights"; the quirky musical score to my superhero civil wars might feature David Soul's "Don't Give Up on Us" or Al Stewart's "Time Passages."

Music transported me far from Chicopee; emotional ballads telling stories of love and loss cut me deep. Those were my stories, ones I needed to tell. I memorized every song, letting the words and melody spin my world, picturing myself inside the lovelorn lyrics, doing what the characters did, feeling what they felt. Music altered my personality, revealed a side of me that craved attention and gave me license to perform.

When my parents threw basement parties, I'd saunter down sporting Ray-Bans and a woman's wig, scour a box of Lincoln Logs for a stick microphone, and file through our record collection, choosing a playlist for a lip-sync concert. I'd skip past Perry Como and Barbara Streisand and Engelbert Humperdinck, leaving them sniveling in disappointment.

I'd pick out my favorite 45s, select an opening number, and flip on the turntable. I'd lower the needle and take my mark in the middle of the carpet. Amid the reek of stale beer and cigarettes, my devoted audience settled into their seats to the expectant static. The cramped confines of the finished basement, with its paneled walls and drop ceiling, had the aura of an intimate nightclub. And I was the headliner. My mom smiled in her metal folding chair up front. My dad hushed the crowd from his station behind the wet bar. The songs played.

Then it was me—not Frankie Valli—reminiscing about the girl I missed and the love I left behind; me dropping to my knees in the dim light, crying how "My Eyes Adored You." And it was me—not Terry Jacks—telling Michelle, my little one, it's hard to die; me closing my eyes, clutching the mic with both hands and reflecting how we had joy, we had fun, we had "Seasons in the Sun." And it was me—not Bo Donaldson, or any of the

Heywoods—relaying how the marching band came down along Main Street; me clinging to the carpeted beam, accompanied by a fife and drum instrumental, becoming a distraught girl pleading to her fiancé, "Billy, Don't Be a Hero."

But it was all make-believe: the basketball games, the drawings, the superhero battles, the songs. Back then, I wasn't brave enough to stand alone in life's spotlight, didn't have the courage to take a risk in the real world, couldn't bear failing. I wasn't a leader, wasn't a star. And I was certainly no hero.

THREE

"Keep Off the Grass"

Fall, 1991

I WAS OUT OF my element, in a fix, under pressure, and overdressed.

Plastic wheels squeaked and squealed and skewed to the right as I pushed a metal cart down the aisle of NBA Entertainment's videotape library. With each revolution, the racket grew louder and more embarrassing, irritating all of my new coworkers. I swung the back end of the cart to the front, hoping to stifle the noise. It skewed to the left.

I continued my crooked course down the corridor, past rows of tapes lined on shelves like soldiers at roll call, neat and stiff as the spanking-new chinos I was wearing. The place had that fresh construction smell, a scent blended with ingenuity and innovation. Dove-white floor tiles basked in the sheen of bright lighting. Sixteen state-of-the-art editing machines whizzed and whirred with fast-fingered producers at the controls. And there I was, pushing a sparkling cart that should have handled like a Maserati instead of one of the rattletraps on my dad's used-car lot. My first day at work, I tried to go unnoticed. Mission: unaccomplished.

Squeak, squeal, squeak, squeal, squeak.

In addition to causing a commotion, I had no idea what I was doing. My self-consciousness was laughable, and a bugging insecurity chewed up my pulpy ego like the Terminator of termites. It was all new: the feeling, the people, the building. And who ever heard of Secaucus, New Jersey?

After thirsting for a career in the sports industry, I'd netted my first full-time job with the National Basketball Association, hired as a videotape librarian in the company's entertainment division. I took pride in my title no matter its menial reputation: equal to toiling in the mail room. Created as a marketing arm of the league, NBA Entertainment produced commercials, home videos, and TV shows highlighting the excitement of pro hoops. Our goal: sell the superhuman talent and mega-personalities of our players to fans around the world.

As librarian, I assisted editors and producers by locating, pulling, and reshelving tapes. The nitty-gritty: know the difference between three-quarter inch, half-inch, and beta tapes; digital and one-inch master reels; split track and mixed audio; features with and without chyron; and the camera angles used during games (e.g., low basket, low opposite, low mid-court, high, and high-tight). The terminology boggled my noggin, and I had a hard time nailing down the nuts and bolts of the job. Technology had never been "my thing," but now I was engulfed by it, and my bosses paid me an exorbitant $16,000 per year to understand it all. To succeed, I'd have to embrace the motto, *Fake It Till You Make It.*

During the interview process five months earlier, I'd dodged questions regarding production and editing, about which I had no experience and little capacity to conceptualize. Born mortal enemies, machinery and I abhorred one another. Recording an outgoing message on my answering machine took the better part of an afternoon, and for an artsy-fartsy right-brainer like me, turning on a VCR was like defusing a bomb.

I was *semi*-qualified to work in NBAE's videotape library though. In addition to my degree in sport management at the University of Massachusetts at Amherst, I had relevant work experience: four years shelving books at the physical sciences library at college; an unpaid summer internship in the Boston Celtics sales department after graduation; and seventeen months selling tickets part-time at the Naismith Memorial Basketball Hall of Fame in Springfield (exactly 9.6 miles away from the Nerf hoop on my bedroom door in Chicopee).

While I'd fudged my way through the production portion of the interview, questions about the league and its players were a piece of cake. An avid NBA fan, I knew every guy on every roster, where they attended college, what year they were drafted, and their career stats, not to mention recent trades, free agent signings, player salaries, and each team's coaching staff.

Plus I knew hoops, had an innate feel for the game, understood what it meant to compete, to be motivated by failure, to dream of being the best and to lay it all on the line for your teammates. I appreciated the joy of winning *and* the pain of losing. I'd been on teams where I rode the pine, and I'd been on teams where I was the MVP. As a fellow baller, and now coworker, I felt connected to NBA superstars like Michael Jordan, Larry Bird, Magic Johnson, Isiah Thomas, Patrick Ewing, and Hakeem Olajuwon, even if I was just a nobody from Western Mass. I'd scored every sport-crazed kid's dream job, and my game plan was simple: work hard and be nice.

I was thrilled for a new beginning but ached for my family and friends back home—as well as my starting second baseman's job on the Chicopee Falls Tigers semipro baseball team. Above all, I missed my girlfriend of the past year, Kiki, now working as an au pair and taking grad school classes in Germany. Saying goodbye to everyone, and everything, would be worth it, I was sure. This was the moment I'd waited for, wanted, and deserved. To blossom in the Garden State, I'd need to soak in each ray of insight my parents shined on me about commitment, responsibility, character, and gratitude.

I was beyond grateful when a friend from the hall of fame, Wayne Patterson, pulled some strings to arrange my initial interview and put me in touch with a pal of his named Steve Michaud, who grew up near Wayne in Connecticut and had been with NBAE for two years. Wayne vouched for "Miche," said I could lean on him for info about the job and help finding an apartment. A month before my move, I made the fateful phone call that set the rest of my life in motion.

"Dude, Steve Miche. Great to talk to you, baby. Congrats on the new gig. That's fantastic. Bottom line: you're gonna love it. Got tons of phenomenal peeps here at the J-O-B and my boy, Wayno, told me you're a super-stud, so you'll fit right in. No problemo."

The whirlwind of words came at me so fast I needed a butterfly net to catch them all. I had no idea what to think and no time to think it. Miche continued, "Yo, I got a couple of buddies looking for a third roommate in Ridgefield. It's fifteen minutes from the office, a straight shot down Route One and Nine, about three bills a month. It's a no-brain-er. You're in. I'll make the call right now. Can't wait to meet you, bro. You got my digits. Hit me up anytime. Long story short, I'm here for whatever you need. Stay safe."

Long story short, I didn't know what hit me. My ears were ringing, and my head was spinning, but when I hung up the phone, I smiled for an hour straight. I'd never met anyone as wacky, or hyper, or charismatic, or endearing. His nuttiness was a lot to process, but his kindness put me at ease. Miche answered every question and helped me find a place to live, but more important, he let me know I belonged and convinced me that leaving Massachusetts was the right thing to do. If everyone at NBAE was as generous and exuberant, I'd be taken care of—and I'd be in for a wild ride.

My conversation, or whatever it was, with Miche confirmed finding new friends in Jersey wouldn't be as challenging as I feared. But no one could replace my boys from Chicopee. Since sophomore year of high school, my best friends had been Mark Nadeau and Mike Kijak. We called Nadeau "Nads" (for the obvious reason) and called Kijak "Droopy" (for a less obvious reason: because he had a pudgy, hangdog face like Hanna-Barbera's jowly cartoon hound). The three of us hit it off the second we became teammates, playing soccer, basketball, and baseball at Comp. We had common interests, senses of humor, and upbringings. Nads and Droopy were a grade behind me, but I'd never felt more equal with anyone. We were inseparable. They were my guys, and I wouldn't swap them out because of a new zip code.

The roommates Miche hooked me up with in Ridgefield were good-natured and relatively drama-free. They also got high a lot. My first day at our apartment, they asked if I wanted to "party" and I politely declined. I'd never smoked anything before and didn't want to start, probably because whenever I was offered a joint, my father's voice raised a ruckus in my head.

When I was in middle school, Dad dropped me at a buddy's house near the bus stop each morning. As I hopped out of the car, without fail my pops signed off with the same sayonara: "Hey, keep off the grass." It was a reminder to be my own person and walk my own path, a subtle poke to let me know he cared, a warning for me to be safe and smart and respectful of the rules. Maybe he just didn't want me to use drugs.

Adjusting to a 3:00 p.m. till 11:00 p.m. shift would take time, but I would've slept in the mop closet at NBAE if the job had so required. That schedule, and the newness of my surroundings, made for a strange and solitary start to this life. Those first few nights at the office, I stayed late to reshelve an overflow of tapes on a wagon train of carts. After punching out, I stepped into a dark, empty parking lot as the sulfurous funk of Meadowland swamps invaded my sinuses. Then I drove back to my apartment, jockeying with eighteen-wheelers in a stinky midnight race across the former pig farms of Secaucus, feeling lonely and alone, wishing I could turn back time.

Early on, I focused only on my library duties, proving my worth, tightroping between "friendly" and "aloof." I didn't open up to my coworkers, kept them a Manute-Bol's-arm-length away, offered only the crib notes to my autobiography. Where'd you grow up? Chicopee. Where'd you go to college? UMass. Any siblings? Two older sisters, no brothers. Lying about Robert and David ensured none of these strangers would know my authentic self anytime soon, and I had no reason to let them in on the secret.

My fourth day on the job, disaster struck. Legendary point guard Magic Johnson revealed he had a mysterious virus called HIV, forcing him to retire from the NBA. As news spread, our office turned into a morgue. We crowded around televisions, mouths agape, watching the surreal press conference in silence. Misinformation about the AIDS epidemic created a foggy reality, and a number of my coworkers, friends of Magic's, weren't sure they'd ever see him again. From what any of us knew, HIV was a death sentence.

My emergency assignment that day was to collect every tape containing footage of Magic. My heart thudding, I scanned the aisles for interviews and highlight reels and B-rolls and home videos and field shoots. I was a never-used sub thrown into action, expected to hit a game-winning shot. The spinning basketball world, slowing to a wobble on the fingertip of doom, counted on me to provide the indelible images of one of its greatest heroes—to remind us all who he used to be. Fueled by grief, motivated by shock, I worked through the night.

I returned to my apartment as dawn fought through the window shades, and I collapsed onto my mattress, mind awhirl. Beside me on the bed, the blue spiral notebook I used for letters to Kiki suggested I document the previous day's events, for posterity, if nothing else:

> *Yesterday, Magic Johnson announced that he has the HIV virus which leads to AIDS. He has to retire from basketball. I feel as if a member of my own family has the disease. This is such a shock to the entire world. Magic will handle the situation with grace and dignity. My heart goes out to him. God surely does work in mysterious ways...*

The pen felt good in my hand. And so each day, I continued to write to pull my surroundings closer, to reconcile the road ahead, to ground myself. Mostly, I wrote to relieve the weight of loneliness, or get around it, or settle into it:

> *In a way this is the beginning of my life. It's time to see what I'll become. Being on my own hasn't sunk in yet. Maybe that's because I consider myself continuing on, not starting over. I refuse to leave my old life behind. I'll find a way to bridge the gap between yesterday and tomorrow...*

> *I've been so lucky with all of this. An exciting job, a great apartment, and cool roommates just appeared right in front of my face. Everything, so far, has fallen into place without my making much of an effort. Someone is looking out for me. What I make of all of this is the question now. I'm ready...*

By the looks of things, I'll be spending a lot of time at the office. It's my only priority now. Until Kiki comes home, most all my time will be spent at work. I believe when I feel confident with the job, I'll fit in perfectly with this company. Strange how dramatically everything has changed. I wonder how I'll cope with the change in myself...

That notebook, bulging with ideas and questions and affirmations, was my copilot on a peculiar journey. Every day during those solitary weeks, in my boring bedroom at 370 Broad Avenue, I sat at my PlanMaster drafting table and explored my feelings on paper. My parents had given me the drafting table as a college graduation gift, a gesture that drudged up the dilemma I'd faced as a teen: pursue a career in sports or apply to art school. But being an artist was never my goal. I dreamed of being the art.

After moving to Jersey, as I spent less time drawing and more time journaling, I began to see life in words instead of pictures, a transition that had been years in the making. The creative writing bug had bitten me during Mrs. Chelte's AP English course in high school, and the purity of poetry left a conspicuous welt. At college, I composed my first poems (more hormonal than ártistic) in a sappy attempt to tell a crush how my heart bled for her. After we broke up, I wrote even more to tie off the hemorrhaging. Now I'd fallen into myself, got stuck under the heaviness of homesickness, and asked poetry to save me again.

I couldn't waste the opportunity. This chance, this career, was all I'd ever wanted. I needed to let go of the past, needed to focus on what might be, not what was. The universe would help but couldn't do the heavy lifting alone. Desperate to express myself, I wrote a poem, a mantra of sorts, pushing me to stake a claim in the world before it was too late:

"The Eyes of Fate"

The Eyes of Fate leer deep and dark but never hold their stare.

A shifted glare from soul to soul fulfills an answered prayer.

The blinded vision of our hope has one lone chance to clear,

For in this life the light is dim, and darkness emits fear.

A captured image in the mind makes no attempt to flee,

But if the dream stays locked inside, the walls are all we see.

When blurried hearts by future's mist discern not love from hate,

Embrace your prayer and fix a stare to catch the Eyes of Fate.

Aristide & Anna

If Dad had told me about his grandparents from Quebec, if I had more to go on than what I gleaned from a few old photos and a subscription to Ancestry.com, then I would've understood my family's origins. If only I'd asked what he knew of those people and why they came to America, there'd be more basis for this immigrant story.

It's 1887...

A scrawny boy—too old to be a kid, too young to be a man—sits in a barren field behind a saggy farmhouse leaning together to hold itself up. A wood and wire rabbit cage rests at his feet. The Canadian sun, not yet risen.

In the front of the house, his mother packs the last of the family's belongings onto a horse-drawn wagon and calls to her son. He ignores her, unfastens the metal hook on the cage, and lets his rabbits free. A gray-and-white-flecked female bounces out, stays by the boy's feet, noses a single blade of grass. A long-eared brown male remains in the pen.

"Go!" the boy commands, voice cracking. "Hurry!"

He rattles the cage, shoos his pets away, clapping loudly. The startled animals scurry across the sandy field and into the darkness. The boy bids his furry companions goodbye with words his father uses when downing shots of whiskey with friends: "*A tout mieux tout,*" loosely meaning "All the best" in their native French. As the alcohol soaks in, his father always adds a cheerful salutation: "*Hiya!*"

The boy knows his rabbits won't last a day in the wild without a fox or falcon making a meal of them. If he could keep them, he would, but his parents allow only bare necessities on the trip to America. He wipes his eyes and whispers the useless salutation again, "*A tout mieux tout. Hiya!*"

His father, this time, calls. "Joseph Aristide! Come now!" The boy stands, dusts off his woolen knickers, and kicks the cage with as much might as his thirteen-year-old body can summon. He runs to the front of the house and hops into the back of the moving wagon. The old mare clops away.

Joseph Aristide Gagne, born to parents Eugine and Mary in the town of L'Ancienne-Lorette—a serene Quebec lumber hub on the banks of the St. Lawrence River, fifty miles north of Maine—is known by his middle name. Derived from the Greek *aristos*, meaning "best," and *eidos*, meaning "species," the title carries grand expectations. The bold boy welcomes the challenge.

For over a century, descendants of the Gagne family have populated the Great White North like snowshoe hares. The surname originates from the Old French *gagner*, an occupational name for "peasant" or "farmer," not to be confused with the verb *gagnier*, meaning "to win." (Peasants and farmers in Quebec are far from winners.) Common as a moose sighting in the region, the name begs the standard joke, *No Canadian need drink alone, because there's always at least one Gagne at the bar.*

He'd been a grower of grain, but Eugine Gagne bailed on

his fields when his crops failed to yield and tested his luck at the lumber mills. When New England states offered higher pay and St. Lawrence millers buzzed south, the lure of the American Dream called. So early that morning, along a dusty road, Eugine shepherds his family past acres of infertile farmland, land given up on by men like him.

The Quebec City train station teems with confusion and excitement. Whistles blow, conductors shout, parents cry for children to keep up while dragging luggage bursting with a lifetime of memories. Young Aristide dodges a blitz of middle-aged women who gallop against the herd, plastering posters on walls warning about the dangers of the smallpox vaccine. The befuddled boy can't comprehend the group's ignorance, their indifference to reading or science. He'd seen the "Red Death" up close, two years prior. The nightmarish epidemic slayed a quarter of the residents in his hometown, including seven classmates, an entire family from the local parish, and his best friend, Lucien.

"Aristide! Come!"

The Gagnes' train of renewal chugs twelve hours south, following the serpentine Connecticut River toward its final destination: Holyoke, Massachusetts. The shining rails hum to themselves something about another world and how to get there. For the duration of the trip, Aristide runs his tongue over a chipped front tooth, busted years earlier by their ornery mare's wayward hoof. Bewitched by the glittery river, he envisions American streets paved with gold, like all the stories say. But when the Paper City's newest immigrants disembark, they step flat-footed onto an ordinary avenue of lackluster bricks. Aristide wonders if his rabbits are dead yet.

In Holyoke, the Gagnes live in a degraded row house with Mary's cousins from Quebec and labor in the factories alongside Eugine's friends from the St. Lawrence lumber mill. Brutal living and working conditions—combined with pay of seventy-five cents per day—test the newcomers' patience and will. But the hearty Canucks grind it out.

Their arrival triggers resentment among local Irish workers who accuse French Canadians of lowering the city's standards and destroying the fragile American way of life. Despite being former targets of anti-immigration prejudice themselves, the nativists decry the uninvited greenhorns, label them "a horde of invaders" with no intention to assimilate. The Gagnes brush off the accusations and become a fixture in Holyoke, another small but significant cog in the machine. The industrious city presses ahead.

At eighteen, Aristide has dreams loftier than any smokestack on any mill. He picks up extra work at night (laying concrete pilings for the Willimansett Bridge connecting Holyoke to Chicopee) and scrooges away his money. His fortunes increase two years later when he's introduced to Anna Quenneville. She's only sixteen, speaks broken English leaning toward dilapidated, hides spunk under shyness, but she knows love when she feels it.

As the only daughter of ten children born to parents Louis Quenneville and Mary Fartan, Anna's treated like a queen in her family but downplays the privilege, toughens up, and keeps pace with her brothers. After arriving in Holyoke from St. Anicet in Quebec at thirteen, she'd quit school to work twelve-hour days in the cotton mills. Trying to keep up with her studies, she fell asleep face-first in her English textbook each night. A beauty with round eyes, olive skin, and hair like corn silk, Anna wears an ever-present shawl to cover up her one physical drawback: clusters of white blotches speckling her shoulders and neck, passed down from her mother. She pays little mind to the blemishes, having been raised to believe, "Things could always be worse."

In 1896, Aristide and Anna marry. Looking to succeed where his father had failed, Aristide purchases a farm in South Hadley. His new wife doesn't love the idea. Her father had been a farmer too, and she remembers how he reaped far less than he sowed. By seventeen, Anna has a house, a husband, and a child to look after. Underlying all that is the language barrier she can't overcome. She understands her neighbors well enough but has trouble expressing herself. Her frustration builds. The eighteenth-century farmhouse has few conveniences. Water is drawn from a well in the center of the kitchen. The stove is fed with wood. Kerosene lamps hang like dim bats from the rafters, doling out little light. The toilet is outside.

Eleven years stagger by, and five rambunctious kids fill the house. The sixth child, one-year-old Wilfred, doesn't develop as quickly as the others and dies of pneumonia. Anna blindly accepts the tragedy as the will of God. She gives birth to a seventh five months later.

Aristide works outstretched hours tending to livestock and toiling over crops. During busy summer months, he takes in orphaned "State Boys" for extra help. Overloaded with kids and chores, Anna gets a minute's rest only on doctor's orders after the difficult birth of her eighth child. As the mouths to feed multiply, Aristide drinks away the commotion, numbing the ache of a backbreaking existence.

In 1918, the Great War produces two powerful enemies: Germany, and an insidious virus close-quartered soldiers spread worldwide. Beginning in early autumn, the influenza pandemic ravages New England and levels South Hadley. Night and day, carriages carry caskets past the old farmhouse on Amherst Road, the incessant clip-clop of horse hooves a constant reminder of the uncontrollable death toll. Bodies pile up on the roadside.

The Gagne children cough up blood. Their temperatures skyrocket. Their skin turns hibiscus blue. Their parents struggle to save the family and the fields, staying indoors whenever possible. Aristide mixes potions of whiskey and lemon to fight fevers. Anna cuts up her cotton shawls, sews them into face masks.

In the heart of spring, on a moonless evening, the Gagnes' youngest and most fragile child, ten-month-old Gerard, dies in Anna's arms. The following morning, in a field of buttercups far behind the house, beyond the unwavering watch of the apple orchard, Aristide digs another small grave for another infant son. Then with no choice but to move on, he buries Gerard next to Wilfred.

In the sweep of eight months, the flu slaughters fifty-thousand souls in Massachusetts, including a sister-in-law of Anna's. The Gagnes take in the deceased woman's two-year-old son and raise him as their own. Grateful to have survived, Anna embraces any amount of extra work and stitches her shredded family back together.

After two more children, the brood totals twelve: six boys and six girls. The eldest son, eighteen-year-old Rheo, respects how hard his mother works without complaint, admires her fight in the face of tragedy. To help her, to *really* help her, he needs to leave the farm. He has big ideas and the confidence to see them through.

Thomas & Elizabeth

If Mom had told me about her grandparents from Scotland, if I had more info than what I'd found on Wikipedia and an outdated website about the Colthart clan, then I'd know why they left their homeland. If only I'd asked Pop-Pop while he was still alive, I could do more than just imagine what that journey, or that decision, was like for his family.

It's 1892...

"Shut up, Coulthartus!" the children of Muirkirk scream, unruly and heinous, like gallowglass mercenaries back from hell.

Ten-year-old Thomas shrinks in his chair as his schoolmates yell and laugh and tease. The mushroom-brown walls of the classroom close in. If it weren't for a severe stutter—tangling his tongue since he first donned a tartan kilt—he'd yell back, maybe take a swing. If using words were an option, he'd stand up for himself. Instead, he withdraws, blaming the father he never knew, the man who left his mother with nothing but a baby to care for and a name to curse.

"Scabby. Smelly. Rotten. Colthart!" The insults crash down on him like frozen waves against the craggy Scottish shore.

In his quest for identity, Thomas has done the research, knows his surname is from the Old English occupational word meaning "colt herdsman." Knows its varied spellings: Coulthart, Colthard, Colthert, Coltert, and Coulthard. Understands that his clan originated from a far-reaching line of poor tenant farmers.

He also knows the alternative story, an unbelievable legend claiming the earliest Coltharts were medieval lords with influence all across Scotland. But young Thomas is no fool. He's aware this lie was generated by a wealthy banker named John Ross Colthart who, desperate to prove his noble lineage, hired a pedigree-maker to fabricate the story of a mountainous Roman lieutenant called Coulthartus. According to the legend, this herculean figure conquered Scotland in 79 AD and married the daughter of a local chief, bearing descendants who are linked to Scotland's most significant historical events. But with no evidence or documents to back these wild claims, legitimate nobles ridicule the Colthart name, reducing it to the butt of a joke.

"You're nothing, Coulthartus. Just a poor bastard," yawp the children.

Thomas Morton Colthart—born out of wedlock to a domestic servant named Margaret Allan Colthart—spends his days alone. He's awkward and shy, charming as a foot cramp, teased for more than his name and its bogus history. Beneath a solemn front, he fumes.

"You shan't fight back," his mother orders. "You must be safe. You and me Thomas, we are all we have."

The boy stays quiet as a mourner, takes the name-calling and cursing and abuse, holds his tongue and his anger inside until the unlikeliest of saviors charges in like a cavalry. Books become his shields, fending off the world's arrows; words and pages, his steady and fierce comrades; literature, his coat of arms.

At sixteen, he moves to Maryhill—"Venice of the North"— to work the mills, but this raucous canal suburb of Glasgow is a poor fit for the introvert. The burly banks appeal to shipbuilding, saw-milling, and iron-founding. The city serves as the center of Scotland's glassmaking industry as well, but it's no place for a breakable boy like Thomas.

Day in and out, he works at the mill then heads straight home to Tolstoy, Hawthorne, Whitman, and Poe. He doesn't carouse. Doesn't imbibe. Never has. Outside grimy pubs, he's pushed around by drunken louts with nothing to lose but a bellyful of haggis and ale. Hooligans fill Maryhill's violent streets. In response to the lawlessness, the UK's first temperance society issues a ban on alcohol. But rules are not for hooligans, and this city's not for Thomas.

Wishing the years away, he fantasizes about an escape, a fresh start, an exile even, to a place where no one knows his name. He's not the only one dreaming. During Thomas Colthart's bleak life so far, a quarter million other Scots—with restless fantasies of their own—desert the glens, moorlands, and isles with sights set on the emerald promise of the United States.

Late in his twenties, with thinning hair and thinner skin, Thomas falls in love with Elizabeth "Lizzie" Doyle, a doting sort from Lanarkshire with a lazy eye and a sympathetic ear. Drawn to each other in the indescribable way a sailor is drawn to the sea, they wed on a New Year's Eve in a soundless courthouse, hours before din and debauchery transform Maryhill into Gomorrah.

Splurging on copper cups of sparkling cider, they toast their future together.

Clunk.

Secure in matrimony, and soon parenthood, Thomas and Lizzie stash away every shilling, pound, and merk with the goal of raising their young family in America. Nine years pass before, at last, Thomas breaks free from Maryhill's shackles and makes his long-anticipated transatlantic journey. He sails from Glasgow to Boston, seeking work in Massachusetts mill towns while Lizzie and her four children wait for word.

Two months later, on a dank May morn, Lizzie receives a telegram from Thomas, as promised, announcing a viable job and secured housing. She and the youngsters—Tom Jr., Annie, James, and Robert—board the *Numidian,* bound for America, huddled among masses shaking off their own shackles, hunting their own futures. Rocked in the Atlantic's turbulent arms, Lizzie comforts her anxious pack in a tiny cabin, setting them adrift in sleep with a time-worn Scottish ballad.

> *Oh ye'll take the high road and I'll take the low road*
>
> *And I'll be in Scotland afore ye*
>
> *For me and my true love will never meet again*
>
> *On the bonnie, bonnie banks of Loch Lomond*

After six days at sea, Lizzie reunites with her husband at Boston Harbor, and the family travels by train, forty miles west, destined for a town called Whitinsville. As the locomotive clickety-clacks through Boston, past the gates of the Huntington Avenue Baseball Grounds, nine-year-old Tom Jr. watches a man on a ladder fastening giant wooden letters onto a marquee: *Tomorrow: Chicago White Sox vs. Boston Red Sox.* He shuts his eyes and dreams about his hero George Chalmers—a Scottish baseball player from Aberdeen—who plays for the Philadelphia Phillies. Young Tom enjoyed soccer back in Scotland, but it's clear to him that America's love is baseball, and he can't wait to join in the game.

Split by the Mumford River, Whitinsville turns a new chapter for the Coltharts. While Tom Jr. shines at school, his father labors grinding tools—quiet and diligent and ceaseless—at Whitin Machine Works, once the largest textile machinery company in the world. Though he's no longer the butt of jokes, Thomas Sr. grows more strict, more serious. No one here knows his heritage, or the true meaning behind his name. No one pokes fun at him. He needn't be ashamed. But the damage has been done. Hard-bitten and distant, he remains true and open only to his books.

With few close friends, the Coltharts keep to themselves, methodically going about their business with the humdrum monotony of entranced bees. Lizzie mirrors her husband's demeanor, tending to her home and her children in machine-like fashion. She scrubs laundry by hand and puts food on the table, all the while insisting her kids mind their manners and their place. She outlaws laziness, discourages silliness, and firmly forbids cursing.

As the years improve, the family marches on in silence, stoicism, and work. At seventeen, Tom Jr. graduates high school and leaves Whitinsville, refuting how his father has shut out the world, rejecting such a narrow existence. He won't be like that shallow man. He'll take advantage of America. He'll travel. He'll enjoy life. He'll speak his mind. He'll be proud.

The wee birds will sing and the wildflowers spring

And in sunshine the waters are sleeping

The broken heart will ken nae second spring again

And the world does not know how we're grievin'

Initially I kept my distance from the crew at NBAE, but they flicked away my Heisman stiff-arm and horse-collared me into their open hearts.

Enticing me to let my guard down, these insta-friends—this multi-striped company of thieves—turned out to be the perfect remedy for my homesickness. All of us were in our twenties or thirties, most of us single and from somewhere else, and we accepted one another fully. Our outgoing band of smart-alecky sports fanatics, our fraternity, bonded like nothing I'd known, and it was exactly what I needed.

Like grade-schoolers, we gave each other nicknames; there was Miche (of course), plus Nooch, Santa, X, Goldie, B-Small, TK, Money, Pod, AT, Clato, and Lep. Some we called by last names only, such as Logue, Koontz, Robblee, Graves, Bornstein, Morgan, and Schwartz. And a select few by first names, like Alvin, Dion, Sean, and Keith. And there were others, many others, too many to name.

I was "Gags" on my first day.

The super-chill atmosphere in our Secaucus office floored me, and the entertainment quotient was off the charts. Along with our emotional cohesion, the physicality of our affection added to the informal vibe and glued us together. We greeted each other with bro-hugs every morning. We busted out ridiculous jokes and puns all day long, jumping into each other's arms, exploding in laughter. When saying goodbye after work, we dapped up and hugged as if separating forever—and we hugged again at a bar an hour later. This secure show of male admiration, this genuine tenderness, hadn't existed for me in Chicopee.

People back home were friendly and helpful, but an old-country stoicism tamped down effusive displays of warmth, especially among men and boys. Dads acted tough and expected the same from their sons. The dourness of their immigrant experience—whether from Quebec or Glasgow or Dublin or Warsaw—flowed in their bloodstreams like intravenous rivers of repression. A cynical undercurrent had Chicopee's foreign-born forefathers holding their breath, reticent to relax, for fear the next wave of immigrants would pour over the horizon and sweep them off the hill that took forever to climb.

In those early days at NBA Entertainment, my friends and I enjoyed an otherworldly interconnection (unlike ordinary earthly relationships) which energized my soul. Like my boy Koontz, NBAE's godfather of Zen, would say: "The cosmic shit we got here is fuckin' sci-fi, man." Pretty much summed it up.

We were a bare-your-soul, fly-your-flag, Technicolor melting pot of every ingredient—Jewish, Christian, Muslim, atheist, straight, bi, gay, Black, Asian, Hispanic, white—intertwined with reliance and camaraderie. We were players on the same team, each of us entrusted with a respected and important role. As corny as it sounds, those diverse people and that new belief system completed me.

In Chicopee, like in tons of white suburbs, Black culture existed everywhere and nowhere simultaneously. Hit TV shows like *The Fresh Prince of Bel-Air* and *The Cosby Show* made themselves comfortable in our living rooms. Michael Jackson, the "King of Pop," moonwalked across our radio waves. *Saturday Night Live* star Eddie Murphy put the boogie in all of our butts with his explosive comedy. And Michael "Air" Jordan defied the laws of gravity—and marketing projections—by throwing vicious dunks on the heads of opponents and stylish sneakers on the feet of an entire demographic.

But those people didn't exist in my *real* life back then. Most faces I saw were the same color as the one looking at me in the mirror while checking for zits each morning. Of the twelve hundred kids in my Chicopee Comp High School, the core were either Polish or French Canadian, a Caucasian collage of consonants and vowels: a Kirejczyk and Szlachetka here; a Boissonneault and Thibodeau there. In terms of racial diversity, there were twice as many syllables in Zigmund Winiarski's full name than African American students in my senior class.

Overt acts of racism were uncommon, but still, the toxins of prejudice and ignorance tainted our waters, ingested by the white man I knew across town, for example, who didn't let his daughters watch Black television programs. And I recall standing among pasty preteens during schoolyard dustups as they egged on opponents with a slur-riddled chant:

Fight. Fight. A N— and a white.
Who's the N— and who's the white?

It'd be easy to say we didn't know better.

When I was sixteen, my sisters had bought me a Run-DMC tape cassette for Christmas. The second I popped that sucker into my boombox, my view of America changed in a flash. With pounding breakbeats and lyrics reading like a PSA, the opening track, "Hard Times," turned the tables on my taste in tunes and opened a window to a wider world. The foundational elements of hip-hop scratched my artistic itch, transformed me with its honesty and freedom of expression, its creativity and powerful messaging, its pure brilliance. And the more I listened, the more embarrassed and angered I became at the injustices people of color had faced forever in the United States.

The political rap group Public Enemy schooled me on Huey P. Newton, Mary McCloud Bethune, Elijah Muhammed, Marcus Garvey, and Malcolm X. (My white-washed history books at Fairview Elementary hadn't touted these giants of African American activism.) KRS-One and Boogie Down Productions imparted their philosophy about how hip-hop was like poetry, innovative and educational. Hitting hardest, Grand Master Flash and The Furious Five rapped a blunt message decrying the broken streets of urban America, places like New York City, a foreign land to me, in an opposite reality.

Now in 1991, I found myself living in the shadow of that distressed city—a three-mile drive across the George Washington Bridge—where I discovered a strange, nourishing, polychromatic world. Awakened to this swath of society, I swam in a sense of wholeness, my world expanding and shrinking at the same time.

Compared to my new crop of buddies, I was a hick off a hay wagon. I didn't swear (much) or drink (a lot) or smoke weed (ever), but those guys respected me. And though I loved who I was, who I'd always be, I stole pieces of my new friends to refurbish myself. Their oversized personalities flavored my heart, outrageous senses of humor tickled my ribs, and eclectic wealth of knowledge challenged my brain. Moving from Chicopee to Jersey was like bolting the sterile studio set of *Leave it to Beaver* and strolling onto the unpredictable movie lot of *Animal House*.

More aptly, I compared my life at the time to the tale of *Peter Pan*, where a group of Lost Boys lived in a fantastical place called Never-Never Land and didn't ever want to grow up. And secretly, my NBA "brothers" and I made an unspoken pact to stay young, and stay together, forever. They taught me how to open up, encouraged me to be bold and boundless, exemplified how to express affection physically *and* verbally. Along with all their hugs, these guys used and reused the phrase "love you" like it was oxygen. My family had never said those magic words to each other, didn't know how. I'm not sure if *any* family in Chicopee did, but I was certain this discovery, this emotional allowance, would change me.

The person I wanted to be had to release his heart, needed

to let it all out. And it was time to open the floodgates, starting with the way I regarded my mother.

During my high school and college years, Mom had lost a brother, sister, father, and a best friend. My sympathy and compassion for her grew stronger then, and when I left home for good, she evolved into a friend whom I cared for, instead of a mother whose care I required. But now we were apart for the first time, and I missed her. Her mom, my nana, was in the hospital toying around with death (she'd tease that poor guy for another ten years), and that uncertainty, combined with "Dad being Dad," sequestered my mother into a dark corner of the sad room that had become her life. I'd abandoned her and our new-found friendship just when she needed me most. A few weeks after I moved, I wrote her a letter to stay connected, to apologize for leaving, and to tell her, finally, that I loved her:

Mom—As I sit at my desk, staring blankly at the bedroom wall, I try to put the words of a poem together for you. I can't do it. Because what I want to express to you, what I feel, cannot be written or even spoken. In a strange way I feel helpless. There are so many things I want to say, to write. Simple words, though, do not do you justice. You deserve so much more than words.

Mom, since I've been away, something has changed inside me. I guess it's a change that comes to most sons and daughters when they finally move away from home. It's a growing pang of sorts, I suppose, a mixture of feelings including loss, pride, shame, respect, and a totally overwhelming sense of love. This all happened because of you.

Moving away from you and the rest of our family was the hardest thing I've ever had to deal with. There was never a question about my taking the job. It was the perfect opportunity and an obvious decision. But, inside, I resented having to leave you all.

Everything is different now. I've realized what I'd always taken for granted, and it's changed me. Don't go thinking that I've miraculously experienced some great metamorphosis. You know, I wasn't such a bad guy before. It's just that colors have a way of changing shade when seen through different eyes.

Now I see how much you did for me, for all of us. I appreciated it then, but I admire and thank you for it now. You put love into every shirt you ironed, every nose you wiped, and every game or practice you drove me to. It's that capacity to love that sets you apart from all other women. No one gives her love more willingly or unconditionally than you, Mom.

You gave me life, and all that I have in this life. I cannot repay you for that. All I can give you is the same kind of love that you've given me for twenty-four years. It's all I have, and it is because of you that I have it.

Now that I've changed, maybe we can start this relationship all over again. There was nothing wrong with it before, but we're on another level now. I won't always be your little boy, but I'll always be your son. You mean the world to me. I love you so much.

In the meantime, I recalibrated my relationship with Dad too. After my initial interview at NBAE, he encouraged me to push for the job and was proud of my decision to move. But when I left, he lost his only ally, the person who understood and tolerated him most. With my sisters also out of the house, Dad had only himself to keep him company and no one to monitor his drinking habit (but the empty nest and a full glass suited him just fine, thank you).

During my visits to Chicopee, he still treated me like a kid, making me Dagwood-style sandwiches, filling my car with gas, bristling in the morning if I got home too late the night before. I humored him, accepted every offering, appreciated every kindness.

The lawsuit filed against Gagne & Sons had bulldozed him to the verge of bankruptcy and threatened to shove him into the pit. Though he had every right to give up, he pushed back. Out of full-time work, and almost out of money at sixty years old, he took charity jobs for little cash but never lost his treasured pride and zany wit. He and I missed each other back then, for unrelated reasons, and he did his best to keep the connection:

Hey, what's up Ken?

Topic: Your Employment

So happy to hear your present position is an enjoyable one. There is no doubt in my great mind that it will lead to unbelievable progress in the future.

Topic: Your Love Life

Are you still hearing from Kiki as often? Are things still difficult for her to adapt? I understand you have your eyes on a couple of cuties at work. Remember abstinence is the best protective measure.

Topic: My Love Life

Topic: Nana's Condition

Unbelievable what this lady has been through at her age and still survives. Mom and Auntie Elaine went last night, and she was doing extremely well, but Mom got a call a few minutes ago from Auntie Gail to say they had to pump her stomach today and put her back on IV. I still feel she will make it.

Topic: My Employment

Still putting a few hours in each week at the consignment house then go home and change in ten minutes and start pumping gas at Legate's for a couple of hours. I expect to put in more hours after the first of the year when Ron's father goes to Florida. Very possible to make $300 to $500 per week.

Topic: Financial and Legal Situation

Too lengthy to explain. Should know more this coming week after meeting with my attorney.

Topic: Bits & Pieces

Linda and I got the tree this past week. It's up in the living room, looks good. Had a drink with Mr. Desormier last night at the Four-Ten then went to Mel's with Uncle Gerry and had a great prime rib. Mom's lying on the couch resting and I'm watching the Patriots & Jets while writing this letter. As soon as she starts snoring, I'll sneak downstairs and have a beer and watch Current Affair. Hope you're able to decipher this great penmanship that I have. I learned it at the University of Hard Knocks, and it wasn't even my major.

Looking forward to seeing you. Stay cool, stay calm, and stay sober. Check your oil and keep your gas tank filled.

Love, "The Greatest"

Topic: Postscript

Keep off the grass!

FOUR

"You Ain't Seen Nothin' Yet"

Spring, 1979

MY SIXTH-GRADE TEACHER, Mr. Burgess, left the classroom with instructions for his students to "silently" read an assigned chapter in our history book. No talking whatsoever.

To ensure obedience, he appointed the upstanding Laura Day in charge of recording the names of any rabble-rousing rule violators. Sturdy in front of the chalkboard, beaming with honor and distinction, Sergeant Day surveyed the room as mild chatter grew among a few students.

My best bud, Craig Patla, and I pushed our metal desks together, unrolled a supersized sheet of newsprint across the top, and sketched an army battle scene. He stationed his men on one side of a cliff, while I did the same on the other. Between us, we shaded in a watery divide. We supplied our cartoon soldiers with an armory of weapons and took turns drawing up military maneuvers against our enemy. In relative quiet, we illustrated tanks and planes, boats and submarines. We exaggerated silly sound effects, our bombs hush-booming and machine guns whisper-rattling.

The rest of the room exploded into chaos. Laura scribbled names on the board as if she were transcribing a high-speed recording of the Magna Carta. The rat-a-tat-tat of her markings flurried all around, chips of chalk spraying like shrapnel. After twenty minutes of unintentional comedy, Mr. Burgess returned to a written tally of eleven misbehaved students, eleven fallen soldiers memorialized on slate, lost to a senseless and selfish crusade. Last name on the list: *Kenny Gagne.*

I turned to Craig. He pulled his desk apart from mine, shrugged, and hung his head, a fortunate survivor, afraid to say "sorry" out loud.

While most of the class read the previously assigned unit from our history book, Mr. Burgess sentenced me and the other delinquents to *write out* the ten-page chapter. I'd never brushed against a trace of trouble at school before, and I stewed at a pariah's desk in the back corner, unfairly accused. As I copied the text, chest pounding, my no. 2 pencil grated the loose-leaf, leaving behind a trail of crumbled graphite.

Mount Vesuvius destroyed the city of Pompeii in 79 AD. Because the city was buried so quickly by volcanic ash, the site is a well-preserved snapshot of life in a Roman city…

For an hour, I wrote…

Because seismic activity was so common in the area, citizens paid little attention when several quakes shook the earth beneath Pompeii. People were unprepared for the explosion that took place shortly after noon on the twenty-fourth of August...

And wrote...

Ash blocked the sun by 1:00 p.m. and the people tried to clear heavy ash from rooftops as it fell at a rate of about six inches per hour...

And wrote...

A glowing cloud of volcanic gases and debris rolled down Vesuvius's slopes and enveloped the city of Pompeii. Most victims died instantly as the superheated air burned their lungs and contracted their muscles, leaving the bodies in a semi-curled position to be quickly buried in ash and thus preserved in detail for hundreds of years...

Writer's cramp locked my knuckles. I slid the nubby pencil behind my ear, shook out the numbness in my hand, and my anger melted into compassion. How selfish of me, upset over my petty penance, justified or not, when these innocent lives had been lost. The sheer sadness of Pompeii's devastation grabbed me, absorbed me into the suffering, and photographs of the victims—their fossilized faces screaming petrified screams—seared into my skull.

I shuffled homeward atop a creepy-crawly carpet of gypsy moth caterpillars laid out on the schoolyard sidewalk. Replaying the unfortunate events of the day, I unwittingly murdered scores of innocuous fuzzies, my Pro-Keds wreaking havoc like weapons of mass destruction. Cleaning bug guts off my sneaker soles was the least of my problems. How was I going to tell my mother I got in trouble? I imagined giving her the note Mr. Burgess had demanded she sign, and my stomach turned. I didn't fully understand the recent radioactive disaster at Three Mile Island, but I guessed Mom's reactor was about to overheat, emitting deadly waves of disappointment, causing a nuclear meltdown.

Approaching our house, I noted a beat-up white Monte Carlo in the driveway, Gagne & Sons sticker prominent on the rear bumper. Why was my father home from work so early? Chin on my chest, I trudged up our steps, pushed open the door, dropped my book bag onto the breezeway floor, and slunk toward the living room, and what sounded like my mother crying. My only thought: the school principal had called ahead.

Then I saw her, barely recognizable, hunched over on the couch, head in hands, chest heaving. This could not have been *my* fault. Assessing the scene, I held my tongue for a second before asking a question I didn't want the answer to: "What happened?"

My father leaned against the picture window, one hand in his pocket, the other holding an empty glass, and waited on his wife to respond. Outside, the Connecticut River flowed quietly in the distance, as if hiding a secret. Trying to compose herself, my mom struggled to speak. Hyperventilating, she wiped her tears with her sweater sleeve and mustered what little strength she had. "David died."

The pain of those two words broke the person who was once my mother, and she wailed. Her soul bent, then cracked, and the fissure sucked in her drastic cries. I turned to my dad for assurance, for comfort, for a cue. He was made of stone, but shame bubbled beneath the stiff surface. We faced each other, father and son, incompetent to rescue the woman I assumed we both loved. And in that moment, I understood what he lacked. Mom didn't deserve this. Didn't deserve him.

Unable to quell the mounting hurt, I settled beside her quaking body. David's life had been a dormant volcano waiting to erupt, his ending inevitable. But we ignored its certainty, leaving us unprepared to deal with the fallout. The sky raining cinders of anguish, Chicopee was our Pompeii, and the burning ash of my brother's death froze our family in time.

One month shy of his seventeenth birthday, David was gone. Much too soon it seemed, but a child born with the severity of his condition had a life expectancy of less than five years. Once he passed ten, the experts considered it a miracle. The cause of death was pneumonia, technically. The doctors told my mother it would end that way. They explained, clearly and clinically, that as fluid built up in her son's lungs, he'd lack the strength and mobility to fight infection. He'd labor to breathe and, eventually, wouldn't survive. But Mom refused to accept the sterile prognosis and hoped against hope, since the day she gave him up, that David would live a lengthy life. He couldn't walk or talk or see or hear, but she prayed her love would keep his heart beating.

And it did. For a while.

Lifting his eyes from what used to be a full glass of scotch, my father scowled at the window like a former assailant. Not the time for joking or teasing, his only alternative was saying nothing. This once-handsome man, balding and overweight, appeared older than forty-eight. Dark-rimmed glasses framing distant eyes, he shifted from leg to leg, as if the subtle movement might compensate for his silence. Behind him, my mother eroded, her sobs intertwining with the clink of ice cubes filling the hollow air.

My dad was a good man, did his best, I was sure. But on this gray afternoon in May, in this blue-collar Western Massachusetts town, his best wasn't good enough. And he knew it.

The doctors had implied this was his fault; Tay-Sachs disease was more common among people of French-Canadian descent. Ever since that accusation, he tried to shake off the shame while struggling to find someone else—or *something* else—to blame.

Absolution was his white whale, but the beast had escaped him under waves of self-pity and guilt. So for sixteen years my father hunted an elusive scapegoat, only to haul up a clean harpoon after each desperate hurl.

I watched him there, staring out the window, empty glass and empty heart, as the diabolical river mocked him to his face, and the force of David's death drove a wedge between him and his wife.

Rheo & Annette

If Dad had told me how his parents established themselves in Chicopee, if I had more concrete knowledge than a few offhand comments from relatives, then I'd realize what motivated my grandparents to succeed. If only I'd asked Memere to share her stories while I had the chance, I wouldn't have to make this one up.

It's 1930…

In the raw of November, the steel joints of the Willimansett Bridge crick and wrench like arthritic elbows, on a night so black it's blank. In the shadows below, near the river's edge, a boat drifts toward two teenagers waiting in the weeds, dressed in dark clothing.

Behind them, on the sloped embankment, a metal door opens in the thicket and a coarse whisper floats out, soft yet prickly, like pine straw carpeting a forest floor. "Let's go, boys. Put some ants in those pants. You've got school tomorrow, and I'm not paying you fifty bucks each to stand around."

"Yes sir, Mr. Gagne," the enthusiastic high schoolers reply, wading into the seamless water and pulling the boat ashore.

Moving with the swift intention of a double-play combination, the boys carry two dozen wooden crates from the barge, up the embankment, and through the camouflaged door, disappearing into an underground tunnel leading to the dank cellar of a well-disguised speakeasy. In the cellar, the teen workers tuck the crates under loose floorboards and behind hidden wall panels. Safely stashed, countless bottles of gin, whiskey, beer, and vodka breathe easy while awaiting allocation throughout Chicopee.

Rheo Gagne doesn't own this place, but he runs the show.

A thirty-two-year-old married man with two young children and one on the way, the entrepreneur's legal business, fixing and trading cars, performs well while his illegal business, importing and selling alcohol, booms. Prohibition proves no match for the clever Canuck, his smuggles courtesy of local fishermen in Long Island, hired to sail into international waters at Montauk Point and await freighters from Nova Scotia, Bermuda, and Cuba. These lawless captains on "Rum Row" transfer the contraband onto secondary crafts for distribution along the Northeast coastline, including a half dozen stops on the Connecticut River. And every two weeks, they deliver to this house skulking in the shadow of the Willimansett Bridge.

As the high school boys haul the last of the cargo into the basement, and Rheo settles up with the rum runner's captain, two police cars skid to a stop in front of the house and spit out four husky men waving flashlights. Rheo recognizes the warning, the squeal and stink of rubber, and hops off the boat, sinking ankle-deep in the muck. "Au revoir," he mouths to the captain, adding a salute and a grin. He's always ready with his next move.

At sixteen, Rheo worked nonstop splitting time between the family farm in South Hadley and the paper mills in Holyoke. As President Wilson sent troops overseas to face down the Germans, the teen hustled for the kind of life those brave men fought to preserve. When the war ended, the soldiers returned with honor—and the influenza virus that killed Rheo's baby brother.

In dogged pursuit of his future, he left South Hadley at eighteen, relocating to Holyoke to work full-time in the mills. Cramped in a rundown flat with other marginalized first-generation immigrants, he socked away most of his eight bucks per week and spent the leftovers on whiskey shots for fellow French Canadians across the bridge, late nights poisoning his liver in Chicopee dissolving into early mornings breaking his back in Holyoke. For six years, he hopscotched across that bridge—from mill to bar, bar to mill—carrying his contagious laugh, infectious smile, and irrepressible taste for alcohol, symptoms of a social epidemic he spread like a plague. He rarely slept, never turned down a bender, and wrung every drop out of every day. Intent on making more of his life than his father had, he left the farm far behind.

On his twenty-fourth birthday, he kicked a hangover to the curb, gathered his guts and his savings, and purchased The Y Auto Exchange in the center of Little Quebec. Two years later, he pulled another bold career maneuver by tying the knot with a feisty, five-foot-nothing twenty-year-old named Annette Gauthier. (Her father, Donat, owned a glass shop in Willimansett, providing his new son-in-law with a hefty discount on windshields.) An ambitious French Canadian herself, Annette hitched herself to Rheo in an equally shrewd business decision. Aiming to assimilate and boost her status, she obsessed with the frills and finery of American culture, her happiness falling somewhere between "more than enough" and "too much." A poor farmer or mill boy couldn't satisfy her expensive tastes. But an up-and-coming auto shop owner had a chance.

With wit and honesty, Rheo generated a loyal clientele and cashed in on his gamble with the fledgling car industry. To combat the exhaustive hours he logged working, *and* playing, he limited his commute by buying a pocket-size house directly across from The Y. While he built his enterprise, his wife raised their children and spent their money.

An ugly bias against French-speaking residents permeated Chicopee at the time, but the locals spared Rheo any mistreatment. Patrons enjoyed chatting with him in the show-room or relaxing with a beer in his back office. He kept a bowl of hard candies on his desk for their kids, didn't correct anyone who mispronounced his last name, and mastered how to laugh at himself and others with equal oomph. Winning people over with a cushy charm that belied his imposing six-foot-two-inch frame, he understood their feelings for him depended, mostly, on how he made them feel about themselves.

The high school boys scatter, hiding in the riverbank brush. Without a ripple, the rum runner vanishes, the low hum of its motor fading in the night. The four burly Chicopee cops burst into the house. An officer with pocked skin and a greasy handlebar mustache whacks the walls with his billy club. "Let's go, Gagne. We know you're in here. We ain't got all night."

"Easy, O'Reilly. He'll come out," the ruling sergeant says, motioning to his troops to head down a hallway leading to the cellar. "He understands the situation."

The basement door swings open, and Rheo emerges from the top step with a wooden case in his arms. "Okay, boys. You got me," he says with whimsy. "Don't hurt me, please." The cops form a semicircle around the perp, sneering with delight at his surrender. The mustachioed officer pokes his club into Rheo's ribs. "Hey, Frenchy, you stupid or somethin'? What's in the box? Better not be what I think it is."

Through the hallway window, the moon shines, darting like a searchlight. Locking a leery eye on the pocked policeman, Rheo bends a knee and places the goods on the floor. As he pulls his hand away from the case, he slides a switchblade from his sock, flicks open the sharp steel, and brandishes it wildly. "Now let's get down to business."

Three of the cops draw their guns, but the sergeant holds up his hand. "Settle down, men. Mr. Gagne is smarter than he looks."

"*Merci*, Sergeant. I'll take that as a compliment." Rheo cracks open the wooden crate with his knife, revealing the precious contents: twelve gleaming bottles of premium Canadian Club rye whiskey. "I assume this'll hold you over. Six-year-old, one hundred proof single malt. Best I've got," he says like a father bragging about a beloved son. "Divvy it up however you see fit, though I'd suggest a little less for your comrade with the anger issues." The greasy cop glares and grunts; his handlebar mustache steers into a sneer.

"Take the evidence to the car, O'Reilly," the sergeant orders. His surly subordinate picks up the case and slinks away. The sergeant smiles and shakes Rheo's hand. "Will I see you Friday at the poker game, Canuck?"

"*Oui*, I never miss a chance to take your money."

Tom & Fran

If Mom had told me how her parents met, if she'd offered more details about that place and time than what I got from a quick Google search, then it'd be clear why Nana and Pop-Pop loved each other so much. If only I'd asked my grandparents to tell the tale, their version would've been different than this one.

It's 1927...

A heavy haze presses against the golden glow of gas lamps lining the cobbled streets of Fall River. Fog horns moan like dead sailors haunting the harbor of the Bay State's bygone whaling village.

Twenty-five-year-old Tom Colthart strolls the sidewalk after finishing his shift as floor manager at the petering American Printing Company, the one-time world leader of printing cloth, when this place was known as "King Cotton." Tom approaches a newsstand, pulls three nickels from his pocket, and purchases a paper. He expects his friend, Bill Dwyer, a writer for the *Herald-News*, to show up any minute for their weekly visit; complete with thick clam chowder, thin cigars, and stout conversation.

While Tom waits, he dives into Dwyer's weekly column, *The Man About Town*, an observant and honest take on life in Fall River, now known as the "Spindle City." Tom pulls music out of the newsman's article, eats the language with a spoon, admires Dwyer's way with words, his witty turn of a phrase. During the course of their friendship, the best storyteller in Bristol County has become a father figure to the kid from Whitinsville. The men share a Gaelic connection, formed the first day they met.

It was six years earlier. A Friday night. These same streets were bustling with wealthy folk strolling to fancy lobster dinners and working men packing into pubs, dumping paychecks into a bottle, or two, or five. Young Tommy Colthart, anxious to get home from work, covered in dust, hung onto a strap off the side of a trolley. He swung from one arm, mentally empty, physically spent. Cloth fibers from the factory irritated his eyes, needled his skin. His feet ached.

At a previous stop, he'd given up his seat to a well-off woman lugging two bulky shopping bags and sporting an expensive hat adorned with daisies. With lace gloves, she clutched a dainty change purse to her chest and stared straight ahead, bags locked between her feet, ignoring the boy who'd insisted she sit.

At Bank Street, the woman hurried off with her bags but left her purse behind. As the trolley moved on, Tommy grabbed the purse. Though his stop was still two miles away, he leapt off, hitting the street running. With an eye trained on the daisy hat in the distance, the teen dodged pedestrians on the sidewalk, bobbing and weaving as if avoiding defenders on the soccer pitches of Maryhill. Finally, he caught her. "Pardon me, ma'am. You forgot this."

At the sight of Tommy's filthy face, the stunned woman ripped the purse from him and stomped off without a word of thanks. Bill Dwyer had seen the entire incident. As Tommy Colthart walked away, sweaty and unaffected, the novice reporter halted him. "Excuse me there, lad. That was a grand thing you did. It's a shame I'm the only one who thinks so." He extended his hand. "The name's Dwyer, from the *Herald-News*. Mind if I ask you some questions?"

After Tommy introduced himself, he gave a few humble quotes, nothing substantial, about returning the purse. The reporter detected a slight brogue in the do-gooder's voice. "Not from here, are you, son?"

"No, sir. From Scotland. Came over when I was nine." Having sniffed out Dwyer's own accent, Tommy followed up. "And you?"

"Ireland. Been here twenty years now." He smiled, impressed by the teen's manner. "You've got character, lad. I can tell. And it's as solid as the granite this city's built on. You a working man?"

"Aye," said Tommy. "Been a cloth dryer at APC for two years." A shade of lowliness colored him, and he examined his boots.

"That's a respectable job, son," said Dwyer. "All a man can do is put in a noble day's work. I'm certain your father's proud." He waited till the boy raised his head. "You know what I think? I think there are no insignificant lives, Mr. Colthart, just inadequate ways of looking at them."

A friendship was struck those years ago. Nearly contemporaries now, the two men meet again, like they do every Wednesday, to rehash events of the week. This day, it's their favorite subject.

"Well, Tom, our last place Sox shocked the Senators today," Bill says, excited to announce the news. He flicks a match next to his young friend's cigar. "Slim Harris threw a gem for the first time in his life. We scored three in the first. Even Buddy Myer got a couple of hits."

"Buddy's been serviceable at short lately," Tom says behind a puff of smoke. "Makes that Pee-Wee Wanninger trade to Cincy look like a stroke of genius. What about the Yanks?"

"Murderer's Row claimed another victim today. Ruth went hitless but Gehrig got a couple of knocks, including a double. He's hitting four-eighteen, you believe that?"

"It's only the first of June, Dwyer. Those wallopers are sure to hit the doldrums once the dog days of summer come barking."

An hour ticks away. Their stogies sucked to stubs and cups of chowder slurped dry, the friends shake hands. "You should alter your route tonight," Dwyer says. "Take Tecumseh. McWhirr's Department Store's under renovation again. South Main Street's a mess." Tom nods, registering the information as if his life depends on it, and walks away. The newspaperman calls out, "Safe home, son."

Son. The young Scot likes when Dwyer calls him that. Peering over his shoulder at his mate in the mist, Tom wishes true family could be chosen instead of assigned. Venturing home, he turns down Tecumseh Street, as suggested. Half a block ahead, a familiar ditty rings out. He reaches the song's origin and finds a fetching, petite lass on an apartment stoop tying a toddler's shoe. On the sidewalk below, three other children skip rope and chant:

Lizzie Borden took an axe

Gave her father forty whacks

When she saw what she had done

Gave her mother forty-one

Defying his sober personality, Tom jumps into the action, hopping in sync with a little girl in pigtails. For a moment, they bounce in song. Drenched in glee, the girl screeches, "Hey Franny, look at me!"

"Well done, Grace, but don't hurt the nice man," replies the lass on the stoop.

Tom whips his head around to the sound of her voice and trips up, his ankles tangled in rope. The kids laugh at the former star athlete from Whitinsville, a perma-smile baked into his overcooked face.

The young woman smiles back. "Careful, it's a dangerous game."

"Well, I could've kept going, but I didn't want to steal all the fun," Tom says, fooling no one. "Plus, I was distracted by that murderous song. A bit ghoulish for these half-pints, don't you think?"

"Appropriate at the moment though," she says. "Or haven't you heard? Poor old Lizzie passed on earlier today."

"You don't say," Tom exclaims, curious that Bill Dwyer hadn't known about the demise of Fall River's most notorious villain. (For the past thirty-five years, since being acquitted of chopping her father and stepmother to pieces, Lizzie had lived as a recluse in a decrepit estate nearby.) Tom joshes, "My mum's name is Lizzie too but, as far as I know, she doesn't own an axe."

The sidewalk kids giggle at the bad joke and the obvious attraction between the funny man and their older sister. "Okay, it's time for you all to go inside and wash up for supper," she tells them. "Ma will be home soon. Go on now, quick-quick like a bunny."

The kids bound up the steps. The street quiets. "By the way, my name is Tom Colthart. And you are?"

"Frances McMellon, but you can call me Fran."

"Okay, Fran, what's your fascination with Ms. Borden?"

"Well, I wouldn't call it a fascination. It's just that my father used to work as a cloth folder at the bleachery for Jefferson Borden, cousin of Lizzie's father, Andrew." Fran shakes off her demure disguise. "I remember my father gathering all us kids around the fireplace, telling the story of how Andrew and his wife were bludgeoned by their daughter. And how Lizzie was found not guilty a year later. Daddy said it was one of the most famous trials in history."

For a fleeting moment, Fran drifts away, daydreaming how Frank McMellon would end his spooky recount by reminding his children that Lizzie still lived in Fall River, cloistered behind the walls of her Maplecroft mansion in a wealthy section of town called The Hill.

"Don't go to The Hill, my wee ones," he'd warn the kids in a whisper, "or Lizzie will getcha with her axe." Then his eyes would widen in horror as he pointed a quivering finger over their shoulders. "Th—Th—There she is!" he'd yell. And the children would flee, like skittish kittens at the growl of a dog, while their father rolled on the floor.

"I miss him and his silly stories. He died in an explosion at the bleachery six years ago. He was only thirty-four. I was thirteen," Fran tells Tom without a hint of reticence. "He was a fine man. I just wish Grace and the others had as much time with him as I did."

The fog clears. A cutthroat sunset drapes its pink and purple tapestry over the rooftops. In the middle of the street, a lone seagull pecks at a mussel shell. Spellbound by Fran's openness and honesty, drawn to her strength, Tom extends his condolences, shuffles his feet, and admits a sudden guilt. "I haven't seen my family in years."

"Don't you miss them?"

Tom balks at the question, as if grilled on the witness stand. Then he turns a key, unlocking long-ago memories. "My father is a difficult man to understand. Takes life quite seriously, barely speaks, just works. Nothing like your father, it seems." Tom falls into Fran's compassionate eyes and admits a basic truth. "I miss my mum, but I had to leave."

Seven months later, the Great Fire of Fall River chars five blocks of a city already asphyxiated by shuttered textile plants. Tom and Fran marry before the smoke clears. They start a family as the Great Depression hits and the town goes broke. After four kids, they relocate fifteen miles east to New Bedford, where Tom works as a personnel manager in American Printing's corporate office. In 1936, a fifth child, Cynthia Grace, joins the Colthart bunch. Soon, Firestone Tire and Rubber purchases APC and welcomes Tom into their fold.

The world watches, aghast, as the German zeppelin *Hindenburg* explodes above a New Jersey air base, and a bold American pilot, Amelia Earhart, disappears somewhere over the Pacific. In the meantime, the Colthart family takes flight, growing in number, soaring in devotion. Clear skies ahead. For now.

∽

As I tried to get my head around the news of David's death, Dad stood apart from me and Mom like we were lepers.

Then, of course. Why hadn't he seen it before? Looking through the picture window that day, past his own reflection for once, my father saw the root of his misfortune, the reason life had turned black: the river. If his great-grandfather, Eugine, hadn't followed the Connecticut River down from Canada to Massachusetts, carrying with him a foolish dream and a deadly gene, then none of this would've happened and Bob Gagne wouldn't be here now. Everyone would've been better off without him, he thought. And in that pall of delusion and self-contempt, he wished he'd never existed.

But my dad's theory, like the rest of him, was flawed. Eugine was just a poor farmer-turned-miller when he made the trip to America with his wife and son. He couldn't have known that, across the Atlantic, two English scientists had recently discovered a genetic disorder that would haunt the Gagne family for generations.

And he couldn't have known that Warren Tay and Bernard Sachs claimed the disorder destroys infant nerve cells in the brain and spinal cord, becoming apparent by six months—with the baby's inability to turn over and sit and crawl—followed by the loss of hearing and sight. Or that children born with this condition are ravaged with seizures, suffer from respiratory complications, and die early deaths. And how could *any* of the Gagnes have known that Tay-Sachs disease is rare in the general population but, for unknown reasons, a vast number of cases are found among French-Canadians from Southeastern Quebec? No one knew.

My mother wept in a room filled mostly with absence. Her trembling hands sheltered burning eyes. Her thumbs pressed hard into cheekbones, crushing her head like a vise. Tears fought through her fingers, soaking deep into the paisley-patterned couch. As she lifted her head to face the window's immense pane—and my father's back—she gasped for air and considered the lack of oxygen a blessing. If her life ended now, it might be for the best.

The world had built walls and fences around her dreams. Now the universe closed them in forever. Giving up her sons to the care of the state had been debilitating. Burying one of them now, sixteen years later, was unimaginable, soul-wrecking. Cynthia Grace Gagne (née Colthart) should've remained in sorrow's grip for an eternity, but that's not what Coltharts do. She'd learn to live alongside her sadness and, in time, smile her splendid smile again.

Now, though, wasn't that time.

My mom mourned more than her son that afternoon. David's death reminded her how my father had ignored David's life. It'd be unfair to say my dad hadn't loved the boy, but the man's runaway guilt trounced what little affection he could show. As I sat close to my mom, I regretted that she had to endure this tragedy alone. My father's son, I said nothing, could only place a soft hand on her back. It shouldn't have been that way. Dad should've been the one sitting beside her, holding her. Even if he didn't utter one word, he should've held her. I stared into the picture window and prayed it would all go away.

For twelve years, what I saw outside that glass represented the freedom, adventure, and limitlessness of an idyllic childhood. Before that day, in our backyard, beyond the swimming pool and vegetable garden, I embraced endless acres of hay fields and sandy hills, rocky streams and frog ponds, berry bushes and skunk cabbage—a natural amusement park for a wide-eyed boy, his sisters, and their neighborhood friends. We spent unending days pioneering this sprawl of land, the terrain unraveling into the Connecticut River Valley; a place of discovery where we built tree forts and lifelong friendships, a place of exploration where we planted sunflower seeds and first kisses. We collected Indian arrowheads by the dozen. We camped out in musty tents, eating junk food, counting shooting stars, telling ghost stories. We flew paper airplanes across the dingle, planes that never landed.

In winter, we blazed legendary sledding trails with giant snow ramps that shot our coasters high into Creamsicle skies. In spring, we clogged a trickling stream with stones and logs, then wrecked our dam to create rushing rapids perfect for high-speed stick boat races. On sun-kissed summer afternoons, we picked blueberries for the following morning's bowl of cereal. At the end of autumn, we raked mountains of fallen leaves and leaped out of trees into an exhilarating crunch of crispy foliage. We shared our wonderland with pheasant, turkey, deer, and fox. All that disrupted our bliss: our mothers' barely audible calls to dinner each evening.

I stared out the window on that suffocating afternoon, and the agony of real life clouded my view. Nothing would be the same. Motionless on the couch, in a disoriented haze, as the playground of my youth faded away, I vowed to return what my brothers had stolen from my parents: the possibility of joy. To smother Mom and Dad's pain, to reinforce a crumbling bridge between them, I switched the default setting on my priorities. Trying to be a "good son" wasn't enough anymore; my mother and father needed more from me. I'd have to live my life for them, give my all for them. And for someone else.

Twenty miles west of our grieving living room, the burnished brick buildings of Monson Developmental Center stood mute and antiseptic, unnatural in their bucolic New England surroundings. The state hospital for the mentally and physically disabled loomed high on a wooded peak, overlooking the sleepy town of Palmer, Massachusetts. (I had been there once, when I was six, with my mother.)

On the face of the building farthest from the road, open windows invited in the scent of spring. But the sounds escaping those windows weren't pleasant, nothing like the laughter of my friends running through hay fields behind my house. These were guttural noises, fractured and unintelligible utterances of suffering patients, cries dancing out of time with the urgent placations of nurses attempting to help in any way. This was the pain of incomplete people living incomplete lives.

A misshapen silhouette, the scribbly outline of a teenage boy, twitched in a second story window. Slouched in a wheelchair, his frail body spasmed while his head, topped with wavy brown hair, bobbed up and down to the broken rhythm of a drum that didn't exist. Unable to see or hear or speak, he said nothing, heard nothing, stared into nothingness. The familiar features of his face: a funhouse mirror reflection of my own.

The boy, Robert Gagne, named after his father, had endured in this place nearly all his life, banished in the leafy hills of Palmer, a short drive, but a world away, from his mother. And earlier this day, behind these burnished bricks, Robert's twin brother died of pneumonia.

FIVE

"Your Wealth Is Your Family"

Winter, 1995

*ET'S SEE. THURSDAY night, Friday night, Saturday night, then
home on Sunday.*

I counted the days on my fingers and tossed the exact
amount of clothing I'd need into my backpack: three pairs of
underwear, three pairs of socks, and two T-shirts. The jeans and
sweatshirt I was wearing, I'd wear the whole weekend. I slung the
pack over my shoulder, locked up my apartment, and hopped
down three flights of stairs. I flew out the door and into my
macho black '87 Camaro, the Palisades Park morning chill nip-
ping at my heels.

Five years earlier, before my move to Jersey, Dad had sweet-
talked one of his car dealer cronies into selling me the Camaro for
a song. The pretentious hotrod wasn't my cup of tea, but it was a
steep step up from my first car, a lemonade-color 1970 Dodge Dart
that coughed and hacked like a yak with bronchitis. A repulsive

chick repellant, the Dart took all the blame whenever one of my dates turned down a proposal to "go parking." After I junked that catastrophe-on-wheels, I took my life into my hands with a clunky Subaru hatchback that met its maker the summer before I got the gig at NBA Entertainment. Now, I'd rely on my Camaro to beat a nor'easter forecasted to hit New England later that afternoon.

It was the first of my favorite four days of the year—the start of March Madness—and I was on my way to Mark's in Wakefield, Rhode Island. Since my buddies and I left Chicopee, the trip had become tradition. Each year, at the start of the NCAA Basketball Tournament, Droopy and I took Thursday and Friday off and spent the extended weekend at Nadeau's, eating and drinking and kicking ourselves for getting too cute with our brackets. This year, my alma mater, UMass, led by super-sophomore Marcus Camby, was the number two seed in the East. I expected this tourney would be special.

I opened the glove compartment and pulled out my crumpled Rand-McNally road map to determine my Rhody route. I'd been to Mark's place at least ten times, and the three-hour trip was a breeze, but I needed a refresher course with the directions. Finally, I was on my way. Before I hit the GW Bridge, I stopped for gas at a Mobile station with an attached Dunkin' Donuts. After filling up, I grabbed a coffee and a corn muffin. As I pulled out of the lot, my balding tires spun out on a patch of ice. I scanned the scene, hoping no one heard the screech or saw me as some lug nut compensating for his sexual inadequacies by peeling out in his "hard guy" sports car.

All clear. I hit the accelerator as lingering gasoline vapors shot up my nose. The fumes reminded me of childhood mornings spent with my father at Gagne & Sons. While waiting for Mom to finish grocery shopping across the street at Perrault's, I'd sweep the burgundy tile showroom floor for a dime and a lollipop. Then I'd watch python-like hoses uncoil from Gulf tankers and inject fuel into the thirsty ground below twin gas pumps that looked like Rosie the Robot from *The Jetsons*.

Using up a couple of vacation days in mid-March was no big deal. I'd been doing good work at NBAE, earning the time off and the freedom to adjust my schedule. After launching my career as a librarian—followed by promotions to logger and production assistant—I now honed my skills as an editor on an international show called *NBA Action*. I enjoyed the challenge of piecing together interviews and music and highlights and sound effects to paint a video portrait of a particular player or team, and I clicked with the creativity of editing. Daily repetition forced me to learn the technicalities, but the artistic angle came easily. Producing a feature required talent I already had and consisted of the same steps I used when drawing a picture: think up an idea, sketch it out, and fill in the details. The edit room was my laboratory where I brought to life all the wild wackiness in my head, winning ego-boosting praise from both supervisors and peers. And those peers had become brothers.

Nooch, Miche, Koontz, Santa, Logue, and Check had been there from the start, but a fresh crew—Tre, H, Teif, Lav, Coulter, Big Bull, and George—had since joined the company. Our gang hung out hard, hitting too many New York City bars, downing too many Hennessy and Cokes, checking in at the Navel Base, the local strip club, to say a quick hello to the ladies, and sneaking in rounds of golf whenever we could. We also played daily pick-up hoops, blacktop brawls where we traded vicious elbows, forged eternal rivalries, and won each other's respect. My sweat-soaked friends and I recapped each day's battle as we sat curbside at a convenience store chugging Gatorade under the setting sun, satisfied and depleted, rejuvenated and exhausted—peace after war, love after hate. It was what I thought heaven must be like.

At the time, rumors ricocheted around the basketball world that Michael Jordan—who retired from the NBA in '94 to play minor league baseball for the Birmingham Barons—might return to the Chicago Bulls. Our NBAE softball team, boasting a few guys who played college baseball, was at least as talented as the Barons. Nooch played center (like he had at UPenn), and I played left (like I'd planned to at UMass before getting cut my freshman year). With his bazooka arm, Nooch gunned down overly aggressive runners on the bases every game, and I hurtled through swampy Secaucus nights, laying out for line drives like a frisbee-catching Labrador. We compared defensively to any out-field duo in the majors, pro comparisons ending with our arms and gloves since neither of us could hit a curveball.

Of all my NBA buddies, George Land was *my guy*. Hailing from South Carolina, by way of Atlanta, with stops at Duke and Morehouse and the Pittsburgh School of Medicine, "G" came from a disciplined and supportive family. Though our child-hoods were nothing alike, *we* were almost identical. As a kid, he withstood slurs and slings while integrating his elementary school in Rock Hill, SC. When I was a kid, I roamed free in my backyard, oblivious to the injustices outside Chicopee. From the start, our friendship was cemented with an unspoken promise to serve and protect. If one of us had only five bucks in his checking account till the end of the week, neither of us spent more than four. At sketchy bachelor parties—where certain "situations" tested the fortitude of Male Code—we vowed to keep each other from doing anything we'd regret. We looked at the world the same way. It looked back at us differently.

George and I agreed on most matters, but none more than the foundational Law of Divine Oneness: that everything in the universe is interconnected and there are no coincidences.

The Garden State Parkway was slick but safe, and my Camaro glided north like a chill-seeking missile. Dying to pass the time, I dialed in and out of random radio stations before landing on 1010 WINS where I waited for an update on the storm. The news anchor—possibly named Jim Crow—greeted me with a bulletin that seemed to leak out of a time capsule: "…and one-hundred-thirty years after its passage, Mississippi today has become the last state in the union to ratify the Thirteenth Amendment, approving the abolition of slavery." I shook my head and thought how the Magnolia State was a sour-smelling late-bloomer, then I flipped off the channel in pursuit of musical relief.

I was forced to reflect on a sore subject (my stagnant personal life) after clicking on the following songs in order: "I Swear," "I'll Make Love to You," "Now and Forever," "If You Go," "I'll Stand by You," and "Always." Adding insult to misery, when "Here Comes the Hotstepper" blasted, I was reminded how, in the dance of love, my contemporaries hot-stepped circles around me. The bulk of my friends at the NBA were married or engaged; Cheryl and Linda, both married with kids; Nadeau, living with his girlfriend; Droopy, set to tie the knot in September, three weeks before he and I would run our third marathon together. For a guy whose love life hadn't budged, I was wiped out.

My parents, financially and emotionally bankrupt, were in way worse shape. If what Dad always told us was true, that "Your wealth is your family," then he'd need to put his money where his mouth was and start saving up because, at the moment, all he had in his heart-shaped bank were a few dusty coins from under the couch cushions. Unable to take stock in her husband, Mom invested everything into her children, spending time with my sisters, checking up on me with weekly phone calls, and paying monthly visits to thirty-three-year-old Robert at Monson. No matter what, she always made those visits.

For my father, the past was the past, and that's exactly where he kept his eldest son. The only routine appointment Dad kept took place during the small hours before sunrise and involved the host of his favorite talk radio show. While his conscience slept, Bob Gagne swilled a heavy dose of provocation—like a shot of strychnine in his coffee—jolting his anger, boosting his fears. Already robbed of his wallet, my pops left the door wide open for a bigoted opportunist to rush in every morning and loot his soul.

Without the means to afford trips on their own, my parents took mini vacations to Vermont and Niagara Falls and Edisto Island with our former pastor and her husband, Ann and John Geer. To make ends meet, Mom worked in the membership department at the Holyoke YMCA while Dad bagged groceries at the Big Y, earning minimum wage for pestering impatient patrons and flirting with Chicklet-chewing cashiers. When he got called onto the carpet for talking more than working, he tossed his apron at the manager and said, "You'll never find another bagologist like me."

My Camaro muscled over the Tappan Zee Bridge, high above the Hudson, then through Westchester and onto the Merritt Parkway. Cars whizzed by, well over the speed limit, as I hugged the guardrail and accelerated to keep up with the flow. I may have fallen far behind in the race for love, but I'd run away with the preliminary qualifiers: friends and family and career. Still, I was alone and incomplete, lapped by the field, nowhere near the winner's circle.

I sped across New Haven on Route 95 through twisting funnels of snow spinning on the frozen highway like wispy, whirling dervishes. Tired of the radio, I took my eyes off the road for a second and leafed through a nylon case of compact discs. *Where is it?... Hmmm... Nope, not that one... Oh... Here we go!*

PM Dawn's *The Bliss Album* was one of my favorites CDs to play on long, isolating drives. I'd fall into a trance listening to those songs—their experimental beats and pulsing rhythms and lush lyrics—and the rest of my trip would flash by at warp speed. Steering with my knees, I removed the disc from its casing and offered it up to the stereo. Like a mechanical aardvark, the dashboard slot pulled the CD from my fingers and slurped it up with thin, electronic lips. Then the opening lines of the album slid into my ears, and I slipped away.

If Dad had told me about his childhood, if he'd said more than, "My mother once threw me down a flight of stairs," then I would've sympathized with the sadness he felt as a boy. If only I'd asked what his family was *really* like, maybe he would've opened up, and I wouldn't have to imagine this story.

It's 1938…

Whispers waft downstairs in his grandparents' kitchen. His father is back; he's certain this time.

Seven-year-old Robert grabs his eyeglasses off the nightstand and adjusts the wires around his ears. Careful not to stir his older brother sleeping next to him, he rolls off his cot like a log of cotton. The bedroom door is open, from when he last checked if his dad had returned. No one will wake from those creaky hinges; a noise Robert likens to the lid lifting off a coffin. His sisters, Constance and Jacqueline, slumber in the spare room across the hall while his grandparents snooze in the bedroom adjacent. The rumble of his Pepe Aristide's snoring wiggles the old farmhouse in South Hadley.

In striped wool pajamas, Robert creeps down the pine staircase and peeks over the rail. It's nearly eleven. The imposing oak dining table is bare, save for two empty bottles of cabernet. A low-lit kerosene lamp sways from a crossbeam overhead. Somewhere in the yard, dogs bark at the autumn wind.

"Papa?" Robert wheezes as he sneaks across the kitchen floor, past the dying coals in the wood stove, toward the open cellar door; the basement is the one place in this house he's never had the courage to explore. He peers down the staircase into the abyss. "Papa, is that you?"

"I told you to go to bed, you little shit!" His mother's growl rips through her clenched jaw, and she snags the back of his shirt collar with both hands. Robert cranes his neck. There's rage in her switchblade eyes, wine on her breath.

"I just want to see P—P—Papa," the boy stammers. "I—I thought I heard him."

"You know your papa isn't here."

Robert braces himself in the doorway at the top of the stairs. His mother tightens her grip on his shirt, her polished fingernails piercing his neck. His sweaty hands slide down the edges of the rough doorjamb as she pushes against his shoulders. She sucks her teeth at his insolence, her anger brewing. She's a stub of a woman, only slightly taller than Robert, but she scares him. Especially when she's drunk. She wears a ghoulish glare and slurs with a ferocious Quebecois accent. "Maybe in the goddamn cellar tonight is where you want to sleep. You want that?"

He tries to appease with his use of French. "*Non, Maman, s'il te plait.*"

Fear always tastes like copper to him, and now his mouth is stuffed with a thousand old pennies. Panting, gulping, he turns from her, his hands inching farther down the wood frame. He stares into the basement depths. A splinter punctures his thumb, sends a toe-curling current of electricity straight to his brain. He shrieks and yanks his hand away from the jamb. Behind the force of his mother's weight he loses his balance and plummets down the stairs. Covering his head, he tumbles over ten wooden steps that bang on his bones like battering rams.

Still as a corpse, face down on the dirt floor, Robert considers—for an everlasting moment—if he's alive. And, if he *is* dead, would his mother even care? Would his father miss him? Would the world go on as if he'd never existed?

He pushes up onto his knees and glides his palms across the dirt, pawing for his eyeglasses lost in the dark. A swollen elbow stiffens his arm. He licks away blood and sawdust from his lip. His head pounds. The house is quiet. The wind dead. The dogs silent.

Blinded by hurt and terror, Robert staggers to his feet, drags himself up the staircase like a limping rodent. At the top, he wrangles his courage and hobbles through the kitchen toward the screen door. He zips past the oak table and the blurry outline of his mother. She's wilted in a chair, her corkscrewed face plastered in contemptable hands.

The boy bursts out the door into the night, demanding too much from his bruised legs. "Robert Alphonse!" Annette cries half-heartedly. In bare feet, he scampers down the dusty driveway and into the protection of the orchard, dodges dozens of broken limbs littering the ground, tiptoes atop a roller rink of ripened Cortland apples. His mother's calls disappear as evening's black blankets him, barren branches shielding his escape. Panic numbs the pain in his elbow and head. He runs deeper into the grove. The farmhouse in the distance, he clambers up a stubby trunk. Nothing can hurt him now.

It's been five days since the "Great New England Hurricane" ransacked Western Massachusetts. Five days since flash flooding on the Chicopee River washed away the Chicopee Falls Bridge. Five days since the Connecticut River rose and cascaded into the streets of Willimansett, pouring in eighteen feet of water, causing five hundred million dollars in damage, drowning two hundred souls.

Robert and his family had been lucky. As soon as his father, Rheo, heard the newsflash, he loaded his wife and children into his truck and headed for higher ground. He dropped them at his parents' farm in South Hadley and then rambled seven miles back to Willimansett, racing galloping gales, to secure his house and business. He helped friends safeguard their homes and families, sheltered their cars at The Y Auto Exchange, and provided food and drink from The Y Café.

Under the watch of his Memere and Pepe, Robert and his siblings picked vegetables alongside frantic cousins and hired hands, saving crops from wind and rain, filling and storing baskets of beans, eggplants, onions, squash, cabbage, and cucumbers. Robert liked being with his grandparents, even as a hurricane loomed, but found no refuge from the deluge of abuse levied by his older brother and sister—Rheo Jr. and Constance—to whom Robert was a hangnail of a boy, irritating and insignificant. Their mistreatment was nothing new.

Robert had few friends, spent much of his childhood at home with his strict and unstable mother. He tried to please her, but she never noticed, only complained that he wasn't as smart or as talented or as handsome as other children. She forced him to take piano lessons and serve as an altar boy, but no matter how he obliged or what he accomplished, nothing sufficed, his mother's unfair comparisons and scathing criticisms robbing him of the few fleeting moments of happiness slipping in and out of his life.

Robert loved his dad terribly but rarely saw him. Though Rheo Gagne worked directly across the street from his house, he dedicated his free time to friends, customers, and local dignitaries. At supper, he'd stay at the table just long enough for a few beers, then grab his coat and hat and tousle Robert's hair on his way out the door. "*A demain, mon loulou*," he'd say. "See you tomorrow, my little one." And every evening, Robert waited for his father to come home as unseen forces pulled on his eyelids like window shades. Sleep always won those battles.

Rheo needed to see the people, needed a pop or two, and doing so often took all night. Well-connected and generous with his money, he bought drinks for the whole town—including the mayor and chief of police. (A shared cocktail strengthened bonds and improved economic status in Willimansett, arguments settled with a bottle of booze and a handshake.) A big man with a bigger personality, he was a go-getter, a guy who got things done. The year Robert was born, Rheo won approval from the

Massachusetts Supreme Court to expand the boundaries of his auto service property. Below the extra plot, he planted a colossal oil tank and erected gasoline pumps above. He ran his business discerningly but with a kind heart, extending loans and making discounted repairs for folks in need, building loyalty, credibility, and respect. His shop, at the epicenter of Little Quebec, was a meeting place where friends and fellow proprietors stopped by to bullshit and share some suds. Rheo's liberality put food on their plates during the Depression and wine in their glasses during Prohibition. Everyone counted on him.

What Robert loved best about his father was how he treated children. Each summer Rheo threw lobster bakes and hot dog roasts for neighborhood kids. And every Christmas he dressed as Santa and brought bicycles and sacks of toys to his many nieces and nephews in South Hadley. All of Willimansett knew the Gagne family had money, but for Annette, it was never enough. It peeved her that her husband gave more than he took, spreading his hard-earned wealth to lift the entire community. In Rheo, she saw a naive idealist unable to give her all she wanted, while Robert saw an admired hero unable to give him all he needed.

The insects of the night whine in rhythm. A chill crawls under the boy's skin as the yelp of a coyote echoes around the Seven Sisters mountain range. No matter, he's safe. The canine's howl in the feral forest pales to his mother's scowl at the kitchen table. Up in his tree, Robert studies each sparkling star in the autumn sky until his eyes ache. The wind rocks his perch like an off-balance cradle, fills him with a familiar dread. Without his glasses, a billion fuzzy twinkles above the orchard become two billion. He looks back at the farmhouse, searching for headlights in the driveway, and recalls what his father once told him: "There are more stars in the sky than grains of sand on every beach in the whole world." He wants to believe.

Two hours pass.

The darkness grows heavier. Emptiness fills the orchard. No rustling leaves. No yipping coyotes. And still no headlights in the driveway.

Robert shuffles back to the farmhouse. He opens the screen door with surgical care and steals inside expecting violent screams and a backhand to his still-aching head. In the quiet of the kitchen, the kerosene lamp is dead, the wood stove cold. The two drained wine bottles remain solemn at the table. A single glass sleeps in the sink.

Robert edges across the floor, bracing himself for a punishment more powerful than any hurricane. He peers into the living room. And the bathroom. Nothing. Aside from his Pepe's snores banging the walls, there's no sound or sight of anyone. He's alone.

❦

I enjoyed driving long distances by myself.

I relished the peace of knowing I wasn't bothering anyone, wasn't needed, wasn't in anyone's way. My favorite place existed inside my head, where I was covered in serenity and comfort, devoid of accountability or commitment.

I'd driven sixty miles on Route 95 in a semi-hypnotic state from the first fourteen tracks of *The Bliss Album*. I didn't recall any of those songs playing, not "When Midnight Sighs" or "The Ways of the Wind" or "Looking through Patient Eyes." And as the opening piano notes tinkled on the final track, "I'd Die Without You," I escaped again, fell into a familiar dream-zone, where I'd visit my sensitive side and take emotional inventory of my life.

Finally making enough money to help my parents pay their bills, I chipped away at an unpayable debt, even sent them on a surprise vacation to Scotland so Mom could tug on a few branches of the Colthart family tree; the financial hit I took was like a love tap with a crowbar, but the thrill she got meeting a distant cousin in Glasgow was worth every cent. Meanwhile, my sisters had moved outside of Chicopee with their families, and I visited often, playing up my role as the energetic and attentive uncle, rollicking with my nieces and nephews. I knew what I was missing, was convinced I'd be a great dad, and wanted a family of my own, but I faced double roadblocks. First: I hadn't found "Ms. Right." And second: I cultivated my relationships at a glacial pace. If I moved any slower with the ladies, my friends joked, I'd be going backwards.

I'd been in love twice.

The summer after my freshman year at UMass, I fell for a doe-eyed teen named Elise when we linked eyes one night at Willimansett's Chip-n-Putt golf course. Ours was a scandalous twosome (she was four years younger than I), but I threw a bear hug around the canyon-sized age gap. Dating a high schooler took pressure off me to move too fast—emotionally *and* physically. A petrified Pollyanna, I plodded along with my fifteen-year-old girlfriend at a safe, comfortable, preferable speed.

A sophomore in college at the time, I skipped weekend frat parties and quad hangouts to be with Elise back in Chicopee. We savored every moment together, starting the second I picked her up on Friday nights (from her waitress job at the Lucky Strike) till the hour we spent kissing goodbye in her driveway late on Sundays. She had me wrapped around every one of her fingers. And both thumbs.

One Saturday evening in January, I hiked to her house for ninety treacherous minutes through a blinding snowstorm because my dad proclaimed the roads undrivable and refused to hand over the car keys. After Elise and I watched a video we'd rented from Blockbuster the night before, I bundled up and marched the three and a half miles back home through foot-high drifts. It was the easiest decision I'd ever made, and not only because the underrated *Teen Wolf* was such a great movie, but because I loved her and would've walked *ten* miles in *ten* feet of snow just to hold her hand. What we had was perfect.

I wasn't ready for an adult relationship—or the drama and responsibility that came with it. I practically needed a Rand-McNally to find my way around the female body, and college girls terrified me. My first week on campus in Amherst, I got caught up in a carnal cyclone with a frisky, fleshy co-ed two dorm room doors down. After dating for a month, she said I'd make a great father—a line that scared the parachute pants off me. I would've rather been trapped in a nest of vipers while handcuffed to the head-spinning, chunk-spewing kid from *The Exorcist.*

Innocent and romantic and sweet, the connection between Elise and me was the epitome of puppy love. Speaking honestly and laughing forever, we poured our feelings out to one another and I learned from her that, someday, I wanted to be with a woman with her peppy sense of humor and easy self-confidence. I needed someone who spoke her heart as openly as she did, someone who stayed true to herself, whether fighting through life's blizzards or relaxing in the calms before and after the storms.

We lasted fifteen months before she broke up with me to go out with a guy her age. It was a sensible move, but I was crushed. For another year, we made weak attempts to get back together, always ending up in the same place: apart. Stuffing a notebook of poetry about her, I held onto an invented hope that we'd rekindle our relationship. The written self-therapy was crucial to my healing and my understanding of love's fickle nature, shining an inner light on my wants, needs, fears, and desires. One particular poem I penned helped rescue me from an emotional wilderness and pointed me home:

"Stages"

So here we are again, it seems we've played this part before,
But now the stage is empty and the spotlight long since dim.
Our hearts have simply changed the acts
that time could not restore,   .
And the leading man no longer fills his costar's every whim.
The tragedy is over, all the tears are shed and dried.
Now the actor and the actress must return for one last bow.
No more will there be lines to miss, nor sudden smiles to hide,
For now we both can be ourselves. Or have we both forgotten how?
The performance was a masterpiece of critical acclaim.
All the audience stood cheering as the curtain took its cue.
Though the crowd was much delighted,
I just could not feel the same,
For the play had not the ending that I would have liked it to.
The romance between characters should not have met its end;
We portrayed the Love too beautifully for such a dreadful close.
Now that the story's over, you are more than just a friend,
But I'm the victim of a fateful twist some heartless writer chose.
So here we are again, two actors cast in two new roles.
Without a script to read and memorize, the words are all our own.
There is no audience to satisfy. The critics are our souls.
So maybe this time when the curtain falls, I will not be alone.

I was devastated without Elise but tried to accept *The End.*
I'd been hanging onto my innocence and needed to grow up,

needed to get over the bitterness, the frustration, and the gut punch of failure. Harboring a grudge or wallowing in self-pity would only weigh me down, and it'd be wrong for me to blame either of us for a relationship that simply ran its course. So with a reluctant eye to the future, I let go.

With Elise, love was a garden to grow. With Kiki, it was a fuse to be lit.

After I graduated college, Kiki and I spent three white-knuckled years on a rip-roaring roller coaster, doomed to fly off the rails. She'd grown up at the end of my street, and we'd known each other since we were kids. A singular force with a spicy smile, Kiki was powered by an imperceptible energy. Our time together was rife with raw emotion, and we were blissfully in love—when we weren't at each other's throats. Reckless, arms up and screaming, we survived blowup arguments, unending fits of laughter, and a car crash in the French Alps.

Long into our relationship, I visited her in Europe for two weeks to meet friends she made while working as an au pair in Germany and relatives of hers in France. One night, while driving to her mother's hometown of Thiacourt, snaking our way around an icy mountain a mile high in the black sky, we lost control of our rented Peugeot and skidded off the road. Heading into the unknown, I braced Kiki with my arm and, for a nano-second, conceded that the world had seen the last of us. Had we slid to the left, we'd have plunged over a cliff, but the gods of the Alps were smiling on us and, out of fluky fortune, we slid to the right, smack into a stone wall.

Shaken stiff but suffering only minor cuts and bruises, we wilted down a walkway to wake a farmer and his wife. Kiki apologized—in French—for their wrecked wall and asked for help. An hour later, a strapping man with a beard and a tow truck hooked up our mangled car and hauled us to the closest village. Finding no vacancy at the lone hotel, we accepted the driver's offer to stay the night with him and his family. With no other choice, we slept six surreal hours on a pullout sofa and enjoyed croissants and coffee with our savior, his wife, and their three-year-old daughter. We spent the rest of the day exploring the quaint hamlet while our car was repaired, then drove back through the mountains to Thiacourt, musing about our odyssey the whole way.

If the crash was a signal our bliss was amiss, I ignored the warning. Lovesick at twenty-six, I predetermined the obvious next step and, without an engagement ring or much forethought, planned to propose to Kiki at the Eiffel Tower on the last day of my stay. On that raw and gloomy afternoon, while I waited for the precise moment to spring my surprise, we became embroiled in a convoluted argument that blew in swift and violent like a waterspout off the Seine, and my not-yet fiancé stormed away. I forgot what the disagreement was about but remember feeling that whatever it was, she was wrong.

Unsettled and upset—yet victorious and free—I leaned over the tower rail a hundred meters above Kiki and watched her itsy-bitsy figure disappear, swallowed by a sea of tourists. I waited, and waited, finally spotting her when she emerged out of the crowd and sat on a park bench. I descended the never-ending Eiffel steps and hurried to reach her. We embraced, said sorry, and agreed to break up (for good this time). Then in one final gesture of devotion, before leaving that park, we promised each other, as our battered roller coaster hissed to a halt, that we'd get back together if we were still single when she turned forty. And we left us, loving us.

Back on Route 95, I loosened my grip on the steering wheel and shook my head with a smile, incubated by vented heat and a warm gratitude for the girl who dragged me into manhood. The upholstered seat fit around my body like a perfectly broken-in bucket hat. Steeped in happy-sad recollections, I lamented the love I'd lost and the love I hadn't found.

After Kiki, I dated a few other girls from Chicopee, two or three from work, and a Chilean cashier named Evelyn who illuminated the Shop Rite across the street from my first apartment in Ridgefield. In typical Gagne fashion, I gathered the guts to ask her out only after she flirted with me for a year from behind the safety of the customer service counter. Besides those women, I got close with smart and spiritual Jocelyn, a friend-of-a-friend who lived in Queens. We hung out on and off for six months and genuinely enjoyed each other's company, rollerblading in Central Park, catching flicks at the Angelika, and meeting up for beers in Greenwich Village. But despite our joint adoration, I never tried to kiss her, sensed she was waiting for someone else. I guess I was too.

With every failed love connection, I recovered like a resilient clover springing back to form after getting stomped. I welcomed each unique lady into my life with an open heart, but something always felt "off"—until I met the woman I knew I'd marry, a first-generation Cuban American named Jackie, in autumn of 1994. George had introduced us at a party he and his fiancé, Lisa, had thrown at their apartment and, from that day, this stranger occupied an entire corner of my mind.

My Camaro hummed as the highway flew beneath me, and I saw the memory of my original meeting with Jackie, far away in itself, reflected in the windshield:

As I nursed a warm Amstel and laughed about nothing with friends, a vision appeared in George's living room, a woman who paralyzed me with ruby lips and mocha skin and deep, dark eyes that drew me in. Her cropped, jet-black hair exposed her delicate, swanning neck. Beside her sculpted cheekbones, studded diamond earrings sparkled, competing with her megawatt smile. Everything about her—this mystery girl from some magical place—struck me as familiar, and I was undone.

"Who's that?" I asked George with uncool eagerness.

"That's Lisa's friend from HBO. Her name's Jackie."

"And who's the guy with her?"

"That's her husband, Chuck. Let me go say hi. I'll be right back, Gags." George walked away sensing, I know, how that word, husband, demolished me.

In a dress made of smoke, Jackie moved about the room with an easy grace, her spider arms expressive as she extended hellos to the group. I sized up her husband, gauged his attachment to her, studied their vibe and connection. Before I overstepped and spoke to her, I needed to be sure Chuck wasn't the overprotective type. He was cordial and polite around George and Lisa and the others, if not totally comfortable, like he would've been happy enough staying home. I saw no hand-holding with Jackie, no gleam in his eye, no playful touching. They acted more like friends than husband and wife.

A Halle Berry clone, Jackie quickly extinguished my burning celebrity crush on Jodi Watley. With no intention of being a homewrecker, I shoved aside my lust and slithered into Jackie's conversation with her, um, husband. After we introduced ourselves and had a few meaningless laughs, Chuck asked if I needed another beer. I told him I was all set and he excused himself. *Now what?*

Normally when with a cute girl, I'd hesitate before speaking, editing my words to avoid offending or coming across as too forward. But since Jackie was married, I faced no pressure to impress, felt no anxiety about how, or when, or if I should ask her out. I had zero shot at her and nothing to lose, lending bravery to my bashfulness, gall to my game. My rap was never better.

"Where you from, Jack?" I asked the married woman. (Full disclosure: to a goody-two-shoes like me, this banal question seemed insanely flirtatious, but the words slid easily off my tongue, and I smiled with nervous confidence, like I had all the answers to an impossible test written on my palm.)

"I'm from Brooklyn, near Coney Island." My knowledge of Coney Island was limited. I only knew it was home to the Cyclone roller coaster, Nathan's Hot Dogs, and one of the best basketball players in the country: Lincoln High School's Stephon Marbury.

"Did you go to Lincoln?"

"Yes, but I'm a little older than Stephon Marbury."

So she's a mind reader. Impressive.

Then Jackie turned the tables. "Where are you from?"

"I live in Palisades Park now, but I grew up in Massachusetts."

"Where in Massachusetts?"

Okay, here we go. I'd been through this drill a zillion times. Whenever I'd tell someone I was from Chicopee, they'd do two things: first make fun of the name, then say they never heard of it. After that, we'd play the "hilarious" game of narrowing down the location of my hometown. It was annoying and boring, but I'd join in any game with Jackie.

"Western Mass," I said.

"Where in Western Mass?"

"A small town near Springfield."

Her eyes danced with mischief as if she had something up the sleeve of her sleeveless dress. "What town?"

I surrendered. "Chicopee."

She took a long sip of her pinot grigio. "I was just there last week."

"C'mon! No way. Are you serious?"

She was wicked serious. She worked in sales for Home Box Office and paid routine visits to cable companies throughout New England. Indeed, one week earlier, she'd attended a meeting with executives at Greater Media Cable on Front Street in Chicopee. She'd been there three times in the past twelve months and joked we might've passed each other on the sidewalk. Impossible. No way I would've forgotten her face.

I was proud of my hometown, held anyone who had the slightest knowledge of Chicopee in the highest esteem. Because of Jackie's ties to the area, I felt a psychic kinship, like she understood what made me tick after a five-minute conversation. So in that West New York apartment, in that tiny living room, as a skylight showered us with warm and wonderful sunrays, we talked about all things Western Mass. She said she liked to stay at the Yankee Peddler Inn in Holyoke then mused how people from my neck of the woods had no Boston accent, lived for Dunkin' Donuts, and called submarine sandwiches "grinders." Finally, when she told me she'd yet to attend Chicopee's annual Kielbasa Festival, I was hooked, holding neither her marriage nor her blasé attitude toward the "K-Fest" against her.

After Jackie left me to reunite with Chuck by the crudités, George wandered back over and jabbed me in the ribs with another Amstel. His smile broadened while his eyes did most of the talking. "Ain't no coincidences, Gags." He was right. This was fate.

As I regained my focus on the road, a sign for Mystic Seaport hollered that I'd be in Wakefield soon. I'd beaten the nor'easter and would be glued to the tourney within the hour, elbow-deep in Nadeau's famous chili. The dashboard clock read 11:11, and I made a wish as the sky turned from blue to black and *The Bliss Album* started over again.

The highway ghost quiet, I zipped across the Rhode Island border. Glancing down to eject the disc, I tugged the steering wheel a tad to switch into the fast lane. I felt the tires turn, but the Camaro continued dead ahead. My eyes widened. My throat filled with fear. The car began to drift sideways. I adjusted, pulled to the right. No response, nothing. I pumped the brakes. Nothing again, helpless.

No, God, no.

Now hydroplaning, mind racing. Fast.

C'mon, Kenny, stay cool.

Now all the way sideways, facing left. Sliding, now backwards, gliding. Trees blurry. Traffic across the median zooming. Same direction, opposite. Yanking the wheel, pumping the brakes. Again and again. Sideways again. Facing right now, spinning still. Faster.

What? Where?

If I were a praying man, I might've had a shot at survival, but I was not that man, never had been. To me, the act of prayer was a selfish endeavor, and I was uncomfortable asking the "Big Fella" for a favor out of the blue. But in this moment, as my world spun away, I pleaded for emergency assistance with anyone who might be listening: *Okay, God, or whoever. I'd like to trade in all those times I did "the right thing" in exchange for a chance. How 'bout it? One chance. Right here, right now. To live.*

After a full 360-degree spin, the car skidded toward a ditch on the side of the road, ripped up chunks of icy turf while rumbling down the embankment, and slid to a halt. I shifted into park and peeled my foot off the brake, my hands shaking. The engine in my chest spurted steam, desperate for a few quarts of coolant. *Where? How?*

It took a few seconds to realize the car was facing north again. I was safe, the Camaro intact, but my mortality had taken a hit, T-boned by a higher power. All previous thoughts of my permanence on this planet had been totaled and dragged off to the scrap heap. Dizzy and trembling, I stayed in that ditch for ten solid minutes. Cars and trucks raced past; no one stopped. I waited for the highway to clear and wormed up the embankment onto the shoulder. I drove steady in the slow lane, keeping my hands at ten and two, and continued my journey with deliberate purpose.

It'd take a while to get where I wanted to go.

SIX

"It Takes All Kinds to Make a World"

Summer, 1980

CLICK. CLICK. CLICK.

The multi-colored LEGO blocks snapped together in rhythm—one after another after another—like the sound of a pocket watch ticking off the remaining seconds of my childhood.

My friend, Jimmy Uszynski, and I sat across from each other on the benches of an auburn-stained picnic table on his back deck. It was only midmorning, but the young Chicopee sun had set the town on fire, the lavalike wood searing my bare feet. Mrs. Uszynski, a cheerful woman with a lemon meringue bouffant, walked onto the deck with two Hoodsie ice cream cups, vanilla and chocolate swirl. I lapped up my cup-o-chemicals so fast the wooden spoon splintered my tongue. "Hurry up and eat it before it turns into a milk shake," I told Jimmy between slurps.

"I will, just gotta find a few more of these big pieces first," my pal said and pushed his cup aside.

AC/DC's "Back in Black" blared from a boombox in the backyard below, where Jimmy's older brother, Dave, and next-door neighbor, Mike Beck, played Whiffle Ball. Pretending to care about my rinky-dink LEGO fortress, I watched the older boys pitch and hit, praying a ball might sail onto the deck, ready to snag it, like gloving a dinger in the Fenway bleachers.

It was a Saturday afternoon, tail end of June. School had let out for the summer the day before, releasing us parolees into three months of freedom. I sure wouldn't miss the jailhouse taupe halls of Bellamy Middle School, named for Chicopee's Edward Bellamy, author of *Looking Backward*, about a boy who wakes from a dream to find himself in a futuristic Utopian society. *And weren't we living a dream here in our Chicopia?*

Jimmy was my best friend on the street, lived a few doors down. We didn't have a lot in common, but he was agreeable and funny and benign. One of only a couple of boys near my age in the neighborhood, Jimmy invited me to his house all the time. Aside from his huge plastic bin of LEGO blocks, he had all the latest toys and gadgets: remote control cars and Transformers and Star Wars action figures and infinite board games. First thing on Christmas mornings, I called to ask what he got because I played with *his* stuff more than my own. Another big draw at their house was the Atari console in the basement, though a disconnect in my brain kept me from mastering the nuances of the joystick. I preferred real games like baseball, basketball, soccer, tennis, street hockey, anything physical.

Sometimes, Dave and Mike asked me to play Whiffle Ball with them. I salivated at the opportunity, diving in the trampled grass for unpredictable grounders, crashing into the chain-link fence for line drives, and whipping around the bases with abandon, sliding hard whenever possible. Those older guys respected my spunky spirit. They were high school seniors, same age as my brothers (well, only one brother now) and I did my best to impress. I wasn't sure how many people on the street knew about Robert and David but figured the adults had heard the story, had gossiped about my parents sending the twins away, had conjectured reasons for David's death. But did the neighborhood kids know? If they did, they didn't hear it from me. I never told a soul.

Jimmy and I were a few blocks from finishing our fortress when my ears perked to the sound of some boys calling my name. "Hey Kenny, you back there?" one of the voices shouted from the front of the house.

"We need you. Let's go," another one finished.

I tilted my head to sharpen my hearing and the kids yelled again. The sound lifted me off the bench, and I looked at Jimmy. "I'll be right back." I hustled down the deck steps to the backyard fence and saw two boys in the street coasting on their bikes in tight circles like vultures. It was Craig Patla and Rob Desormier, my buddies from school, who lived nearby.

Craig saw me and beamed. "Hey KG, a bunch of us are gonna play Whiffle Ball over in your church parking lot. We need you to make even teams. Let's go."

"Oh, okay. Hold on," I said trying to keep my cool. "I'll be back in a sec." I zipped across the yard, skipping on air. Who else would be playing? Whose bat would we use? Would they want me to pitch? I bounded onto the deck where Jimmy fumbled with a couple of ill-fitting LEGO pieces. I picked up my empty Hoodsie cup, brought it into the house to throw away, then came back outside as Nazareth's "Love Hurts" played on the boombox.

"Um, I gotta go," I said, my chin on my chest.

"I know."

"I'll call you tomorrow to see if you want to do something."

"Okay."

Jimmy didn't look up, and as I walked away, in the lie of it all, I knew I'd never play with him again. In a sad, cruel ending to a sweet, innocent friendship, I abandoned him, let him melt away like ice cream left out in the sun. But I had to move on, had to grow up and expand my world beyond the limits of Langevin Street, needed to test myself. And to do that, I'd leave everything behind.

While I set off to find my independence, my mother, now forty-four, prayed for hers. Dad criticized her every move back then, and she'd go days without speaking to him. On the rare occasion they tried to hold a conversation, it'd end in an argument. David's death a year earlier had been a world-shifting event riddling me with guilt, infusing me with a desire to please my parents at any cost and live my life for my surviving brother. But being the perfect son wasn't easy, and I shoved Robert further back in the closet of my mind. It was hard to make my mom and dad happy those days. I tried, but they were too angry, too distracted. And it was impossible for me, or anyone, to do anything for my brother.

At the church parking lot, Craig, Robbo, and I hopped off our bikes to find five boys waiting for us. I recognized all of them from school and rec sports teams, but I didn't know them well. That was about to change.

Basketball was Craig's best sport, but he was a decent baseball player and an above-average overall athlete. Charismatic, confident, and inclusive, he was tall and strong and a natural leader. Rob "Robbo" Desormier was a French-Canadian hit machine, a lefty who laced liners to all fields. Short and stocky with superior hand-eye coordination, he was the youngest of our crew, only in sixth grade. Steve Geoffrion was a reliable hitter and okay fielder. In seventh grade, like me and Craig, he lived on the street parallel to Langevin. He was short and good-natured and sported a loose blond Afro, which the elementary school girls went gaga over. Tommy Rivet, an eighth grader who lived near Patla, was one of the fastest kids in Chicopee. Rivet flew like he had

Canadian falcon in his blood. He was an average baseball player but a great soccer player with more muscles in one calf than I had in my entire body. Dave "Fitz" Fitzpatrick, a thoroughbred athlete with Scottish roots, was also in eighth grade and the only kid in town who could dust Rivet in a footrace. He had an imposing physique and a quiet demeanor and *actual* facial hair. Kenny "Howie" Howard, another eighth-grader, owned a quick wit and all the albums by the Beatles. The right-handed version of Robbo, he was a technical hitter who served outside pitches to right field in his sleep.

Then there was Pat Hall (a.k.a. "Feeble"), a loner who rarely said a word. When he did speak, I detected an English accent. Age unknown, he was wafer thin with pasty skin and whitish hair hanging over sheepdog eyes. He was supremely uncoordinated, lacking the slightest ability to hit or catch or run, but he lived across the street from the church, meaning the guys knocked on his door only out of convenience. When I said hi to Feeble that day, I called him Pat.

Craig commandeered the title of Whiffle Ball czar and, confiding his personal scouting report, divided the talent equally. He took Geoffrion, Fitz, and Howie on his side. I joined Robbo, Rivet, and Feeble. From what I gleaned of everyone's athletic ability, Craig had given himself a slight edge.

Geoffrion spray-painted bases on the asphalt. Fitz set up a lawn chair to use as a strike zone, and Howie announced the ground rules. "Okay, it's four-on-four. We'll play with a pitcher, one guy in right, one in center, and one in left. If someone hits a grounder and you get it to the pitcher before the guy gets to first, the guy's out. Anything over the fence in left or right is a homer. Anything landing in the grass in left center is gone too. Anything that gets past a fielder and bounces into the grass is a double. Anything hit above the church windows is a triple. Got all that, you fembots?"

I nodded and jogged to left field. Better not mess this up, I thought, or tomorrow you'll be back on Jimmy's deck making another dumb LEGO fortress.

Cynthia Grace

If Mom had told me about her childhood, if I had more evidence from her young life than one of her sixth-grade writing assignments and a letter she once received from her father, then I'd know why *family* meant so much to her. If only I'd asked about her hopes and dreams, I wouldn't have to assume how she felt back then.

It's 1948…

A noisy wooden bird pops out of a grandfather clock, suggesting with alternating cuckoos that time has come a bit earlier, or stayed a bit later, this Sunday evening. In her cotton nightgown, belly flat on the wood floor, twelve-year-old Cynthia pulls a knitted blanket from the couch and covers her bare feet. She bites her lip, taps a thoughtful beat on the side of her head with a pencil, and stares into the blank pages of a school notebook. "Can you help me yet, Daddy?" she asks with polite eyes.

"Yes, right after I figure this out, young lady," her father says while fiddling with the antennae on the Colthart family's first television set. He gnaws on his cigar like it's rolled in shoe leather and slides an end table aside, clearing a path to the TV's posterior. As he maneuvers into position, he bumps the table, knocking over a stack of books he's been reading. *The Poems of Robert Louis Stevenson* falls first, followed by *A Farewell to Arms* and *The Biography of Jefferson Davis*. The hardcovers carom into the legs of a nearby tray table and rattle the pieces on a chess board, slaying king and queen and pawn alike, postponing the war Tom had waged against himself.

His wife, Fran, checks on her mate. "What's all the racket,

Daddy?" she yells over the splashing of tub water, her hands lost in a sea of soapy suds on her young son Alan's head.

"Nothing at all, dear," Tom fibs, unsure of his amateur gambit.

Cynthia's teenage brother, glib and gangly Glenn, snickers into the pile of potatoes he's peeling at the kitchen sink, while in the hallway, younger sisters Elaine and Gail bicker and shuck corn on a rug of newspaper. Even with the two eldest Colthart boys away in the service, the apartment is hectic and cramped, barely enough room for a string of cigar smoke. But Tom's wife and kids are his heartbeat, and the tight quarters keep the family close.

Their move to Holyoke six years earlier, in the fall of '42, had been daunting but necessary. Back in New Bedford, Fran had ahold of seven children under age twelve, and Tom had been satisfied with his job as a manager at Firestone Rubber. But eight weeks before Japanese fighter planes raided Pearl Harbor, an inferno broke out at a Firestone factory down the road in Fall River. The all-night blaze caused millions in damage, cost thousands of jobs, rendered Tom Colthart's livelihood all but unsalvageable. And as the cloud of war cloaked each American family, Tom and Fran searched for the light, protecting their children from leaked news of Nazis corralling Jews into concentration camps, distracting from reports of gas chambers and mass graves and the extermination of millions of innocent lives.

Within a year, Tom found another job, and the family relocated a hundred miles west to a thriving mill city on the banks of the Connecticut River. In Holyoke, they mourned the death of President Roosevelt; celebrated Germany's surrender; and cringed in horror when the U.S. dropped atom bombs on Japan. They chuckled collectively as the Slinky sprung off toy store shelves; gawked when bikinis hit the beaches; and cheered when a Black man broke baseball's color barrier. Now they've called this city "home" for a half dozen years, and each member of the family has an assigned role in the Colthart ecosystem.

Overlooked and often taken for granted, Cynthia helps her parents however possible, tending to the younger siblings, deferring to the old. Asked to care for Aunt Grace, her mother's sickly younger sister in Rhode Island, Cynthia answers the call. A tough-as-nails stickler, Grace is childless and chilling, known mostly to Fran's kids for barking about manners and etiquette. Still, Cynthia forfeits her summer vacation and busses a hundred miles east to fulfill her duty. Midway through her stay, Tom writes to his amenable daughter, catching her up on the happenings at home:

Cynthia Sweet—Boy, are you having a time. First thing you know you'll have us all jealous of you. Well, I'm glad to know you're enjoying yourself and Aunt Grace says you are behaving very well and that you are good company. I'm glad to hear that too. Make the best of it. You never know when we'll be sending for you to come home as Ma has lost her best babysitter. I was glad to hear Aunt Grace did come home on Saturday. Tell her we said a prayer for her. I hope she's feeling better, and you help her all you can.

Alan's picture was in the paper this week, dressed up as Jesse James. What a hot sketch he is. The kids started Bible School this week, I guess they like it. Jane has a part-time job at Walgreen's Drug Store on the soda fountain and we received a letter from Donald yesterday. He arrived in San Antonio last Thursday and had a swell time on the train. He said he has a porky hair cut so I guess he's a happy man. Glenn hasn't really started to work steady yet, so he's taking care of the children for Ma. I go out early most days, so Alan and Gail are asleep when I leave.

So, you haven't even been to a show yet? How do you live? I thought you had to see the movies at least once a week. How are you fixed for spending money? I'm putting a little in this letter, but don't expect me to write to you too often, because that will prove expensive. I take it that you haven't been into Fall River very much although we haven't had any mail from Nana. Have you caught any fish yet???

Glad to hear you're getting acquainted with everyone down there. That way you should have a good time. Send my regards to Aunt Grace and Uncle Sammie and tell them we'd like to see them soon. I know we won't though because you'll want to stay down there.

Well, keep on behaving yourself and maybe Aunt Grace won't be sending you home.

— Daddy

"Do you remember when you were a little boy in Scotland, Daddy?" Cynthia inquires, still wrestling with her seventh-grade homework, a paper about her family's history, while her father focuses on the finicky television set. As he twists the antennae, the in-and-out picture of a female singer shows through snowy static.

"Wait one moment, sweetheart, I think I just about have it." The muscles in his face scrunch as Tom turns a knob behind the tube with the steadiness of a safecracker. Then, like a miracle from above, the image of Sarah Vaughan crystalizes in the glass, her angelic voice blessing the speakers. The family rushes around the TV, fawning over *The Ed Sullivan Show* as Ms. Vaughan wraps up "It's Magic" and Ed introduces an Egyptian magician named Gali Luxor, who produces live chicks from his assistant's trousers. The Colthart children chuckle and cluck along, but

Cynthia ignores the silliness, deliberates instead on her yet-to-be-written essay. Her father—typically a serious Scot—places his cigar in a tin ashtray, sits beside her on the floor, and softly sings:

Oh ye'll take the high road and I'll take the low road

And I'll be in Scotland afore ye

For me and my true love will never meet again

On the bonnie, bonnie banks of Loch Lomond

"My mother would sing that to me whenever I was anxious," he says, resurrecting his long-lost brogue. Then he strokes his daughter's satin hair and dictates wistful recollections of his past. In perfect penmanship, Cynthia writes about her father's childhood in Scotland, his family's journey across the Atlantic, and their adjustment to America. Like a sailboat on placid seas, her pencil flows over the page until the wind dies and the once-enthusiastic girl drops her head.

"What's wrong, dear?" her father asks. "Don't you trust my memory? Haven't I told you enough?"

"You have, Daddy. It's just that, well, there's something else I have to write about, and I don't know what to say."

"What is it, sweetie? I'm full of ideas tonight."

The hoo-hah around the TV declines. The air in the smoky room clears. Cynthia's soft eyes meet her father's. "I need to write what I want to be when I grow up."

Tom gapes into the heavens. "Well then, let's think about that one," he says, scratching the stubbly dimple on his chin until the eureka moment hits him. "Well how about that, I've got it! It seems clear to me that you'd surely fashion an extraordinary career for yourself if you mix together all the wonderful things that make you such a special young lady. The way you comfort others. The way you care for everyone. The way you're always looking to help. Those qualities are a gift, Cynthia. Use them and do something with your life that you truly enjoy. I wholeheartedly believe that you, my dear, have been put on this Earth to share all the love that's bursting out of your heart."

"But what can I be? What should I do?"

Her father leans in and whispers, "Be yourself, and do something that lets your light shine." Cynthia smiles; the wind fills her sails once again.

"Who Am I?"

Scotland, the land of heather and bagpipes, is the place that gave my ancestors birth.

My father and his parents, my grandparents, were all born in Scotland. In March of 1910, my grandfather sailed from Glasgow to the United States. Arriving in Boston, he found employment at Whitin Machine Works in Whitinsville, Massachusetts. This firm manufactures textile machinery. Two months later, in May 1910, he sent for his family: my grandmother, my father, and three other children. Both my paternal grandparents have resided in Whitinsville since arriving in this country. My grandfather is sixty-six years old and is still employed by Whitin Machine Works, his first and only place of employment since coming to America. He became a U.S. citizen at the earliest date possible and has never regretted leaving "The Old Country."

My father was brought here when he was nine years old. He has worked in many places, but right now he is employed at the American Thread Company. He has worked there for the past six years. He and my mother were married in Fall River,

Massachusetts. My father still remembers some of his early years in Scotland and is proud of his country of origin.

I made my first appearance on August 8, 1936. I was born in New Bedford, Massachusetts. I came to Holyoke when I was six years old. I then started at the Lawrence School and went from the first grade up to the third grade. I was then made to change schools and went over to the South Chestnut Street School. I went there for three more years and now I find myself back at Lawrence where I started. My ambition when I am older is to become a schoolteacher.

Can you guess who I am?

⌁

Wobbly waves of heat radiated off the asphalt, turning the church parking lot into a mirage.

While we played Whiffle Ball, I tried to keep cool, but a bundle of out-of-control nerves cranked up the thermostat. Afraid of doing or saying the wrong thing, I copied Craig's actions and reactions. He wore a continuing smile and teased the others with cold-blooded affability. I studied Craig's technique, how he'd ridicule one of the guys then cackle his Pied Piper cackle on the heels of the joke, disarming his victim, who'd laugh right along. More impressive, he could dish it *and* take it, hooting even harder when someone made fun of him. The group's jeering was stimulating and unrelenting, a test of solidarity, a leveling of the playing field, confirming us as equals. I was hooked.

"I've seen better swings on a gate," Craig cracked after Rivet swung and missed at a knuckleball. Boiling inside, Rivet tried to connect on a pithy comeback but whiffed again. Strike two.

"Nice one, Patla. You got an arm like a leg," Robbo chirped

after Craig launched the next pitch, a side-armed slider, eight feet over Rivet's head.

"Hey Feeble, you play that piano or just carry it?" Howie ranked as Pat struggled to get under a skyscraping fly to right. When he dropped the ball, the fellas doubled over in hysterics. I hid my smile.

We played on a loop into the unwinding afternoon. Our sweat-soaked skin glistened under a fanatical sun as we hit and ran and caught and threw, all the while listening to a Red Sox game through a tinny transistor nested in Craig's balled-up Seals & Crofts T-shirt.

Heaps of pressure burdened me, and I couldn't shake the tension, scrapping and straining to prove my worth as if I were trying out for the bigs. I hadn't hit well in five or six games, grounding out or popping up nearly every at bat. I played okay in the field and scored a few runs but didn't drive in any. As my audition flopped, the odds of my getting a callback dwindled.

In the last inning of the day's final game, Robbo knocked me in with the go-ahead run, but Craig's team had last licks. With two outs and a runner on second, Rivet served up a meatball to Fitz, who lashed a rocket to left-center field. My eyeballs bulged, and I turned sprinting to where I thought the ball would land. But a jerky pine branch interfered and swatted the fly downward.

I planted a foot in the grass and reversed course, unwilling to accept a loss at the hands of a fluky homer. In slow motion, I hoofed toward the ball as it laughed in my face and taunted, "If you don't catch me, you'll never play with these guys again!"

An inch before it hit the ground, I dove forward and tipped it up, buying myself another second. For an eternity, the snarky sphere hovered above me, suspended by fate. I flipped from my stomach to my back. With no time to reach out with my hands, I splayed my legs apart like a set of human tongs as the ball descended, and I locked the final out between my knees.

Game over!

We called ourselves the "Fairview Gang." And during that magical summer of my initiation, we played Whiffle Ball every day, popped wheelies all over town, and splashed in my backyard pool, where my new friends hoped to catch a glimpse of my sunbathing sisters. We played tackle football and tennis and pickup hoops at the park. During basement sleepovers, we roughhoused and peeped nudity-laden movies, guzzled gallons of Dr. Pepper, and pulled pranks on whoever dozed off first. On humid evenings after rainstorms, we carried empty coffee cannisters and flashlights to a field near Patla's house and yanked stingy nightcrawlers from the earth. At dawn the next morning, we skewered the beefy worms with fishhooks, flung our lines into the South Hadley Reservoir, and waited with bated breath for nibbling pumpkinseeds to rip our bobbers out of sight.

Some days, we hopped on our bikes before our dads left for work and roamed the not-so-mean streets of Chicopee until our moms got tired of calling us home for supper. We rode into Willimansett, past the Spalding Factory, where baseball pro Albert Spalding established his sporting goods company a century earlier. We rode over the "Singing Bridge," which straddled the roaring rapids of Chicopee River, clarifying why the Nipmuc Indians called their *Chickuppy*, "the place of the violent waters." We rode around the MacArthur Monument, a seven-ton granite ball honoring Chicopee's famous Civil War general, the Union Army's Arthur MacArthur, father of WWII's General Douglas MacArthur. And we rode to the Fairfield Mall to feed the Pac-Man machine at Just Fun Arcade and slobber over Farrah Fawcett and Loni Anderson busting out of scant swimsuits in the poster rack at Spencer's Gifts.

The mall opened in '75 to accommodate an influx of families moving to Westover Air Force Base, a five-minute bike ride from my house. It was the country's largest reserve base, carved out of twenty-five hundred acres of former tobacco fields. Westover had been a storage facility for nuclear weapons, and when Russia attacked, our teachers said, Chicopee would be a primary target. And so, every week at school, we hid under our desks during bomb drills.

The families from Westover never stuck around long. I'd known only one kid who lived there, a friend in kindergarten named Tonya, the first Black person I ever met. I remember she stole my mittens one day, and Mrs. Moynihan made her apologize. Tonya said she took them because she just moved from Texas and didn't have any warm clothes. She told us her mom hadn't had time to shop for any since her daddy left to work in "Toyland." She said he'd been gone for seven months, two weeks, and three days. I said there must be mittens in Toyland that he could mail to her. Mrs. Moynihan told me her daddy was sent to Thailand, not *Toyland*, and it was on the other side of the world, and it was very hot there. The next day, I brought an extra pair of mittens to school. Tonya moved away in the spring.

In the summer of 1980, while the Cold War got chillier, I found my hot spot: hanging with the Fairview Gang. Those brash boys swore freely, spoke lewdly about girls, and "borrowed" Playboys from their dads. Pledging their crew was like stowing away on a pirate ship, and the farther we got from shore, the more I wanted an eyepatch and a parrot. Until then, I'd never been myself for *myself*.

At the back end of August, as my buddies and I revved up for another school year, the members of my family motored ahead—away from one another. My sisters sputtered with the workload and cliquish drama of high school. Dad chugged into his third decade at Gagne & Sons, teaming up with his brother selling and repairing cars. To earn extra cash and get out of the house, Mom cruised into a part-time job as a secretary at a Holyoke printing company. Heading into eighth grade, I accelerated and flew (almost literally) into the world of sports..

When I was five, my mom had enrolled me in an acrobat class where I learned to jump and bounce and stretch and fall in impossible ways. I spent every Monday night for three years at Larder's Dance Studio practicing flips, cartwheels, round-offs, and somersaults. I could walk on my hands and stand on my head and bend over backward with Gumby-like flexibility. Between those lessons and running the hills in my backyard, I developed the agility of a ninja and the endurance of an Olympic marathoner.

Pint-size and slow compared to most athletes in our town, I compensated with the stamina and shiftiness of a caffeinated chipmunk. A freakish science project MacGyvered with pipe cleaners and Silly Putty and spit, I manipulated a sinewy body strung with elastic tendons. Flinging myself around local fields and courts, I was an indestructible superhero, hell-bent on not letting anyone down, competing with a head of steam. In basketball, I led the league in floor burns. In soccer, I turned the slide tackle into an art form. And in baseball, I dove to catch every ball like it was a grenade about to blow all of Chicopee to smithereens.

My aggression unleashed an anarchist fighting to outdo opponents and teammates alike. As a runt, I had to fight to survive, spurred by a tenacity to prevail. I fed my inner under-dog, cheated and took cheap shots, tripped guys and pulled their jerseys, faked injuries to elicit foul calls. I played heated and angry, determined to destroy my enemies with the toothiness of an irritated Doberman. Civil and diplomatic off the field, like my parents raised me, I gave myself moral license to prowl the sporting arena with nastiness and malice. An alter ego emerged, an audacious avatar, out to prove I was better than the rest.

Like drawing before, sports offered an escape, and though I liked being known as an "artist," I treasured my new identity as an "athlete," running free, connecting with myself, getting lost in the singular act of "doing." One passion complemented the other. Whether dreaming up a cartoon or chasing a ball, I locked into the only two things that mattered: creating and playing.

My mom and dad loved watching me compete back then, never missed a game, saw how I gave more effort than anyone else, and were proud. Finally someone in the family willing to fight for something, they may have thought. But my "fight" wasn't allowed to leave the field, court, or pitch. And so I left it all out there, where it belonged. Then I stepped over the sideline and into my second self, an ordinary kid quietly battling against invisible forces tearing his parents apart.

I was thrilled to be part of the Fairview Gang, but as much as I enjoyed the cool new me, they were a mischievous posse, and I suspected trouble around every corner. I could fake a hint of rebellion, but I was no outlaw. The strength of my character tested daily, I continued to follow Craig's example. My best friend wouldn't lead me astray.

The eve before Halloween, "Beggar's Night," the crew devised a dastardly plan to peg houses in my neighborhood with rotten tomatoes. At dark, we crept through Old Man Keeler's vegetable garden to fill paper grocery bags with squishy, rancid rounds of artillery. I spent most of my time hiding from passing cars, taking cover in the leaf lettuce, and ended up meekly armed compared to the rest of the troops.

The crescent moon hid behind skeleton trees as the seven of us (Feeble wasn't invited) mounted our bikes. Dressed hat-to-shoe in black, we soared down Langevin Street in a V-formation like naughty Canadian geese navigating the night on instinct alone. I brought up the rear, excited but conflicted by our uncivil disobedience. Crickets chirped a futile warning of the bombardment as we glided past my house and the silhouette of my mother washing dishes in the kitchen window. I stopped pedaling. Did she see me? Was she wise to our plan?

The fevered tempo of baseball cards tick-tick-ticking in my spokes slowed like a decelerating roulette wheel, and my charcoal Huffy drifted far behind the rest of the armada. In the middle of the road, I coasted to a stop. Then, as the other boys seeped into the night, their bikes wandering away from the streetlight's vigilant eye, I turned around and went home.

SEVEN

"Your Mind Is a Computer"

Winter, 1988

A COMEBACK WAS IMPOSSIBLE.

On a bitter January morning in Chicopee, during the closing minutes of a men's league basketball game, my team—the Druid Ridge Warlocks—packed it in against a squad of older guys from the Four-Ten Lounge. The enemy featured two of my childhood role models: Langevin Street's Dave Uszynski and Mike Beck. I was twenty now, and they were twenty-five, but I still felt like a pipsqueak next to them, still a runt looking for approval.

The Four-Ten had man-handled us all game and, late in the contest, we fell behind by an insurmountable twelve points. It was a familiar situation (down by double digits) in a familiar setting (the same Comp gym where my high school basketball career had fizzled). Bored on the bench, waiting out the final sixty ticks, I gathered my sweats and jacket, kicked back, and fantasized about the Egg McMuffin in my future. But Eddie Medina fouled out, and I subbed in.

I wasn't programmed to admit defeat, no matter how bleak the outlook. So the first time I touched the ball, behind the three-point line on the left wing, I rose for a jumper. Mike Beck closed out to challenge my shot, and I let my leg drift a bit to the side. As he ran past, his foot clipped mine and I faked losing my balance, letting out a yell and exaggerating my fall. After the ball clanged off the rim, the ref blew his whistle.

"Are you serious? How is that a foul?" Mike screamed. "He stuck his leg out on purpose." But the seventy-year-old official making twenty bucks to not break a sweat saw the play differently.

I pulled myself up off the floor, grabbing my hip in faux pain. With fifty seconds left, I hobbled to the foul line and sank three free throws. Down by only nine now, Druid Ridge had hope. What happened next would go down in Chicopee recreational sports lore.

Despite holding a comfortable lead, the more experienced Four-Ten players caved to the momentum swing, got tight as piano strings, and threw away the inbounds pass. I seized the loose ball and swished a three from the top of the key. Losing by six, we purposely fouled their steady redheaded point guard, whose name I always forgot, to stop the clock. He missed his free throw. With under half a minute remaining, my buddy Craig Patla made a tough reverse layup and got hacked in the act. He calmly hit his foul shot to draw us within three.

On Four-Ten's next possession I drew a charge on Mike Beck, fooling the ref again, this time with a fantastic flop that would've been the envy of a Hollywood stuntman. Mike slammed the ball next to my flattened body, which lay stiff and mangled like the chalk outline of a homicide victim. "Screw you, Kenny," he muttered. Our ball with ten seconds to go.

We called time-out and drew up a play for our quiet go-to guy, Steve Sawa, who hit a clutch three at the buzzer to tie the game. The Druid Ridge faithful—one set of sleepy parents and a couple of hungover girlfriends—ditched their Styrofoam cups of Dunkin' Donuts coffee and hollered like crazy. (They were already nuts, having shown up at a freezing gym at 8:00 a.m. just to sit on rock-hard bleachers for two hours as we weekend warriors relived our high school heydays.)

In overtime, we eighty-sixed the Four-Ten. Our miracle comeback complete, my mates and I slapped high fives and lined up to shake hands with the bad guys. Mike Beck angled toward me. I braced myself. He steamed and huffed, red-faced and riled. I half expected a punch in the mouth. He snatched my arm and pulled me into his chest. His breath smelled like revenge. "Great game, jerkoff," he said with a wink, tousling my hair like he used to during Whiffle Ball games in the Uzsynski's backyard.

"Thanks, man," I said before slapping him on the backside. "You taught me everything I know." I strutted away to join my teammates in celebration having never felt more respected, and hated, as an athlete. It was a feeling I'd continue to chase.

Ten hours later, I'd again summon my acting skills. This time, in front of my parents and best friends at Chicopee's famous Polynesian restaurant and lounge, the Hu Ke Lau, the predominant cultural experience in our town outside of ordering takeout from Millie's Pierogis.

The house lights dimmed. Hula dancers and fire-eaters hot-footed off stage as the emcee's announcement boomed through speakers baked into the ceiling. "Ladies and gentlemen, it's time to be mesmerized." A roomful of puckish patrons scorned their scorpion bowls, nixed their chopsticks, and pooh-poohed their pu pu platters. "Please welcome the spellbinding R-rated hypnotist, Burt Borello."

For Christmas, my parents had bought five tickets to this show and looked forward to a rare evening of levity, hoping Kijak and Nadeau and I would volunteer to get hypnotized. Mike and Mark were on break from Union College. I was in the middle of my junior year at UMass—and still heartsick over Elise. I welcomed the distraction of a night out, but all I knew of hypnosis was from the old-time movie character, Svengali, the mangy soothsayer who forces a woman to fall in love with him. *Oh, Elise.*

I'd volunteer if the opportunity arose but would be shocked if Burt Borello could put me in a trance. No one had ever talked me into doing anything against my will, and I doubted this raunchy huckster would be the first.

Just weeks away from turning "legal," I'd yet to taste a drop of alcohol (not counting the occasional beer my father fed me when I was a kid). My mom had begged me not to drink, and I obeyed out of duty and fear: fear of throwing up and making a mess and needing my friends to take care of me; fear of kissing a girl without permission or getting into a fight; fear of doing anything out of character or disappointing anyone. Temptation was all around, and I stood firm. But not without help.

Keeping me on the straight and narrow was the budding friendship I shared with one of my college roommates, Mike Zdrojewski (pronounced phonetically exactly as one might imagine: Mike, like bike), a working-class kid from Woburn with an endearing snaggletooth and a side-splitting way of calling a Pop Tart a "Pauwwp Tauwt." After a semester at Tufts, he'd transferred to UMass and moved into my dorm spring of sophomore year. The following fall, we were roomies in an off-campus apartment with Patla and another kid from Chicopee named Kevin Garvin. Like me, "Z" wasn't into partying, a core requirement for most majors at UMass. He and I bonded over hoops, not Heinekens.

During pickup basketball games, we were unbeatable when paired together, competing with the same unselfish, mind-melding style, anticipating each other's moves as if we'd been teammates our whole lives. But when we played one-on-one, we were programmed killers, dueling Bond villains in tube socks. After our battles, we'd sometimes refuse to speak to each other for hours. Or at least till the blood dried.

Like Kijak and Nadeau had done for me in high school, Z boosted my self-esteem. I felt smarter and funnier around him, a little taller sometimes. We riffed off of each other like jazz musicians, freelancing without judgment. By simply being himself, he showed me it was okay to be honest and emotional and vulnerable. We were bizarro twins. He was left-handed; I was right-handed. He had two younger sisters; I had two older ones. His parents weren't together; mine shouldn't have been. He spoke openly about his hang-ups and fears, cutting seriousness with humor, and I learned to do the same. He was my mirror, one I turned to before heading out into the world; his reflection gave me confidence, telling me I looked okay—even if skinny ties were "so last year."

Hanging out with Z fortified and inspired me but did little to take my mind off my ex-girlfriend. I was whipped and, like a loyal pup missing its master, fell asleep every night next to Elise's picture in a frame. I'd dumped my soul into our relationship, and the weight welded me to my youth. Under her spell, I was helpless to move on. Someone had to snap me out of it.

"Hey, how's everyone doing tonight?" The R-rated hypnotist said, sauntering across the stage. An engaging man with saucer-sized glasses, sweaty hair, and a triple chin, he dragged the microphone cord behind him like he was walking a dead pet snake. I stuffed half a cold eggroll into my mouth as Mr. Borello got down to tacky brass tacks. "When we're babies in our mother's womb, we're resting in a dream state that instructs us to be who we're going to be."

Oh, brother. Time for some sweet-n-sour chicken.

"Hypnosis is a way of hacking into this dream state, into our limitless imaginations, and reprogramming us to do or say just about anything."

Hmm, how about some fried rice?

"You see, your mind is like a computer."

Hold up. What? That's what Dad always says.

Across the white linen tablecloth stained with soy sauce, my father sat back in his chair, a devilish grin on his wise-alecky face. "See that. I tried to tell ya, Kenny!" He was in his glory. All my life, the man stacked up tiny bricks of confirmation biases like this to stand over me on a platform of supremacy. (He wasn't nearly as tall as he appeared.)

Burt asked for volunteers to come forward, and I sprung from my seat. But Mike and Mark didn't budge.

"Hey, let's go. We said we were all going to do this, right?" I asked. My buddies shook their heads and sat on their hands while I stewed in a soup of agitation. "C'mon. This is why we're here. We can't just watch everyone else up there. This'll only be fun if we all volunteer."

"Or at least if one of us does," droned Droopy in his waggish monotone.

Dad backed me up. "Don't be a wimp, Nadeau. Get up there Droops, you zero." My friends just laughed.

"I don't believe this." I shoved my chair in and headed to the stage to join thirty other volunteers in a wacky mind control experiment.

I stood on the end of the line, farthest away from Burt, as he showed us guinea pigs how to relax. "Take three deep breaths," he instructed. "Now allow your eyes to blink twice very slowly." He snapped his fingers once, and then again. "Feel your eyelids getting heavy and allow them to close."

I did as I was told.

"Sense them melting into your cheeks as they close tighter and tighter." It sounded like he was gargling with syrup. "They are heavier and heavier. And now when I count to three, you will open your eyes."

Really? This is it?

"One... Two... Three!"

I opened my eyes.

Burt scanned the line. "If your eyes are open you can go back to your seat." I slammed my eyes shut; no way I was going back a failure.

The flunkies who couldn't cut it mumbled and shuffled off stage. I snuck a peek; there were ten of us left.

"Now take another deep breath. Relax. And sleep."

No problem, Burt.

Denying this cut-rate spellbinder's hocus pocus would be child's play. I specialized in pulling the wool over the world's eyes, and this Hu 'Ke Lau caper was right up my alley. The spotlight beamed in from the back of the room, my Bat Signal calling on me to save the city from boredom, to make everyone happy. I pulled on my mask.

Those I knew best labeled me naïve, pegged me as a Polly Purebred who'd never lie or cheat or steal. Scammers would stomp all over me, they figured, because I trusted everyone. That was partially true; I assumed most humans were kind-hearted givers like my mom, but I was no rube. My blind trust was a cold, calculated matter of efficiency. Believing in everyone from the start required way less energy than picking all the bad apples out of the bunch. It took too much brain power to spot the rot, so I made quick judgments on folks and opened up. If anyone took advantage and made a mark of me, that'd only prove I was the better person. Those fraudsters and swindlers were yin to my yang, showing me what *not* to do. I learned trust from the untrustworthy, kindness from the unkind, politeness from the impolite.

To feign hypnosis, I had to trust Burt Borello and play along. I knew impossible when I saw it, and this wasn't even close. That sweaty-haired joker had no idea the award-winning actor he was up against. My self-control was too much for his amateur-hour sorcery. Falling into a fake trance would be easy; all I had to do was pretend, and I'd been doing that my whole life.

Bobby

If Dad had told me what he was like as a teen, if I'd known more than the fact that he'd been kicked out of two high schools, then it'd be no mystery why he praised my average report cards. If only I'd asked about his disappointing academics, I wouldn't have to guess how it affected his sense of self-worth.

It's 1949...

Headmaster William adjusts his bifocals, sighs, and reshuffles a neat stack of papers on his desk. Tired eyes, sagging jowls, and age spots dotting his wrinkled head tell the tale of a man worn out from his job, specifically, and the priesthood, generally. In the back corner of the oaken office, Brother Ricardo, dean of discipline at St. Benedict's Preparatory School, poses prim and proper, a decade of secrets hiding behind his buttoned robe and zippered lips. Outside, a steady spring rain falls.

Seated across from the headmaster, eighteen-year-old Bobby Gagne languishes, belligerence dripping down his face. Beside him, his father Rheo's burly frame tests the structural integrity of a plush chair. His wet fedora rests on the desk; a puddle forms. Bobby waves away the stink of damp wool as if a muskrat were tickling his nose. Rheo taps his wooden cane on the floor, and the echo dominates the room.

Whap! Whap! Whap!

Raising his gaze above his glasses, Headmaster William says, "I'm very sorry, Mr. Gagne. We certainly appreciate the generous contributions you've made to this institution. And we do realize your eldest son graduated from our school five years ago. But you must understand there is nothing else we can do here." He squints and pans to Robert. "Certainly not in this case."

"Well then," says Rheo, "seems our business here is done." He pushes himself up from his creaking seat, the chair and headmaster equally relieved. The hulking Canadian dons his still-soggy hat and nods to his son. As Bobby stands, Rheo pounds his cane into the floor.

Boom!

Brother Ricardo jumps out of his collar, shaken by the sudden clap of man-made thunder.

"Thank you both for your time," says Rheo. "Good day."

"Is there anything else I can do?" Headmaster William offers before reorganizing his stack of papers.

"You've done enough."

"Brother Ricardo can walk you out."

"No need." The Gagnes are already at the door, finally leaving the school Bobby never wanted to attend in the first place.

The campus grounds are more pretentious in the rain. Boys in matching uniforms walk to class with an entitled ease, bone-dry under expensive slickers and umbrellas. The chapel bells gong as father and son drive under the front gate's iron awning and into the town of Danvers, formerly Salem Village. A familiar pain stabs Rheo's abdomen, reminding him he needs a drink.

Under darkening clouds, Danvers basks in an unbecoming light. A thousand moons ago, it was home to a notorious coven of teens who wrongfully accused a dozen townsfolk of witchcraft. In mass hysteria, the village's frenzied residents showed the obtuse symptoms of a mad fever: the chills of blame, the aches of ignorance, the rising temperature of vengeance.

And on this day, that madness festers still. The demons of the haunted town have thrown a hex upon Bobby. He's been expelled for delinquent behavior including, but not limited to: failing grades, insubordination, vandalism, drinking, and fighting. Those same sins had led to his expulsion from Chicopee High School two years earlier, triggering his banishment to St. Ben's Prep. Now, eight weeks before graduation, he faces exile again.

Rheo's car slushes through town, heading west, as the

windshield wipers chant an incantation. Father and son sit silent as an old photograph, neither wanting to address the elephant in the DeSoto. Finally, Rheo unloads. "They told me you broke almost every rule at that school. I assume that's an exaggeration."

Bobby watches the raindrops collecting on his window. Each one trickles on its own—stopping and starting and stopping again—before joining with another and racing down the glass. He hasn't seen much of his father in the past year, and he's happy enough sitting beside him now. His craving for the man's attention is an out-of-reach itch and, like the acne on his back, it'll scar if left untreated. Wordlessly, Bobby pleads for the love his dad heaps on everyone else.

"Don't you have anything to say?" Rheo asks.

Bobby stares out the window.

"Answer me, boy."

"No," says Bobby.

Rheo's voice ratchets up a level. "What was that?"

"No, sir. I have nothing to say."

"Destroying school property. Disrespecting teachers. Booze. Fights. It's always the same thing with you." Rheo flicks his cigarette over the tray separating man and boy. A nub of ash blows onto Bobby's leg; he brushes it off, leaving a gray stain on his tan trousers.

They pass a grassy mound called Gallows Hill. A carved wooden sign on the roadside commemorates the site where thirteen victims of the Salem Witch Trials were hung, scapegoats for the trespasses of a gullible town. Bobby tries to make out the year on the sign, but his blurry eyesight fails him. It's been that way since grade school, when a punch from a kid twice his size crushed his glasses. Fed up with her son's behavior, Annette Gagne refused to replace the spectacles.

"And what about your grades?" Rheo continues. "Were your subjects so tough that you couldn't pass any of your exams?"

On this topic, especially, Bobby's at a loss. He wishes the rain would wash away the conversation.

His father demands an answer. "Did you even try?"

"Yes, sir."

He can't tell the truth, that there's no use in studying, that taking a test causes his heart to pound so hard it drowns out his thoughts and ignites an anger in his belly. Bobby's never been able to pay attention in school. Words and numbers confuse him. He can't sit still, can't do the work, assumes he's just a dummy like all the kids say. He can't make decent grades, can't even fake being competent, so he creates conflict—in *and* out of class—to stimulate listless synapses. For a cheap rush, he picks fights and starts arguments. He'd tried to put his energy into football at St. Ben's but forgot the plays and butted heads with the coaching staff, who saw him as just another spoiled kid. His parents paid little attention to his struggles, offered scarce support, leaving Bobby to fend for himself.

After two tense hours on the road, the car crosses the Chicopee town line and rolls into Willimansett, where Bobby's future hinges on one of two imperfect options: pump gas at his dad's auto shop or enlist in the service. "So, what's your plan?" Rheo asks. "Now that you've thrown away your best chance to make something of yourself." The words are cruel, but Bobby accepts the criticism and hopes, in time, they can repair this fractured relationship. Pretending to be friends would be enough, even if neither called it "love."

When they pull into their gravel driveway, Bobby spies his mother standing stern in the parlor window, arms crossed, glaring. He slides down in his seat. Another twinge zaps Rheo's gut. "Hey, son, grab me that Canadian Club out of the glove box, will ya?" Bobby hands over a half-empty bottle of whiskey. His father twists off the cap, takes a grown-man swig, and lets out a satisfying belch. He smacks his lips and gives the bottle to his boy. "Here, you're gonna need this." It's more an order than an offer.

A tout mieux tout. Hiya!

⁓�§

As part of his cheesy act, The R-rated hypnotist had roles for us volunteers to play, and instructions to follow.

He suckered two elderly women into thinking the guy next to them—a biker with a Fu Manchu—had intestinal issues; I couldn't help but smirk as the biddies gagged on the suspicious stink of fictitious farts. Then Burt Borello convinced four middle-aged men they were world-class ballerinas, and we all watched them proudly lumber about, performing one ungraceful pirouette after another. And he somehow induced two cute girls wearing Jordache jeans into forgetting their last names. I waited at the far end of the Hu Ke Lau stage as those nine simpletons made fools of themselves. Were they actually hypnotized? Was I the only one faking?

Burt strolled up to me. "And what's your name, young man?"

I flashed an eager smile and chuckled. "Ken."

"This is all pretty funny to you, isn't it Ken?"

Shining under hot floodlights, I was hyped to show off my skills. "Yeah, these people are clowns."

"Well, Ken, let's find out what they think of you," the sweaty man said into his sweaty mic. The audience buzzed as Burt laid out his plan for me. "You see, we all know that two plus two equals four. But you, my fine fellow, you believe that two plus two equals *five*. And you're going to prove it to the ladies here on your left."

The two cute girls who couldn't remember their names wore giggling grins. "Hey Ken, are you good at math?" one of them asked.

I puffed out my chest and ran my fingers through the flowing locks of my sublime mullet. "Good enough to know you two are both tens."

"Wow, thanks. Can you tell us what two plus two equals?"

"Um, duh. It's five." The crowd roared, and without skipping a beat, I threw a look toward the cheap seats and demanded, "What's so funny?"

Laughter rained on me, and I strained to stifle my pleasure. Acting confused, I stretched my arms out and yelled to the audience, "Hey, what's going on here?"

The tight-jeaned girls were hungry for more. "So two plus two equals five, huh?" the other one asked, playing right into my hands. "Can you show us with your fingers how that adds up?"

"Are you kidding? You two are ridiculous. Hot, but ridiculous," I said. "Okay, it's like this." I made a peace sign with my fingers. "Two." Then I flicked out two others. "Plus two more." Then I popped out a condescending thumb to present an open hand. "Is five."

The crowd was in stitches. The girls laughed their pants off. "Ha ha! What a dunce!" I let the moment breathe.

Like a mongoose toying with a quiver of charmed cobras, I prepared for the big payoff. Emboldened behind my mask of hypnosis, I plunked my hands on my hips, waited for the room to quiet, and let the tension build. Then I stared the cuties straight into their patronizing, pretty eyes and demanded, "Last names, please."

The place erupted with sharp delight, chiseling the girls into speechless statuettes. I tried to steal a glimpse of my parents— between the tiki totem and giant plastic ferns in the back—but the stage lights were too bright.

Burt ended his hokey routine and dismissed his volunteers, but before we left the stage, he primed us for the grand finale. "Now when you go back to your seats, you'll still be hypnotized, and you'll have no recollection of what just happened here. Oh, and one more thing, when you talk to the people at your table, you won't be able to speak English. You'll *think* you're speaking English, but it'll just sound like gibberish to everyone else."

I focused on Burt's commands like he was an air traffic controller instructing me how to land a plane; my parents and friends expected a comical touchdown, and I aimed to deliver.

"Only when I say the magic word will you wake from your hypnosis and speak English again," he said.

Okay, I thought, got it. No, wait. What's the magic word?

"And the magic word is... *supermarket.*"

My ruse nearly complete, I headed to my seat with fifteen seconds to decide the most credible way to babble incoherently without blowing my cover. Facing the moment of truth, determined not to gag, I casually settled into my chair and began blabbering whatever nonsensical, multi-syllabic verbiage I could dream up.

"Was it fun up there?" asked Droopy.

"*Shecka kenalke rooba niliak tripundapop sura doop.*"

"Do you remember anything?" asked Nadeau.

"*Fossum bobart nishy oopatip convalack.*"

I played those suckers like ukuleles, performed my ploy to perfection. They bought it all, hook, line, and *stinker.*

Containing hysterics, my mom covered her mouth and buried her head in my father's shoulder, and he placed his hand on her knee while trying to keep a straight face. It'd been years since I saw them laugh together, since I looked at them and saw more than their brokenness. I wanted it to last forever.

Unsure how much longer I could keep up the scam, I prayed Burt would spit out the magic word and break my "spell." The Polynesian island gods answered my plea and, finally... *supermarket.* I flowed into English mid-sentence without a stutter.

Now, back to living another lie.

At that point in my life, I wasn't sure who I *needed* to be or who I *wanted* to be, and I debated whether to follow my mind or my heart, with no idea which was more important. Mom and Dad were proud I'd gone to college and let me decide my own path. Once I realized I wouldn't be a professional athlete, I figured the next best thing would be a career in the sports industry (seemed like a sure-fire way to *not* work for a living). My parents trusted my choice to major in sport management, a suggestion I took from my high school coaches, and they had faith in my landing a job. They knew that when I did, I'd give it my best and find a way to be happy, which is all I'd wanted for them.

With me at college and my folks home by themselves, Dad was more callous and Mom more unreachable. That was the main reason I traded in UMass for Chicopee every weekend. As marital referee, I toned down his brash bark, dulled his cheeky bite, and sidetracked his constant attempts to demean my mother. His behavior toward her was a tired act, but one I'd understood only recently. When I was a self-absorbed kid, I'd sensed the tension in their relationship but denied the toxicity and ignored the evidence: the Alcoholics Anonymous pamphlets, the marriage counseling paraphernalia, the frigid shoulders. A bumbling Inspector Clouseau would've connected the dots in minutes, but I was clueless. Now their troubled marriage, made worse by Dad's money woes, came into crystal clear focus.

The EPA's lawsuit against him siphoned dollar after dollar and emasculated my father, the stress and embarrassment eating at him like roadkill maggots. Adding to his helplessness, the "family" in the family-owned business turned its back on him. For years, he ran Gagne & Sons with his brother, but when Uncle Rheo retired, my father took over the biz. Now as the sole owner, and defendant in the case, Dad got stuck with the bill. A last-ditch chance to save face, if not cash, fell away when my uncle bailed on a court appearance, refusing to testify on his little brother's behalf, and the suit crawled toward its ill-fated outcome. The EPA wanted its man; the lawyers wanted their dough; and my father wanted no part of the inevitable—something called chapter 7.

For her part, my mother took a behind-the-scenes stand as a character witness and drafted a letter to the judge presiding in the case, throwing herself on the mercy of the court, resurrecting the memory of the man she'd known her husband to be:

Dear Judge Murphy,

I am writing to you on behalf of my husband, Robert A. Gagne, who has no knowledge of this letter.

I know I cannot change facts or laws leading up to your conclusion of this trial. I can, however, make a statement about this good and kind man who has never willfully and/or intentionally deceived anyone in the twenty-eight years I have known him. But for whom he is in conflict now, I can name many friends, customers, neighbors, and more in our church and home communities who would testify to this fact.

My husband is a good, honest, and caring person. He has never hurt anyone but, rather, helped many. While I know you have to make a just and lawful decision, I am asking you to be as kind as possible to him. He has already been destroyed financially. I am only asking that the spirit of life left in this man not be destroyed as well.

Thank you for reading this letter and also for allowing me to write it.

Sincerely,

Cynthia Gagne

Trying to rebound from the legal hit, Dad acquired his real estate license at age fifty-six, accepted a hookup from a pal at a local agency, and became their top seller (a prestigious honor that included a gold cup emblazoned with *Realtors Need Closure* on its base). A swaggering salesman with a renegade's moxie, my father did things *his* way, but that rarely synced up with the company line. Eventually, his lack of acumen and etiquette rubbed his boss the wrong way, and she evicted him from the office. He left the trophy.

While Dad reprised his role as Willie Loman, my sisters struck deals and formed partnerships of their own. Cheryl revoked her prized independence and got together with a friend of mine, Mike Labrie, my former American Legion baseball coach. When I played for him, Coach believed in me, and after I aged out of Legion ball, he kept believing and made me his assistant, a vote of confidence that carried me whenever self-doubt gave me a charley horse. A former star athlete at Comp—and now a popular lawyer and successful high school basketball coach—Mike was Chicopee's favorite son, and I idolized him like I would a big brother. He'd tell me, "You gotta talk to the people, you gotta see the people, and you gotta mix it up for the people." I heeded his advice and appreciated his allegiance. Then and always.

Linda followed Cheryl's lead and got her groove on, dating a silky-smooth R&B front man named Kevin. His popular group, New Star, sang and swang and did their thang for jammed dance floors all over Springfield. Sometimes I'd go to those trendy clubs with Linda sporting acid-washed jeans and a sapphire V-neck, swimming in Drakkar Noir and nonchalance while Kevin threw me shout-outs from the stage, boosting my coolness factor a notch. At the end of their sets, New Star bandmates dapped me up and gifted me not-yet-released cassette copies of the latest soul records. I was never more fly, fresh, or dope.

In the meantime, Mom forged ahead, poring over the

classifieds, looking to provide my father some financial aid. In a laudable show of sisterhood, dear friend Susan Cassidy wrangled a full-time job for my mother in the membership department at the Holyoke YMCA. From behind the front desk, Mom greeted every guest at the Y with that easy smile of hers. Her longtime Holyoke cronies—classmates and old flames alike—burned more calories cavorting with Cindy each morning than they did in their Jazzercise classes. Susan and the rest of the staff, plus every camp kid and member, became my mother's second family.

And she loved them like she loved us.

I never told my parents the truth about my phony Hu Ke Lau hypnosis act. I enjoyed watching my mom and dad laugh together that night and didn't want to sully the memory—in my mind or theirs. I liked being the entertaining jester, liked making them smile. I never told Kijak or Nadeau the truth either. It felt good to outsmart them for once. In their eyes, I was a blissful knucklehead, perpetually fooled, the guy who fell for anything. A sucker. Even my best friends didn't know the *real* me. If they had, they would've understood I didn't mind wearing their sympathetic labels. "Poor Kenny," everyone said, and I soaked up the pity. Playing into that narrative relieved the pressure to be anything extraordinary. No one expected much from me. Or *of* me. And I was sure I could deliver on those expectations without letting anyone down.

EIGHT

"I Could've Written This Thing"

Spring, 2002

OUT OF THE corner of my eye, I studied Jackie's profile.

She was focused, intense, contemplating a response to a situation heavier than any we'd faced together. I watched and waited, like I waited for her divorce from Chuck; like I waited a month to kiss her after we started dating; like I waited for her at the Willowbrook Mall Park & Ride with an engagement ring; like I waited for her with the Reverend Ann Geer at the end of a garden path behind an old inn deep in the Berkshire mountains on our wedding day.

Dr. Murray, a genetics counselor with caring eyes and a cream-colored sweater, sat opposite us at a glass desk in a small-ish office at St. Barnabas Hospital. The place felt like held breath. A beacon of empathy, trained to inform and comfort during life-shifting scenarios, the doctor adjusted the band of her watch and curled a quasi-smile. The desk's dim lamp and window's half-drawn shade gave the aura of a confessional booth. Though neither my pregnant wife nor I had sinned, our penance was severe.

A slash of light from the window heckled us and beckoned April's renewal, succeeding as a weak metaphor for irony. Outside, budding maples framed the parking lot and irrepressible tulips sprouted along the sidewalk. Perky robins shook off winter's chill and pecked at the still-thawing ground. Brave blades of grass stood tall.

Dr. Murray gave it to us straight. "Tay-Sachs is a neurodegenerative disorder of the central nervous system that most commonly affects infants. It's a progressive disease that, unfortunately, is always fatal." Her cold and pointed words hung on a string of quiet, like icicles on a frozen wire, before breaking loose and stabbing my brain.

I grabbed my knee to settle a hyper jitterbug. "No one's sure, but that might be what my twin brothers had," I said.

Our second child would be a girl, but five months into the pregnancy, a blood test showed the baby had Tay-Sachs. The news shattered us. I couldn't fathom enduring the same trauma that tore my parents apart. Jackie and I held on to a shred of optimism when her ob-gyn said the result might be a "false positive." But only a procedure called amniocentesis would tell for certain. During amnio, doctors would puncture the womb with a hollow needle and draw fluid from the uterus to detect chromosome abnormalities or genetic disorders such as Down syndrome, cystic fibrosis, and Tay-Sachs. But along with that knowledge came the risk of a miscarriage. Jackie was in her twentieth week, the cutoff date for the procedure. We had to decide that day.

Dr. Murray handed me a few medical pamphlets. "For whatever reason, Tay-Sachs is commonly found in Ashkenazi Jews and French Canadians from southeastern Quebec."

"My dad's whole family is from Quebec," I said growing numb to the conversation.

"Well, the final choice to go through with amnio is obviously yours, but if you want to be sure of what's in store, I suggest you seriously consider this." Jackie and I locked eyes.

From what I knew, doctors couldn't peg my brothers' affliction on Tay-Sachs. Children with the disease typically died by age six; David lived to sixteen and Robert, still at Monson, was almost forty. The math didn't add up, the facts pointing to an unknown culprit, a shape-shifting fugitive on the lam for four decades. How could *no one* know the truth?

Dr. Murray added to my confusion and fear. "There are different types of the condition, with different life expectancies. The most severe type is infantile Tay-Sachs." She leaned forward and folded her hands on the desk, narrowed her eyes. "Most affected infants have nerve damage in utero, before birth, with symptoms usually appearing between three and six months."

"I think that's when my mom noticed something was wrong."

"It includes deafness, blindness, decreased muscle strength, seizures, and delayed mental development. Progression is rapid."

"That sounds like what happened." But what did I know? The past was a black hole and the future obscured. All I knew for sure was *now*.

At the time, life in our magical Maplewood was a bundle of busyness as we settled into our fledgling family of three. Caleb, weeks away from his second birthday, was a precocious delight with a ceaseless supply of zest. To stay home with him, Jackie had stepped away from her longtime position at HBO, a decision she didn't regret. My job took me to various NBA cities all over the country twice a month. I didn't love being away from my family but had a blast interviewing players—like Grant Hill, Vince Carter, Chris Webber, Steve Nash, Dikembe Mutombo, and Shaquille O'Neal—as a producer for a Saturday morning

TV show called *NBA Inside Stuff*. When I wasn't on the road, I was back at NBAE editing with proficiency and exuberance, as if artificially designed for the job.

Once a week, I'd give Jackie a break by staying home with Caleb during the day and working all night. After telling him a bedtime story, I'd drive fifteen breezy miles to Secaucus screaming down the highway like a runaway thrill-seeker in a Springsteen anthem. I'd tear into the office lot, dash out of my car, and skip steps leading into the building. Then I'd cut, snip, slice, and splice hours of footage, compressing it all down to three or four minutes. Near dawn, I'd watch my finished feature again and again, fine-tuning along the way. Then I'd sit back in amazement, thinking how—like all those fantastical pictures I drew as a kid—my latest masterpiece had stemmed from a small-seeded idea and crystallized in mere hours.

Those weekly winning outcomes shouldn't have shocked me. All that was good in my life had unfolded the same way: I imagined it, then I worked at it. I followed that blueprint to the letter and enjoyed the results. Like Dad used to say whenever he guessed the next line on a TV show: "I could've written this thing." It was all so predictable, so possible. The one hiccup now was the disease our unborn child might have. Well, that, and Mom's cancer.

In the summer of 2000, soon after Caleb was born, my mother experienced stomach problems, symptoms synonymous with diverticulitis. But a colonoscopy foretold a darker diagnosis. The crushing news drifted down casually when Mom, sixty-four at the time, took my sisters to lunch and announced—after ordering an iced tea and Cobb salad—that she had stage III colon cancer. The prognosis? A fifty-percent chance she'd live five years.

My parents could've called it quits then, but they teamed up well, managing the rigors of Mom's chemotherapy and radiation treatments almost as if they were a dedicated, loving couple. Dad had forever been a malignant polyp on her heart, his removal requiring invasive surgery. But when she got sick, he stepped up as a willing and helpful assistant. On his best behavior, afraid of losing her, he made the most of the days they had left, made her comfortable, made amends. Before her shift at the Y, he'd chauffeur her to appointments at Holyoke Medical Center, then take her to work, pulling over for vomit breaks as needed. She lost fifteen pounds and most of her hair but maintained her cheery spirit. After a year, she had cancer licked; at least that's what she told us.

Mom's health was our only concern till the fall of 2001, when the events of 9/11 overshadowed all else. On that surreal morning, huddled in a small office with George and Miche and Santa, I watched in horror as the Twin Towers fell, could almost hear the screams reaching across the Hudson. I remember wondering if the country were under attack. And if anything would ever be the same. I drove home that afternoon with George following close behind. "Let's stick together," I told him. "You know, just in case."

The darkness of terrorism, the specter of cancer, and the uncertainty around Jackie's pregnancy endangered our days. To deal with these crises, I had the perfect partner. If war came to America's shores, we'd rally. If tumors consumed my mother, we'd cope. If our unborn daughter had Tay-Sachs, we'd raise her and love her until she died, or we could terminate the pregnancy. We'd float the possibilities and wait for them to land. We'd handle all this, together.

Pragmatic and focused, humble and driven, Jackie was born of Cuban immigrants who raised her to work hard and keep her nose down. Her parents, Vincent and Hilda Rowe, had been teachers in their homeland, defecting from the island when Fidel Castro confiscated their schoolhouse. Risking more than their dreams, they snuck off to Jamaica—claiming the bogus need to settle a real estate transaction—then bolted to Brooklyn with no possessions, little English, and less money.

They worked menial jobs while Vincent (endearingly called "Tooncy") attended night school for a bachelor's in education. But metal detectors at his first teaching post in the Bronx set off alarms in his gut and impounded the passion he had in Camaguey. Disheartened, he traded in his lesson books for a mop and took a job cleaning the cafeteria at Ex-Lax Corporation. From there he scaled the company ladder, becoming an attendant in the "monkey house." And years later, an office manager.

For her part, dogged and diligent Hilda worked in the kitchen at Ex-Lax before Chase Bank hired her to whistle through the graveyard shift and keep the books at a local branch. Though saddled by shaky English, she was a whiz with numbers and a valued member of the Chase family. At a noisy Coney Island subway station, Hilda handed Jackie off to Tooncy every evening as husband and wife crossed paths to and from their jobs, connecting one day of struggle to the next.

Sponsored by Tooncy's white boss, the Rowes discreetly secured a modest apartment in Trump Village, a battalion of seven high-rises overlooking the Atlantic in the Jewish neighborhood of Brighton Beach. When a lawsuit accused Trump Real Estate of racial discrimination in '73, none of the kids in the complex had Jackie's complexion, and out of sixteen hundred units, the only Black tenant was her father. But after escaping Castro's thuggish dictatorship, the Rowes were on top of the world raising their only child in Fred Trump's ivory tower.

Tides rose and fell for these castaways, this mixed-race family striving for the American Dream, while Tooncy handled nightmarish bigotry with an uncommon grace his adoptive country didn't deserve. The United States offered the Rowes freedoms unavailable in Cuba but demonized Tooncy's Blackness.

In turn, he kissed the ground each day and channeled his conflicted resentment into an impossible love for Jackie. Endowing her with his character and discretion, he passed down a chameleonlike ability to blend into any environment without making waves. But a fire burned inside them both.

At the hospital, Dr. Murray spoke of decisions in front of my wife and me, and I considered the obvious questions: What if the amnio result was positive for Tay-Sachs? Would it be too late for an abortion? If we had the baby, how would we deal with the devastation to follow? I fought back a future sadness, an uncertainty not enough tomorrows away, and feared the day I'd have to say goodbye to my little girl. I turned to Jackie, reading one final question on her face: Would our marriage survive if our child didn't?

Invisible words hovered in the room, avoiding my ears. I picked at a crusty scab on my elbow—the result of a head-first slide during a softball game—and tore off its rough coating. A wellspring of blood uncorked and plummeted down my forearm like the dye in an icehouse thermometer. Without breaking eye contact with Dr. Murray, I pulled a tissue from a box on her desk and dabbed my arm clean. Another scab would form, and then a scar in time, adding to the zigzagging roadmap scratched across my body. Life was nothing but a sport to me, bruises, cuts, and scrapes all part of the competition. The unknowns flying around our daughter's future was a deadly game of dodgeball, but I was confident we'd navigate the gauntlet. Fooling myself into believing the universe was on our side, I'd do what I do best: visualize a positive outcome and will it into existence.

We wanted the truth and scheduled the amnio test for later that week. We'd have to wait fourteen excruciating days after that for the results. Jackie grabbed my hand as Dr. Murray logged our appointment in her notebook. We'd hope for the best. We'd stay strong. We'd remain optimistic. Just like Mom.

Cindy

If my mother had told me about her teenage years, if I had more to rely upon than her high school portrait and a box of love letters she'd saved, then I'd understand why she always followed her heart. If only I'd asked what she saw in her future, I wouldn't have to fill in so many blanks.

It's 1954…

Seventeen-year-old Cindy takes off flying from one end of Jackson Parkway to the other, her saddle shoes barely touching the sidewalk. Her ponytail swishes, dusting off her shoulders. Her plaid skirt waves in the April breeze. The six quarters she's earned from her after-school job—babysitting for Miss Christine's three mildly behaved children—clink in her change purse. It's past five o'clock. The mail should've arrived by now.

A postman rolls alongside beeping in his Jeep. "Well, hello there, Cindy."

"Hi, Mr. Sullivan!" Cindy yells flapping her arms like a novice orchestra conductor.

"Expecting anything from me today, are you?" the jovial codger asks, a grin fanning out under his bushy mustache.

"Um, I was hoping so," the teen says.

"Better hurry on up then and get home. There's another air mail letter waiting for you. But you watch out for those servicemen, young lady." Mr. Sullivan wags a finger. "They might seem all grown up, but they're still just foolish boys."

"I know, Mr. Sullivan," Cindy says. "I'll be sure to watch out. Thank you." She's out of sight before the mailman can doff his cap.

In front of her apartment, she crosses her fingers and pulls open the mailbox. Dopamine floods her skull. She's sure the letter's from Hank Britton, a former classmate at Holyoke High with dimples for days and a movie star jaw. He's with the air force now and has written her every week since September. His notes are filled with dreamy details from exotic locations, but his words are cryptic, his feelings for her unclear. And nearly indecipherable penmanship adds to his mysterious intentions.

Cindy peers inside the box; her sun-drop eyes cloud over. Nothing's inside. Her heart sinks. Deducing her mother already retrieved the mail, she bursts into the apartment and tears down the hall with renewed hope, slamming on the brakes when she hits the kitchen table. She shuffles through a pile of bills, leaflets, and letters, none addressed to her.

"Whatcha looking for?" The high-pitched snark shoots out of nowhere. It's Cindy's twelve-year-old sister, Gail, a cutie with a mess of molasses hair and a freckled face disguising a sinister sneer. Like an evildoer from *The Shadow* radio show—a Colthart family favorite—Gail's a menace.

"You know what I'm looking for," Cindy demands in the nicest possible way. "And you know where it is. Now give it to me. Please!"

"It'll cost you a penny," Gail says, sticking out her tiny, bratty hand.

Cindy shakes her head, rolls her eyes, reaches into her change purse, and forks over the copper ransom. "Now where's my letter?"

Gail inspects both sides of the shiny penny and drops it into her pocket, satisfied with the negotiations. Then she puts a finger to her cheek. "Oh, I think I saw your dopey letter in the bread box."

"Aargh." Cindy stomps toward the tin bin on the counter, discovers her envelope between a loaf of banana bread and a French baguette. But the letter isn't from Hank Britton. It's from Melvin Coogan, a sweet and awkward boy from high school who's now an airman stationed in Germany. Cindy murmurs, "Gosh, Melvin, why are you writing to me?"

She retreats to her room to find Elaine hammering out homework on their shared double bed. Cindy rummages through a desk in the corner. "Have you seen the letter opener? I know I left it here yesterday."

Without lifting her nose from a bunch of books tangled in the sheets, Elaine says, "I think Alan took it earlier."

After a quick sweep, Cindy finds her little brother in the bathroom, teetering on the edge of the tub, whittling a bar of soap with the opener. The ten-year-old whips around and proudly presents his scented sculpture. "Hey, look, Sis. It's my initials. Neat, huh?"

"You should not be playing with that, Mr. AC. You might cut yourself." Cindy furrows her brow. "Now can I have that, please?"

"Okey doke, I'm all finished anyway," Alan says, handing her his carving tool.

"Thank you very much." Cindy steps into the hallway and slices open the envelope:

Hi Cyn—How's the family? Tell your mother I was asking for her. I think she's swell. I bet you are surprised to hear from me. You'll even be more surprised at what I have to say...

"Cindy play now! Cindy play now! Cindy play now!" The squeal comes from the lowest ranking Colthart, two-year-old Heather, who's stormed down the hall banging an iron soup pot with a wooden rolling pin. She's wearing two different colored socks and demanding fun from her eldest plaything.

"Not now, Heather," Cindy whispers firmly. "After I read this, okay?"

"Cindy play now! Cindy play now!" The shrieks madden Cindy like the buzz of a mosquito exploring the cavern of her ear.

Their mother barks from the kitchen. "Cynthia, take your sister outside and play with her, please."

A three-ring circus performs on Cindy's face before she thinks up a fib. "I will, Ma," she yells, "but I have to go back to Miss Christine's for a minute. I forgot my sweater."

"Okay, but quick-quick like a bunny. And don't forget to put your babysitting money in the jar," Fran Colthart yells back, apparently fooled.

"Yes, ma'am." Cindy shoots Heather a smirk and, with letter tight in hand, starts toward the front door. On her way through the kitchen, she plucks six quarters out of her purse and deposits them into a jumbo pickle jar in the center of the table.

The family has banded together in recent weeks, ever since Tom Colthart lost his job at the American Thread Company, at age fifty-three. To make ends meet, he sold donuts door-to-door until a broken ankle laid him up. Cindy's older brothers, Tom and Donald and Glenn, are away in the service; her big sister, Jane, is married and out of the house. The Colthart's five-bedroom apartment—the biggest in Jackson Parkway—stretches the monthly budget, but their accordion family of eleven has always begged for extra space.

Since the end of the war, the future of Holyoke, and the country as a whole, points toward prosperity, but times are still tough. Despite the loitering hardship, Cindy's adolescence in the Parkway has been memorable. Kids from all over the city congregate to play at McKenzie Field, the high school park across the street. The grounds teem with activity year-round. Cindy's mother can't get a minute's rest from neighborhood ragamuffins asking if one, or two, or all of her kids can come out to play. On cool Indian summer nights, Parkway tots bake potatoes in front yard coal pits while watching movies projected onto bedsheets hanging from trees. Afterward, they remove hot bricks from the fire, wrap them in towels, and take them to bed.

Cindy is the oldest sibling at home; in charge of youngsters Alan, Gail, and Heather. Elaine helps out sometimes. Cindy handles the thankless chore with natural patience, cleverness, and wit. She abides by her parents' rules: no swearing, smoking, or boyfriends in the house. Tom and Fran demand and enforce proper manners from their children. Disobedience, of any kind, is prohibited.

Cindy is tender and pretty, spirited with personality plus. She's filled with possibility, but the contents of her heart are sealed; she's an unopened letter of a girl. She wants to be a schoolteacher, wants to capitalize on her connective quality with kids. And she longs to fall in love. Far from accomplishing either goal, professional or personal, she hopes that, someday, life will make sense to her and hopes she'll make sense to someone.

Melvin Coogan also has questions regarding her future. Escaping the chaos of the hectic household, Cindy takes his letter outside, slips around the corner of the apartment building, and sits in the shaded grass under a clothesline. Sheets and shirts undulate in the breeze, ventilating her from above. She continues reading:

> *I won't beat around the bush. I wanted to tell you this when I was home, but I didn't because I thought it best to wait till you were ready to graduate. That's why I broke that date. Are you still curious? I've been thinking about this for a year and figure now is the time to say it. You're about to leave school and, undoubtedly, you'll be asked the same thing, or you probably already have been asked. This is what I want to know. Would you consider my marriage proposal?*

Cynthia presses a finger to her lip and shakes her head as the words on the page sink in:

I've always been crazy about you, but you seemed so cold, etc. Was there a particular reason? I think you loved me too, but you thought I could never get serious because of our religious differences. That's not true. Now you know just how serious I really am.

You'll probably say I haven't been around and out with girls enough to know. Maybe this is a stupid thing to say, but I think you should know. I've never even touched a girl besides you. That's the God's honest truth. You probably don't believe me, having been out with me, but that's as far as I've ever gone with anyone.

I wish I knew what you are thinking now after reading this far. I hope you're not laughing. I'm dead serious. More serious than I've ever been about anything. I love you, Cynthia, and want you always.

I'm nineteen now and will be twenty in July. You probably think I'm too young to think so seriously, but I don't think so. Have you thought at all about getting married? I know you've got your family to think of. If you tell me that you will consider me, I'll be the happiest man in the world.

Do I rate a page in your diary? I remember you told me you kept one that day outside your house. The time we talked all afternoon. I was supposed to be at practice. I knew then that it'd always be you, but we were too young to talk like this.

I should be out of the service next year at this time. I don't know what else I can say to persuade you. It's up to you now. I hope you say you'll consider me, Cynthia, because I love you more than anyone else in the world.

Cindy slips back into the apartment and into her bedroom.

She opens the closet and stuffs Melvin's letter inside a striped corsage box along with a hundred other letters from a dozen other suitors, their dashed hopes stashed away forever. She's a wanted woman who wants none of what these boys have offered. What she *does* want is a mystery to everyone.

🙞

While waiting for our amnio results, Jackie and I fumbled around to find normalcy. We lived those days with a seriousness, acknowledging the stress, enjoying fewer silly moments where our love always felt most comfortable.

Caleb's second birthday was around the corner, and we decided to take a weekend trip to Chicopee to celebrate with my family. We wanted to check on Mom, and Jackie needed the change of scenery. Spending time with my father would provide more than enough distraction. When they first met six years earlier, Jackie didn't know what to make of my dad. But once she got used to his nutty act, she loved him. Like a pimple, the man was bothersome but harmless, and he had a way of growing on people.

On that quiet Saturday, the neighborhood dozed as I eased down Langevin Street and pulled into the driveway behind my father's caramel Ford Focus. Since I moved away, the street lost more sparkle each time I visited. After I unbuckled Caleb from his car seat, he bounded out of our Outback like a kangaroo, hopped up the three concrete steps, and waited for me at the breezeway door. Above him, perched on the edge of the roof's brittle black shingles, against a backdrop of blue, four curious finches bobbed and flinched.

I twisted the doorknob and engaged my son's excitement. "C'mon, Cay, let's go find Grammy and Grampy. Where could they be?"

Muffling his giggles, Caleb tiptoed into the house. He stood quiet while his tiny sneakers sank in the shag carpet and the bouncy ringlets of his hair dangled like springs on a busted couch. Then he called, "Gwammy? Gwampy? Wharrrr you?"

From inside the coat closet a few feet away, a deep voice boomed like the Great and Powerful Oz. "Who's in my house?"

Startled for a second, Caleb gawked and then strutted toward the closet door, hands on hips. Sure of his little self, peering through the thin wooden slats, he squeaked, "Hi, Gwampy. Isss me, Caywub."

My dad pushed open the door and, with unusual agility, scooped up the tyke. Caleb laughed and threw his stubby arms around "Gwampy's" chubby neck. I smiled at the sight of my father. A brown leather belt barely held closed his red and blue striped bathrobe. His chest hair poured out like gray waves of wire. The loose-fitting robe also exposed an aqua bathing suit (a quizzical fashion choice since the pool was still covered). White tube socks and the $11 Target slippers I'd bought him for Christmas topped off his madcap outfit.

"Nice look, Dad," I said.

"I'm just wearing this so Yacky can drool over my sexy bod," he replied before leaning over and blowing into my wife's ear. "You guys are lucky. You caught me right before my nap."

My mother's faint voice floated in from the living room like a forgotten song. "Uh-oh, is Caleb here? Where's my big boy?"

Caleb screeched, "Gwammy!" He wriggled away from my father and darted into his grandmother's sugary embrace.

"How's she feeling, Bob?" Jackie wrapped her concern in a whisper.

"Good days, bad days, peaks and valleys," he answered.

Dad's glibness aside, my mom wasn't feeling great that weekend. She hardly had the energy to stand, and her face was so drawn, it seemed the Grim Reaper had sketched it himself. Without an appetite, she munched only on saltines, their blandness combatting the metallic taste in her mouth, courtesy of chemo. Those treatments took their toll, but she refused to complain. She believed in her oncologist and remained buoyant while a sinking feeling torpedoed the rest of our family.

"Belief is half of the healing, Kenny," she'd tell me. "Belief in the cure, and belief in the future."

Later that night, after everyone else was asleep, Mom and I watched TV on the same couch where I found her crying the day David died. I considered telling her about Jackie's amnio and our discouraging blood test, but I stayed quiet. Had I broached the topic, I'd be obligated to ask if she thought the twins had Tay-Sachs. Why recall those memories? What difference would it make? Our unborn daughter either had the disease, or she didn't. What we decided to do about it was our choice.

After Mom went to bed, I poured a bowl of cereal. Putting the milk away, I glanced at a handwritten poem stuck to the refrigerator door, the yellowy paper held in place by a magnetic picture of my brother Robert in a wheelchair. I knew the poem; Dad had written it more than ten years earlier, considered it his greatest creation. I ignored it at first, wanting to get back to Winona Ryder's monologue on Saturday Night Live, but the words called to me and persuaded me to look again:

"What Choice Have I to Live or Die?"

My mother has conceived, my body starts to grow.

I have no real name. I'm known as embryo.

My heart begins to pump, my brain starts to think.

Different colors are my skin and eyes that start to blink.

Nestled in my mother's womb, secure as one could be,

Not knowing that my little life could suddenly end for me.

I start to think what I could be, a doctor or a nurse,

A minister or scholar, a tiller of the earth,

A senator or president, a rabbi or a priest,

A leader of a country, or maybe I could teach.

My thoughts have somehow ended, a pain I could not bear,

When a light shined upon me with a voice that I could hear;

Fear not my child, you're with me in skies of ocean blue;

And you must forgive those people for they know not what they do.

Their judgment day is coming, no reason you should cry,

Their sentence will be based upon your choice to live or die.

That was *his* opinion.

After church the following day, my sisters arrived with their kids and filled the house with balloons, presents, sweets and treats for the "birthday boy." Caleb was the guest of honor, but Mom was the main attraction, the celebrity in high demand.

When my son opened the last of his gifts and we all had more than enough cake, Mom gathered her six grandkids in a circle. "Who wants to go on a special walk with Grammy?" she asked in the bewitching way none of them could ever resist.

The kids grabbed their jackets and ran into the breezeway. Oldest cousin Jason helped the youngest ones, Aidan and Caleb, with their sneakers while Brooke, Makenzie, and Quinn waited eagerly outside. I pulled back the lace curtains on the kitchen window and laughed as Mom played mother duck, waddling and quacking down the street, ducklings in tow. From his lookout on the front steps, my father lit a cigarette and watched them walk away.

By sundown, my family and I were back in New Jersey; I

had to catch an early flight to LA the following morning. My assignment: shoot a feature with Laker veteran Mitch "Rock" Richmond after practice on Monday, and then produce a camera crew to capture Game 5 of the NBA Western Conference Semifinals between Los Angeles and the San Antonio Spurs on Tuesday.

With Jackie's test results due any day, I didn't want to go away. But Tay-Sachs had made a fine career out of picking the worst possible time to deliver the worst possible news to poor saps like us. Staying home wouldn't matter. I went to bed feeling like my subconscious was hopped up on Red Bull and cocaine. To call it the worst night's sleep I ever got would imply I got any sleep at all.

During the flight, I splayed my notebook across an icky tray table and plotted my afternoon with Mitch. I closed my eyes and watched the finished feature in my head, imagining what shots I wanted to capture and what I needed him to say. I storyboarded the entire shoot, planned it to the minute. And I pared down the interview questions since the Lakers wanted us to get it all done in a half hour.

Rock met me at an El Segundo beach around noon, and we sat beside the ocean for a not-too-deep conversation about the ebb and flow of his career. We filmed a fun bit with him finding messages in bottles from teammates Kobe Bryant and Shaquille O'Neal. (In advance, I'd carefully written the notes in my best calligraphy, rolled them up, and squeezed them into empty plastic Gatorade bottles before tossing them into the waves.) Mitch gave thoughtful answers during the interview and was receptive to my corny message-in-a-bottle idea. The whole day went as anticipated, and I got the exact results I'd imagined.

The next night, pregame at Staples Center, while I posted up a throng of reporters waiting for Kobe and Shaq to emerge from the training room, my backpack rattled and buzzed like it held a coffee tin of hornets. I reached into the bag and pulled out my massive Motorola cell phone, a Radio Shack special I'd purchased early on in Jackie's pregnancy. The clumsy cell, as big as a Cracker Jack box and heavy as a brick, was an upgrade to the beeper I used to bring on road trips. My heart dropped when I checked the phone. Missed call from Jackie. My neck got hot. I charged out of the locker room to call her back, but there was no cell service in the bowels of the arena.

I told my cameraman and friend Vic Smith about the situation. "Hey, man, can you do me a huge favor and go to the Spurs locker room and grab some sound from David Robinson and Coach Pop?"

"Sure, Gags. Whatever you need."

"Thanks a lot. I gotta give Jackie a quick call. I'll be back in a few minutes."

I rushed up the stairs and racewalked through the concourse toward the main entrance. After flashing the security guard my credentials, I hustled out the doors into a microwave oven powered by the LA sun. On the arena steps, with the last of the fans filing in, I punched in our home phone number again.

C'mon, please pick up. Please pick up.

"Hey," Jackie said. Her tone told me nothing of the news to come.

"Hi. Is everything okay?" I blurted.

"We got the amnio results back."

"And?"

"They were negative."

"Really? Oh my gosh, that's great."

"I know, so great." We enveloped each other in a virtual hug.

"Did you speak with the doctor?"

"Yes. She said our kids could still be Tay-Sachs carriers, and they should be tested when they get older but, for now, everything's okay."

When I got home—with the weight of a thousand Shaqs off my shoulders—Jackie and I kicked around baby names. We liked Rose, Charlotte, Georgia, and Rachel but settled on Lucy, meaning "light," with the middle name Grace, same as Mom's. Perfect. We'd stonewalled my parents from our Tay-Sachs scare; whether we should have or not, I wasn't sure. We'd done it for their own good, but I felt guilty for not revealing such crucial news, such personal turmoil that a parent would want a child to share. I should've at least told my mother, should've trusted her willingness to talk about the twins, could've helped her shoulder the emotional load. But I didn't want to hurt her anymore.

As far as she and Dad were concerned, everything was fine. I'd held the darkness at bay, and it retreated, but it would come back. It always came back.

NINE

"I Don't Miss Too Much"

Winter, 1970

I SLEPT IN MY crib till I was four. Mom told me not to climb out, so I never did.

In my early childhood, recurring nightmares blended with hazy days that followed and absorbed together, all at once, into an ocean of time. My first memory—or what I construed as a memory—included that nightmare: a dream of dark shadows surrounding me, pulling me, making me feel small and lost. A dream that always left me with a little darkness inside.

I woke to a devious December draft sneaking in under the windowsill and smacking my flushed cheeks. The warm, sweet scent of crepes crept in beneath the door, filling the air, chasing away the chill. Constricted by outgrown footy pajamas, I kicked away the crocheted blanket entwining my legs. My sisters' voices, pacifying and merry, pogoed on the other side of the wall. I rubbed my tiny, tired eyes. The sun yawned.

My pupils dilated, adjusting to the brightness in the room. I clutched the crib's wooden rail and labored to pull myself up, the extra luggage of a soggy diaper adding to my strain. Wobbly and impatient, I cried for my six-year-old sister.

"Owl. Owl. Owwwwwwllll."

Unable to pronounce "Cheryl," I conflated her name with that wise bird, that all-knowing spirit animal. Did I request help out of my crib because I was hungry for breakfast? Or did my subconscious call on "Owl" for guidance after another upsetting shadow dream? An owl would know what the shadows wanted. An owl would spot both predator and prey hiding in the darkness.

"Owwwwwwllll."

Cheryl opened my bedroom door and bounced into the room. "Good morning, Mr. Man. How's my baby brother today?"

Like Santa hoisting a sack of toys off his sleigh, she fastened her arms around me, lifted me over the rail, and lugged me into the living room. Linda, perky in her PJs, played on the carpet with the foursome of Dressy Bessy, Dapper Dan, Raggedy Ann, and Andy (all hugged to tatters). I let out a coo and Linda smiled, thrilled to have a real baby doll to primp and pamper. The colored lights on our Christmas tree twinkled.

A kind of swirling atmosphere in my eyes, instead of two tiny humans, my sisters teased me and tickled me, swaddled me, sang to me. They changed my stinky cloth diaper, dressed me in itchy overalls, and hog-tied my cowlicked hair with sparkly barrettes. More than a brother or a plaything to them, I was an exercise, a drill, preparation for the future. With me, Cheryl and Linda applied what they learned from our mother and practiced her most vital lesson, the fundamental key to life: how to love a child.

Later that morning, Mom lowered me into a playpen in the living room so she could help my sisters get ready for school. Safe in mini-jail, I pushed around a plastic fire engine, its battery-powered siren and lights wailing and winking. After Linda got dressed, she returned to the living room and lured our puppy, Bambi, onto the couch. Then she tied a winter hat onto the poor dog's head and wrapped a scarf around her neck. Bambi possessed similar features, but the opposite nature, of her fox cousins stalking pheasant in the woods behind our house, and I empathized as she dutifully played dress-up.

While my sisters walked to school, I lapped up a plate of cottage cheese and fruit cocktail, getting more on my cheeks than in my stomach. After I finished, Mom stripped me of my grubby bib and sat me on the counter beside the sink. With the efficiency of a NASCAR pit crew, she wiped my face and arms with a warm facecloth, shampooed my tangle of hair, and rinsed out the suds with the sink's silver sprayer, all without inducing one tear. Then she bundled me up for an adventurous afternoon of errands.

In the mythology of my youth, I bathed in the light of each day, surrounded by adoration and discipline and trust. My mother gave me the care I needed; my sisters provided the attention I craved; and my father regarded me with pride and reverence, the way a king in a castle window beholds his domain. Back then, our home teemed with whimsy and gratification and a mystic synergy. We were engulfed, mostly, by goodness.

But from a young age, I sensed something else. An unrest. A disquiet. A grim absence lurking in the corners. I was sure everyone felt it, that cold and dark uneasiness, like the uncertainty of storm air. My brothers were there. It was them, Robert and David, all around, begging to be remembered. Mom and Dad's decision to send the twins away haunted us all. And those shadows lived with us in that house. Always.

Bob

If Dad had told me about his days in the army, if he'd offered more of his time in France than thin allusions to a girl who loved him there, then I'd understand why he pushed me to live each day to the hilt. If only I'd asked him about that girl, I'd know her to be real and not this mythic, cautionary figure.

It's 1955…

She moves behind the bar with purpose and grace, energy and efficiency, the way a hummingbird hovers and darts and floats, its heart racing and wings fluttering so fast they don't move at all. A wisp of chestnut hair sweeps in front of her face. Behind her head, a red kerchief restrains long locks. Corporal Gagne sits in the back corner of the tiny café, fixated on the lines of her shoulders and neck. He loses himself in her. She catches him staring.

His fellow servicemen—a boisterous and raging wrangle of testosterone packaged in pressed khaki uniforms—squabble over drained pitchers of beer. Their conversation devolves into the number of sexual conquests they've made in the fourteen months they've been stationed in France. Unfiltered cigarettes dangle from chapped lips as they boast and argue. The Korean conflict has bored the men, reducing them to heartless automatons.

"Tell us again, Gagne. How many babes have you bagged? Two? Three? We lost track." The drunken leader of the ugly Americans teases while his cohorts laugh and belch. Bob's eyes and ears have glazed over. The scathing words drift away with the smoke.

"Hey, get a load of Babyface Bobby," the lout shouts. "He's goo-goo for that skinny thing tending bar. Her chest is flatter than this beer." Two tables away, a middle-aged French couple stands and walks out.

A neglected cigarette burns between Bob's fingers. Ash falls to the floor.

"C'mon fellas, let's split," the leader slurs. Then he staggers to his feet, slurps backwash from his beer mug and slams it onto the dusty oak table. "There's gotta be a little action somewhere in this goddamn village. Come find us after you get shot down, lover boy."

As the brutes leave, one of them whacks the side of Bob's head so hard it nearly knocks off his crew cut. Another one slaps him on the back, sending an electric current rocketing up his spine. Bob whips his face away from the bar. Hunched over and cringing, he presses his eyes shut, grits his teeth. When the pain subsides, he turns, finds the girl watching. She flicks a towel over her shoulder. The corners of her mouth pinch, turning upward into what he's certain is a smile.

The fire colors of the summer sky fade, and dusk covers the sleepy town of Toul. Except for Bob, the six barstools and four tables in Café a la Vierge sit empty. Distant church bells and playful shrieks of children slide through the open windows. A sidewalk musician passes; his horn recites a brassy poem. The scent of fresh baked bread waltzes in the air.

In the low light and stillness of the evening, the girl behind the bar glides like an apparition. Bob musters the courage to approach her, sure of his phony confidence. "*Bonjour, mademoiselle,*" he offers with a raised eyebrow and casually leans against the bar. "*Tu es une belle femme.*"

She raises an eyebrow of her own, sucks on her lips, and dampens a snort. Bob rocks onto his heels. The girl places both palms on the bar and moves in close. "So you think I am beautiful, eh? Why don't you now again tell me in English?" With a stern puff, she blows the strand of hair away from her face, keeping eye contact with the unnerved army man whose heart is now pumping faster than any hummingbird's heart ever pumped. He doesn't respond.

"May I give you another beer while we wait for you to speak again?"

Bob teeters, intoxicated by the potent mix of the girl's accent and wit and charm. "I–I think I need something stronger," he finally says, extending a clammy hand. "*Je m'appelle* Bob. Bob Gagne."

"*Bonjour*, Bob. I am Josiane."

At a table in the back, the two strangers lose themselves in loose conversation. The street outside quiets for them; the walls of the bar draw nearer to listen. Bob lets his guard down, and the sensation exhilarates. He's relaxed and funny and flirtatious. For once, he's himself.

He tells Josiane LePettite he's a radioman in the army, stationed in Toul as part of the American effort to prevent the spread of communism from Russia. He says President Eisenhower plans to send U.S. troops to Vietnam to provide military training to the South Vietnamese. He tells Josiane he's a lover, not a fighter.

"Gagne is a French name. You are French, no?" she asks.

"My grandfather is French-Canadian, from Quebec," Bob replies. "But I'm a red-blooded American."

"I would like to go to America someday, to see New York City and the Statue of Liberty." Josiane's voice trails off. "But it seems like a dream. I do not think I will leave this town."

"You never know," Bob says.

"I do love your American music. Nat King Cole. And your movies too. The one called *High Noon* is showing at the cinema in our village."

"I was just thinking that you're the spitting image of Grace Kelly."

"And I was thinking, Bob, that you look nothing like Gary

Cooper." They laugh together. Sweetness and innocence join them at the table.

Josiane tells him she just turned twenty. Her father owns the café. They're originally from Caen, in Normandy, but moved to Toul in 1944.

"What about your mother?" Bob asks.

Josiane's speech softens. "Maman died on the day you call D-Day when the Americans came to rid us of the Germans. I was nine. I was at school. Papa was at work. Maman was home with Milo, my baby brother. The bombs fell, and the house was gone. We called for them. We listened. But there was nothing. We found Milo's body the next day. The city was destroyed."

"I'm sorry," Bob says, sympathy strangling his heart. "I only knew about the soldiers who died that day. No one ever talks about civilian casualties."

"Papa says the first casualty of war is always the truth." She looks straight through him. Her smile returns for a moment. "I remember, when I was a girl, before I went to sleep, Maman would tell me many fantastic stories about America to, how do you say, *divert* me from the occupation."

"You mean, *distract* you?" Bob says, intent on her every word.

"Yes. The Germans humiliated us. When the Americans came, they were heroes to much of France. But Papa never forgave them for what happened to Maman and Milo. So many innocent French people died then. And now I see American soldiers only with heads like pigs. They come in here and look at me like I am nothing." Josiane pauses. She moves her hand across the table and touches his. "But you are not like them, Bob Gagne. I know this."

Behind the bar, Josiane's father appears out of nowhere and sizes up his daughter's companion. "I don't think your father likes me," Bob says.

"And now you know why." Josiane laughs. "But what of your father? What about *Monsieur* Gagne?"

Bob stiffens and says, "He died not too long ago." Then he snaps his fingers. "Died, just like that."

He spares the details. Doesn't tell this foreign beauty exactly how Rheo Gagne died, two winters prior, from cirrhosis of the liver. Leaves out the grotesqueness of his father's diseased skin, like cracked leather, barely holding in his bones, the color of a half-dead forsythia. Doesn't mention the itching and the bleeding and the bruising. Or how his hero wasted away. Or how the man's love of whiskey superseded his love for his family. And the young American doesn't talk about his own anger. How it bubbled up in him like the bile in his father's intestines.

But he admits to being at his dad's bedside in Chicopee a week before leaving for basic training at Fort Dix in New Jersey. "I remember the last thing he said to me," Bob tells Josiane. "*A demain, mon loulou.*"

He looks into her dark eyes and waits.

"See you tomorrow, my little one," she says.

Bob's drunken friends return from their carousing, yelling that it's time to go. He's connected with Josiane more than he expected. She wants to see him again. He doesn't tell her that he's being discharged and sent home in two weeks because of a chronic back injury. Doesn't tell her the following weekend would be their last chance to meet.

"I'll be back on Saturday," Bob promises. "I'll take you to the cinema. Tell your father he can come too." His smirk and his vow make Josiane giggle and swoon. She flies toward him and kisses his cheek. Church bells clang. He turns to walk away, takes one step and then looks back. She brushes aside the defiant strand of hair, and he drowns in regret.

The following weekend, Bob doesn't go back to the café in Toul. Why say goodbye again? He's tired of goodbyes.

He relinquishes his grip on everything he'll never know and returns to Chicopee with his heart aching far more than his back.

In his childhood home once again, it's only Bob and his mother now. His siblings are married and out of the house. Questioning what to do, what to hope for, he considers the priesthood. He's curious about philosophy and the universe and the convention of religion. Catholicism has been the most stable part of his life. And men of the cloth are prohibited to marry, which may not be the worst thing.

He pities himself and goes to work at Gagne & Sons. His brother Rheo Jr. is president; Bob becomes treasurer, selling cars all day, buying drinks all night. His buddies at the American Legion are his bond and his belonging. But his friends find wives, and one by one, they leave him. On a shrinking island, Bob dates many women but doesn't reveal his heart, never comes close to real commitment. He doesn't want to feel the world; he wants to be *felt* by it.

Josiane LePettite becomes a fictional character in his mind, a presence that lingers, a reminder of love's possibility. And its pain. He won't forget her. He'll frame her like a painting in the mournful museum of memory for the remainder of his days. He'll remember every detail of her face, every inflection of every word she spoke. And he'll remember, always, how she looked at him, how she saw something the rest of the world never would.

❧

The day passed quickly, like all my toddler days.

I clung to Mom's housecoat and followed her around the kitchen as she prepared for supper. She tidied a wild stack of papers littering the table: shopping lists and junk mail, overdue bills, coupon clippings, and written reminders on torn pieces of loose-leaf. She moved the pile to the counter, extending its survival for at least another week. This particular stack had lasted months, migrating from surface to surface like lice hopping head to head. My mother bent to pick up one of the items that had fallen to the floor, a homemade birthday card she'd given my father when he turned thirty-nine earlier in the year. The inscription on the inside was in her handwriting but seemingly from another woman:

HAPPY BIRTHDAY, HONEY! We all want to wish you the best year ever and it will be, I'm sure. There isn't a card I could buy that could express the love that I have for you. The love that we have, and we share, means so much to me. I know you'll have a good day today, and a great year, because I'll be there to tell you I LOVE YOU.

HAPPY, HAPPY Birthday!

All my love,

Cynthia

She tossed the card into the junk drawer and shut it away. Then Mom grabbed a box of cellophane, tore off two pieces, and covered one bowl of black olives and another bowl of sliced cucumbers in vinegar. She placed them on the table and quizzed me on the operation while reciting a play-by-play account.

"And after we put the bowls here, we're going to put these little shakers in the middle of the table. Do you remember what's in these shakers?"

"Salt."

"Salt. That's right. And what's in the other one?"

"Peeper."

"Right again. Pepper. Put some pep in your step with some pepper."

She brought me into the living room and placed me in the playpen so she could finish her work. Gazing out the picture window, I listened to the glass groan as it staved off a bitter frost.

The mountain was a dark gray hulk in the distance. Beside me on the floor, my sisters took turns popping in plastic glow pegs on a Lite-Brite board, spelling out K-E-N-N-Y in giant multi-colored letters. The showy wreath above the fireplace flashed its crimson bow. The cinder-block planter was draped in silver garland. The house smelled like pine and comfort.

Our dinner of roast beef, mashed potatoes, and green beans had been ready for thirty minutes. Dad wasn't home yet, though his workday had ended hours earlier. My mother knew he was at the Legion with his friends, attempting to keep them in their stools a bit longer by throwing a few twenties onto the bar. She knew how two beers became five. Then nine. Then eleven. Then fourteen. Then he'd leave.

Outside, a car engine gagged and choked. Through the glow of electric candles on the sill, Mom peeked out the kitchen window. A husband-shaped object staggered out of the car and up the snow-covered driveway. The streetlight glared. The thing bumbled up the steps and kicked the tin box in which old Mr. Begley dropped off glass bottles of milk for our family on Mondays and Fridays. (Lucky for us, this was a Tuesday.) The sound of rattling metal reverbed down the street, chased by echoes of "Goddammit!"

The clumsy object pushed through the breezeway door, hobbled past us all, and dipped into the basement, leaving behind a track of slushy footprints on the kitchen floor. It grabbed a Schlitz from the fridge, cracked it open, and stomped back upstairs into the living room. Then it lifted me out of the playpen without spilling its more cherished cargo. I pawed at its face and knocked off its glasses. I picked at its sideburns and untamed seven o'clock stubble. The thing stunk of a vintage motor oil liqueur. I ran my finger along the surface of its denim work shirt, tracing the letters of its scripted name on a stitched patch over where its heart used to be.

Jealous shadows in the corner watched as Daddy plopped me onto his lap, facing me toward a grandfatherly man on TV warning of a worrisome war. Holding me loosely with a woozy arm, my father guzzled his beer in one gulp, deposited the useless can on the coffee table, and tossed a yell over his shoulder. "Dinner ready yet, Cyn?"

"It was ready an hour ago."

He grabbed the beer can, squeezed another drop down his gullet and dismissed my mother's remark, as if she hadn't said a word. The little crime pierced her soul, yet another pin in an overcrowded cushion. Time had done a number on him. The good man she married was nearly gone, existing only somewhere between the seconds. A decade earlier, he'd aligned himself with her, with her goodness, in hopes of rising. She couldn't pull him up, so he tried to pull her down. From the bottom, he couldn't fall from grace. But my mother, elevated at a supreme level, faced the constant threat of plunging into despair.

My father let out a disgusting burp. Fed up again, Mom served him the usual. "Bob, you know you have a problem with alcohol."

"You're right, Cyn, I do." He tapped his empty can on the coffee table. "I don't have any. And *that's* a problem."

Out of instinct, Linda interrupted the brewing argument. "Daddy, guess what we did today?"

"Why don't you tell me?" He humored his daughter while trying to light a cigarette with multiple flicks of a stubborn Bic.

"We played with Kenny and went to school and went shopping with Mommy and went to visit Nana and Pop-Pop," Linda said, overly excited.

"And we helped Mommy vacuum, and I swept the floor," Cheryl chimed in, less excited.

"Sounds like fun. Who wants to get me another Schlitz?"

With three small children at home, plus nine-year-old twins

secluded in a facility for the mentally disabled, my parents' hands were full. Mom had grown up with strong parental guidance, a sense of discipline and responsibility. She was capable of handling this unfair and unruly situation. But Dad's parents hadn't provided a durable foundation or instilled in him the confidence to deal with disorder, so he made himself scarce, working and drinking during the week, golfing and drinking on weekends. In a vain attempt to appease his wife, he joined the Massachusetts Board for Mental Retardation. His attendance in the program was exemplary, but his attention and enthusiasm skipped the monthly meetings. Seeking a hopeful future, he blocked out past failures while sabotaging present successes.

Life outside our Langevin Street bubble rushed silently past, like ultrasonic waves, as Mom and Dad kept their heads above water and their marriage afloat. They barely noticed, at the start of the year, when the Beatles broke up and the Apollo 13 spacecraft exploded. Or in summer, when the National Guard killed four anti-war protesters at Kent State and ten thousand women marched for equality in New York City. Or even in autumn, when Jimi Hendrix died in London at age twenty-seven and Janis Joplin followed suit in Los Angeles sixteen days later.

I was on my father's lap, happy and safe. Footage of machine guns rat-a-tat-tatting and bloodied boys fighting and falling flashed across the TV screen. My father blew a funnel of cigarette smoke and halitosis onto the nape of my neck. I coughed as the spikey fumes shot up my nose and down my throat. Slurping on another beer, he bounced me on his knee. I was his flesh and blood, his replacement son, a chance at redemption and a way to forget.

He began to sing: "Kenny goes to Boston. Kenny goes to Lynn—"

This was my favorite game. Bopping up and down on Daddy's lap, with his strong hands holding me tight under my arms, I squealed and thrilled and braced for a surprise fall. I sensed it was coming but wasn't sure when.

"If he's a naughty boy he's gonna fall—"

I won't be naughty. I won't be naughty. Here it comes.

"Right—"

He won't let me go, will he? I won't be naughty. Please.

"IN!"

His knees yanked apart, and his lap disappeared. His grip under my arms loosened and I slipped away, free-falling and terrified. My stomach dropped as I reached out to grab his legs. It was too late. I was gone.

Before I could scream, his hands clamped onto my ribcage, and he pulled me back up. While I gasped for air, some of my trust in him escaped. I wondered if a time might come when my father's grip loosened forever, a time when he didn't catch me. I'd never be naughty, but I feared someday he'd let our whole family fall.

TEN

"Yesterday's History, Tomorrow's a Mystery"

Fall, 2005

OU NEED TO come home, Kenny." With those six words, Linda ended our phone conversation, and I fell apart.

It was a Monday, around noon. I was at work, half-expecting that call. After hanging up, I laid my interlocked forearms flat on my desk and buried my head in a pillow of skin and bones. I slackened, smothered in hurt, as gravity tugged tears from my eyes.

My buddy John Marion rose from his next-door cubicle, moved behind me, and rubbed my back. "It's okay, Gags."

I sobbed facedown, wanting to believe him, wanting to disappear. Somehow, I managed to speak. "I don't know if I'll ever see my mom again."

His hand stayed strong. "It's all right, I've got you."

I cried harder.

"It's going to be okay."

John had heard me talking with my sister and empathized. I'd kept him updated on my mother's health since her diagnosis five years earlier. He was a rock with a compassionate ear who'd lost his mom to cancer when he was just twenty-two, and he'd told me how he struggled to pick up the pieces after she was gone. I'd always admired him for the bravery he showed at such a formative age. I wished for an ounce of his mettle.

Another friend, Bob Santarlasci, wrapped me in a hug and offered to drive me home. I thanked him but declined, knowing I'd need to pull myself together and get back to Chicopee quick. I had to say goodbye to my mother. Time was running out—for both of us.

In a daze, I drove from Secaucus to Maplewood, tossed a handful of clothes into a backpack, kissed Jackie, jumped back into my car, and sped off for Massachusetts. I tore up the Garden State and jetted over the Tappan Zee, zipped along the Merritt through Connecticut as a million fiery leaves hang glided above my car like swatches of burning lace. Memories of my mother battered my mind. I chased away a pack of morbid thoughts and tried to control my speed. But Mom couldn't wait forever. I hit the gas. Highway exits whooshed past.

It'd been a year since I traveled these same roads to say good-bye to a family member. When Robert died at forty-two, my family held a casual memorial service for him at Monson. The ceremony was surreal and forgettable, just a few words spoken by a few people. I remember I'd written something to share but decided not to, kept the paper folded in my pocket:

Some people might feel angry today. They might say my brothers never got a fair chance. The physical abilities Robert and David went without have us thinking they were cheated. Some people might feel sad today. They might say Robert and

David weren't able to live full lives and never knew what was going on around them. All of that's true.

It's true that, without sight, they never saw all the wonderful things the world has to offer. All the things you and I often take for granted. And, without a sense of hearing, they couldn't appreciate the laughter from those whom they brought joy to every day. It's the same laughter we're sometimes too busy to notice.

But I believe Robert and David led full lives. Because the most important sense we all have—the sense that makes us feel alive, the sense that makes us feel loved—is the sense of touch. And with the loving hands laid on them each day— from doctors, nurses, therapists, and caregivers—I believe my brothers felt more love than any of us could ever know.

And I know, above all else, they felt the unconditional love of their mother—a woman whose strength, attitude, and perspective had to have touched their hearts. They must've felt it. They must've known.

That's what fulfills us. It's not the blue of the sky or the chirping of the birds. It's the love that comes from a simple, caring touch. That's all we long for; that's all we need; and that's what Robert and David had.

When the service ended, a nurse handed Mom a box of my brother's belongings, clothes mostly. My mother asked if I wanted anything. I took a gray T-shirt with a tag on the collar that read: *R. Gagne, Hoskins* (the name of the building where he lived). I brought the shirt home and stashed it in the back of my bedroom closet. The part of my life when I knew Robert seemed like it belonged to someone else, nothing like my life now.

In the fourteen years since I left Chicopee, I'd found near perfection in New Jersey: a fruitful career, an incredible wife, and a wide circle of loyal friends. The heart of my existence? Five-year-old son, Caleb, and three-year-old daughter, Lucy. I welled up, regretting that my kids would never see their Grammy again. It wasn't fair; they hardly got to know her. I could only hope her magic had touched them, embedded a spark in their souls. And I prayed her essence had soaked into their memory.

When I got to my parents' house, the street was dead, the chilly day on its last legs. On the front steps, two shrimpy pumpkins huddled together, protecting each other from nibbling squirrels. Taped onto the breezeway door, a cardboard Broom Hilda sneered beside her cauldron, stirring up more commotion than anyone inside the house. I walked in knowing that when I walked out, I'd be a different man.

Mom slept peacefully in her bed, having fought off a legion of seizures earlier that afternoon. Dad took his daily siesta in the room adjacent, the one Cheryl and Linda used to share. At the kitchen table, my sisters and I drank tea with a hospice nurse named Mary, who offered advice and imparted wisdom with the serenity of a sensei. She showed us how to replace Mom's morphine drip and control the level of her medication. She explained, in sensitive terms, the assault on our mother's tumor-ravaged body and assured us all we could do now was make her comfortable. We understood.

After speaking with us for twenty minutes and noticing how well my sisters and I got along, the nurse pulled on her sweater and said, "I've rarely seen a hospice patient in better hands than your mother is with you three. It's so important you're all here and that you have such support for one another. You won't be needing me. I wish you all the best."

I walked Mary out and thanked her. She hugged me and said, "Your mother's a lucky woman to have her family surrounding her during this journey. Just being with her now is the most meaningful thing you can offer."

I didn't want the kind nurse to leave but was honored she trusted us. "This is going to be hard," I admitted as she opened her car door. "We all love Mom so much."

Mary paused and touched my arm. "Oh, Ken, I know," she said. "And believe me, your mother knows that too. You and your sisters are special people. It takes an incredible amount of love to watch a parent die."

She drove off. I waved goodbye from the steps, staying outside until the car curled around the bend, its taillights out of sight, its engine a low drone. Brimming above the rooftops, a blood-red moon intimidated the sinking sun into setting sooner than planned. Night had come.

Like wildfire, the tumors in Mom's colon had metastasized, creeping around her pelvis, up her spine, and into her neck. She endured ungodly pain but never complained, just as she had never griped about her original diagnosis, or the radiation, or the chemotherapy, or the surgeries, or the colostomy bag. She didn't fight cancer; she tolerated it.

Unsure how long she'd last, I'd planned to stay at least a couple of nights. I didn't know what to expect but figured the first evening would be the most difficult. A little after eight, my sisters went home to their families. Dad arose from his extra-long nap and adjourned to the couch. He didn't say a word to me, more interested in a tumbler of Wild Turkey than a conversation about his dying wife.

Seeking more positive energy, I slid into Mom's room and lay down beside her weedy frame. Her nightshirt rippled along with the sighs of an oscillating fan in the corner, and her wilting face wore the bravery of a garden flower in the eye of a storm. The flattened mattress welcomed me, as it did in the early mornings of my youth. On those hallowed days, after Dad left for work, I'd crawl under the covers with Mom and tap her leg with my foot. After she tapped mine, we'd take turns tracing words on each other's backs with our fingertips, every new letter combination somehow spelling out "Love." Then we'd play an ingenious guessing game she invented—called What Do You Like Better?—which bought her fifteen extra minutes of rest before she'd need to face the day.

"Do you like rabbits or monkeys?"

"Monkeys."

"Do you like pork chops or meatloaf?"

"Pork chops."

"Do you like rainy days or snowy days?"

"Snowy days."

The fan blew colder. I watched my mother sleep for a long while, the hum in her throat starting and stopping like a one-note nursery rhyme. Part of me wanted her to wake up, to talk to me, to remember us. If she did, I would've told her, honestly, son to mother, how scared I was, and that I didn't want her to leave. And she would've told me, honestly, mother to son, that everything would be okay, that she'd always been proud of me. But the person I most loved, the woman who defined my world, was somewhere else, on her way to whatever comes next.

I rose from the bed, walked around to her side, and pulled the comforter over her ashen shoulders. A letter I'd written to her a few weeks earlier rested on the nightstand, its blue ink smudged, as if stained by tears:

Mom—It's funny, I felt like I had to write this to let you know how I feel about you, but as I'm sitting here, I can't think of anything you don't already know. That's a good thing.

Let me just say how much I admire you after all you've been through over the past five years. You told me yourself how lucky you feel to have had that time, knowing that many people in your situation don't get that long. You approached those years in typical Cindy fashion. You were determined. You wanted them. You made them happen. Yes, these five years have been a blessing. But they're also a byproduct of your love and respect for life.

You're the greatest person I've ever known. That's not just a sympathy compliment. In fact, it's the opinion of more people than you can imagine. You're the example the rest of us try to follow. It's not easy, but we try. We see how you look at life and we smile, and we understand, and we emulate.

You know, if we were having this conversation face-to-face right now, you'd feel incredibly uncomfortable and attempt to deflect these flowery comments. Sorry, but that's not going to happen here, so grin and bear it.

Now, where was I? Oh yeah, the greatest person ever stuff. Well, you get the gist. I'll let you off easy this time.

I love you so much, Mom. When you weren't feeling well last week, I was so desperate to talk to you, to see you. I was thinking about how much you mean to me, to all of us, and how you play so many roles in our lives. You're a mother, a wife, a sister, a friend, a confidant, a pillar, and a beacon. Facing a day when I'll be without you doesn't scare me. I'm not afraid. But I'll miss you so, so much. You and Dad made me who I am. I've always been honored to be your son. And that honor is the greatest gift I'll ever receive.

Thank you, Mom, for all you've taught me and for lighting my way.

Two hours later, I stretched out on the couch while the night sky spied on me through the picture window. Dad was back in bed, his whiskey-powered snores rumbling out of my sisters' old room, shaking the whole house by its neck. Somehow, through the racket, a flock of mumbles escaped Mom's bedroom and fluttered down the hall. I hustled into the kitchen, grabbed a pad and pen off the counter, then sat outside her door for a closer listen.

Under a shellacked wooden portrait of Jesus (that Cheryl had crafted in Sunday school another lifetime ago), I leaned against the paneled wall and recorded my mother's broken sentences as the baseboard vent threw faint heat up my shirt. During relentless seizures of the past week, Mom had repeatedly gnashed on her tongue, and the swelling inhibited her speech, challenging my effort to decode her words.

"Underneath... crank, crank, crank... You gotta be kidding me, Mary... Yvette, Yvette, Yvette... Pick me up... I fell... I'm having goofy dreams... You're home?... I go through there?... I'm coming up... I'll be down here for a while..."

Clearly, she was holding a conversation, or multiple conversations. But how? Was a lack of oxygen leading to hallucinations? Had I accidentally upped the level on her morphine drip, creating a delusional state?

"She's an old woman, about eighty-six... And an old man... I keep falling... Hi, Lorraine, I haven't seen you in a long time... Anyone want an old-fashioned peanut butter and Fluff?... I'm Cindy from the Y... Have a good summer... Is that really you?... You didn't look so good before..."

Who was she talking to? Her friends Mary Loftus and Lorraine Gaffney were dead. Her sister-in-law Yvette, Uncle Rheo's wife, was dead. The elderly couple she spoke of, perhaps her parents, were dead. Were these people assisting her transition from our world to the next? Were Robert and David there too, waiting for her somewhere beyond?

After she quieted, I tottered back into the living room and flopped onto the couch, an emotional wreck. I'd always been skeptical about the concept of heaven—or an afterlife of any sort—but Mom's illusions twisted my arm, warming me to the idea. I'd been thrown off course in life's mystical maze, and now she appeared as a guide, dropping breadcrumbs for me to follow, helping me focus less on where I was going and more on who I was going with.

I thought of Jackie and our serendipitous relationship, how we'd formed a respectful and loving team in our seven-year marriage. I thought of my friends from Chicopee and college and the NBA, how they'd kept me grounded and pushed me to be more. I thought of my sisters and their families, how Cheryl and Linda had continued Mom's magical way with children and taught me to do the same. And I thought of my father, his peripheral role in the dynamic, located in the soft center of us all.

At 2:00 a.m., another seizure rocked my mother, and I rushed to comfort her.

"What happened?" she asked.

"You had a seizure," I said.

"Why?"

"Because your body is reacting to the cancer and trying to fight it."

"Were you nervous?"

"A little."

"Was Linda nervous?"

"A little." (Neither sister was there, but I'd never had a clearer conscience when telling a white lie.)

"But Cheryl wasn't nervous, was she?"

"She was a little."

"No, sir."

"Yeah, she was."

"Really? Wow. I'm going back to sleep, honey."

That night went on forever, and my mother made good use of the extended time, had lots more to say. Just before dawn, I was back in my hallway hideaway on another stakeout, bending an ear as Mom spoke again with a roomful of unseen specters.

"You're looking at me like you know me or something... Cynthia Colthart Gagne... I remember I saw you when I was fourteen... I'll be back in an hour... I'm falling all over the place... Okay, Cheryl, I'll buy that for you... Come on, let's go to the swimwear department... Hi, Ginger!... Don't you recognize me?... Hey, listen, we're gonna drop by tonight..."

At that moment, she began to moan with a discomfort I hadn't heard before. I bounced up from my seat on the carpet, pushed open the bedroom door, and stood over her. "Are you okay, Mom?"

She looked at me and yawned, sucking every molecule of air out of the house, and said, "Oh, here it is, right on top of the page. It's all about fate." Then my mother shut her eyes and left our world once again.

Cyn

If Mom had told me about the guy she almost married, if I'd known more of this mystery man than what I learned from a bundle of sappy postcards and notes, then it'd be obvious why she ditched him and ended up with my dad. If only I'd asked about her first love, she would've recalled the beginning and the end, and I wouldn't have to dream it all up.

It's 1958...

Thunder and lightning boom and flash in the sooty sky as streaks of rain pelt the inky streets of Holyoke, infiltrating the air with an ear-splitting hiss, like the grating reverb of dialed-up radio static. Surrounded by the violent soundscape, Cynthia and her boyfriend, Joey Stiles, idle in a car in front of the Colthart home. It's a Saturday evening, early spring, well past the young woman's curfew. Joey's in the driver's seat and drunk again.

The door on the passenger side is dented, its window smashed. Taking inventory of her bloody hands and arms, Cynthia tries to remember what happened. She recalls Elvis Presley's "Young Dreams" blaring. She remembers Joey speeding through a stop sign and then swerving to avoid an oncoming car. She remembers screaming. She doesn't remember slamming broadside into the utility pole.

Joey gropes and paws, trying to wipe blood off Cynthia's arms with his shirt sleeve. Fragments of glass stick in her hands, raging like fistfuls of bee stings. A jagged laceration on her head kills. After the dance on Dwight Street, Joey threw down a six-pack of Piels in the parking lot. Now beer curds gurgle up into his mouth as he splutters the unintelligible beginnings of an apology.

Cynthia is upset and hurt, tired of it all. Reality slaps her cheeks, adding to the pain. In her youth, she believed in somewhere else. Now *here* is all she knows. Her best friends, Lorraine Gaffney and Mary Ellen Loftus, have married respectable young men. Cynthia itches to join the club, but she's not desperate.

She's been waiting for Joey to finish his studies at Curry College, a two-year school in Milton, Mass. They've been going steady since the previous summer and planned to marry after he graduated the following spring, when they'll both be twenty-three. Early in their courtship, they saw each other on occasion, whenever he could bum a ride the hundred miles back to Holyoke. They danced at sock hops and frolicked in the river and held hands during double features at the Suffolk Theatre. Sometimes, the precocious lovers stole a few fervent hours alone at Ginger Carlisle's house, only if their friend remembered to hide a spare key under the milk box on those weekends when her family escaped to their Cape Cod cottage.

Cynthia has been loyal to Joey; maybe he's been loyal too. Weekly letters fueled their long-distance romance until he scraped up the cash to buy a '49 Ford, which he lovingly named "Rusty Rita." Whenever possible, between exams and football practices, Joey hopped into that baby and squeezed in trips to Holyoke, cruising the Mass Pike, windows down, singing along with Rita's radio. He was over the moon for his "best girl." And he really liked Cynthia too.

Now she's had enough. Enough of the heavy drinking and the self-pity and the complaints about money. On top of all that, Curry recently switched to a four-year college, putting the Stiles/Colthart marriage plans on hold. Waiting two more years for Joey is no longer an option, especially since Cynthia doesn't love him anymore. She loved the boy he used to be but wasn't fond of the man he'd become. He's strung her along, spinning the relationship into a confusing web of uncertainty, tense and sticky, just how spiders like it.

"I can't do this anymore," Cynthia exclaims, wearing a poorly fitting scowl, not her style at all. Her blitzed boyfriend slumps in his seat. The rain falls harder. The car is a prison cell.

Joey was a Holyoke High football star, charming, with matinee idol looks. They were sweet on each other when they were teens, then reconnected after his three-year tour with the air force. His father, a lifer in the paper mills, wanted more for his son and convinced him to use the G.I. Bill to enroll in college. Joey vowed to Cynthia he'd provide the financial stability he desired and the love and laughter she sought. But now he's incapable of accommodating her half of his promise.

"It's over," she says.

"Cyn, you dunno what yer saying," he slurs.

Besides his drinking, Cynthia finds his interests wearisome and worrisome. Strange obsessions and insecurities betray his decent qualities. He's infatuated with guns and oddly fascinated with TV westerns. Worst of all, his braggadocio about leading panty raids through the girls' dormitories at Curry is caddish at best. Now, this accident has pushed her over the edge. She has to end things tonight. The sky cracks open, and the storm pummels the car roof.

"I said it's over, Joey."

"But I love you so much. You gotta gimme another chance. I can change, Cyn. Can we just talk about it tomorrow when you're not hysterical?" He grabs her forearm. She winces, pulls away.

"You're drunk. I need to go." She jerks the door handle. It's stuck. She can't get out. Her knuckles turn bleach white, her stomach flips. She'll have to get past him to leave. A clap of thunder stamps an exclamation point on the thought.

Kaboom!

"I need to get out," Cynthia says corralling her composure.

He clutches her wrist and babbles, "Wait, just wait, lemme clean off the blood. You know I love you so much. So, so much. Yer so beautiful. Can you just stay here so we can talk?"

"Joey, I really need to get out. Please let me go," she says, terrified now. He stares at her with eyes that aren't his own. He scoffs and releases his clamp on her, opens his door and stumbles out, tumbling onto the soaked street. In an instant, Cynthia scoots across the ripped leather seat, out the door, and into the downpour. She sidesteps the man-boy lying in a puddle. He swipes at her skirt.

"Cyn, I—I—I'm sorry." He lunges again.

She jumps back and sprints up the walkway, splashes toward the house. She reaches the porch. The light's burned out. Hands shaking, she fumbles with the key. She's a mess, wet tassels of hair splattered across her face like soggy spaghetti thrown at a wall, her shirt drenched, streaked with blood. She unlocks the door and pushes it open. Praying her father is asleep, she tiptoes into the house. Rusty Rita rattles away. Cynthia cringes, certain the noise will wake the neighborhood.

Tom and Fran Colthart downsized from their roomy apartment in Jackson Parkway to this modest house when their four eldest children moved out. Of the five kids remaining, Cynthia sits atop the totem pole, babysitting for her mother and working as a clerk at National Blank Book. In his mid-fifties, Tom holds a managerial position at the Electric Game Company in Holyoke, while umpiring in local softball leagues and playing pickup soccer with his mates. He commands a strict Scottish household, and his children respect him, abide by his every rule. They don't swear. They don't imbibe. They don't smoke. They don't spend frivolously. And they certainly don't get into car accidents with drunks.

Slouched over the bathroom sink, Cynthia wets a cloth and wipes her face and arms, sure to wash away all traces of blood when she's done. She stares into the mirror, doesn't love what she sees. Then she creeps down the hall and into her bedroom, trying not to wake Elaine in the twin bed just inside the doorway. But her stealthy efforts don't matter. As Cynthia unbuttons her ruined shirt, a whisper emerges in the dark. "Hey, I saw you and Joey through the window. What were you arguing about?"

"Nothing, Elaine. Go back to sleep," Cynthia says.

"It looked like you were really upset. Did you find out he was cheating on you or something?"

"No, it was nothing."

Her younger sister, eager for the scoop, switches on her nightstand lamp. "Oh, my goodness, Cynthia! You're hurt. What happened?"

"Keep your voice down, Elaine. I'm all right, just a few scrapes," Cynthia explains, bloody shirt in hand. "I'll tell you everything in the morning, but Daddy and Mother can never find out. Please promise you won't say anything." She's sure Elaine won't tattle, trusts her more than anyone, still can't believe she's kept a five-year secret about the cigarettes she found in a pencil case under Cynthia's desk.

"Of course. I promise. But are you sure you're okay?"

"I'm fine. We'll talk about it tomorrow." Cynthia scooches into her bed, covers up, and eases her aching head onto the pillow. Her heart in traction, her body stiff, she lets the rhythm of the rain soothe her mind. She sleeps without dreaming.

∾

The next night, Tuesday, I got cozy on the couch. Down the hall, Mom hung onto the last strands of her life.

While watching Game 3 of the World Series between the Houston Astros and the Chicago White Sox, I heard my mother mumble like she had the night before. Once again, I jumped off the couch and sat outside her door.

"Oh my gosh. Hi, how are you?" she said to someone.

As I jotted the words in my pad, Mom started to pant and groan, in the grips of another torrential seizure. I hurried into the room. Her convulsions were frightening. The deteriorated muscles remaining on her bones tightened and twitched as if they were trying to break free from a straitjacket. I waited out the storm. Her spasms tapered, and she opened her eyes. When she turned to me, I tried to act composed.

"Did I have a stroke?" she asked.

"No, you had a seizure."

"I did not."

"Okay, you didn't," I joked.

"Am I sick?"

"You have cancer."

She tripped over her swollen, sarcastic tongue and blurted, "I said I'm sick, and he says I have cancer. Ha!"

"Do you feel okay?"

"My tongue feels thick. I can't help it." She patted her fingers around her face like she was searching for a misplaced set of car keys in the dark.

I took a facecloth from a bowl of ice water on her nightstand and wrung it out. "Here, I'll put this on your forehead. Maybe it'll make you feel better."

She flinched. "Oooh, that's cold."

"Sorry, I'm just trying to help."

"Well, you're not!" She laughed, and I did too; she wasn't normally that snarky, and we were both proud of her wisecrack.

She nodded off again, and I stood over her in the darkness, watching her dying, pretending she wasn't. I stayed for a long while, yearning for an unreachable past, a time when life was never-ending, when we didn't need to say goodbye. A time when I wouldn't give up on her. She'd always protected *me* from the evils of life, always found the energy to embroider fibs about what was absent and present in the world. Now I was protecting *her*.

Now I was the one lying.

Like a zombie, I staggered back to the living room where the series dragged on. The White Sox had won the first two games but were losing this one 5–0 at the end of the fourth. It looked like the feisty Astros might grab a win and make things interesting. Mom had another seizure, and when she woke, I was with her again.

"What happened? I've never been sick."

"You had a seizure from your cancer, but now you're okay."

"You came home? They called you?"

"I wanted to make sure you were okay."

"Thanks. I love you, honey. I'm going to sleep."

"Me too. I'll go back to the couch."

"With Dad?" she asked.

"Ha, I don't think so."

"Yeah, I know. I'll pass too." Again, we laughed hard. She closed her leaden eyes, and as I walked out the door, she said, "There are blankets and a pillow in the closet."

On the couch, I barely kept my eyes open as the White Sox came back against the Astros in the longest World Series game ever played. True to their motto that season, *Win or Die Trying*, Chicago scored twice in the fourteenth inning and prevailed 7–5, putting a stranglehold on the series. I turned off the TV and rolled onto my side. Keeping a drowsy ear open for Mom, I faded to sleep.

Two short hours later, I was back by her side. Dad joined me and parked himself at the foot of the bed. He tickled Mom's blanketed legs, trying to get a rise out of her one last time. She seemed not to notice and asked, "Did you know Ernest Hemingway is an old man?"

I couldn't imagine a more random comment and gladly played along. "You saw Ernest Hemingway?"

"Yeah."

"Is he a good guy?"

"He's a great guy."

I tried to make a cosmic connection between my mother and the eccentric, swashbuckling Hemingway (who took his life with a shotgun blast to the head a month after my parents' wedding day). Maybe her "old man" description referred to the author's final novel, *The Old Man and the Sea*, in which he wrote: "Now is no time to think of what you do not have. Think of what you can do with what there is." Those words could've been carved on her gravestone. But no Hemingway quote suited Cindy Gagne better than this one from *For Whom the Bell Tolls:* "There is nothing else than now. There is neither yesterday, certainly, nor is there any tomorrow."

I picked up the facecloth again and let the water drip for a minute. Then I put the cloth back in the bowl and placed my cool hand on her forehead. "It's late, Mom. Go to sleep. See you tomorrow."

"Okay, Kenny. It'll be tomorrow before we know it." And with the last of her powers, she touched my hand.

The next day we ordered an adjustable hospital bed and set it up in front of the picture window, where Mom could look out at the pool and the yard and the mountain and the river, that endless, changeless river. It was noon when we transferred her from the bedroom to the living room. Once there, she passed out before anyone could even offer her a blanket.

It was time for me to go. I stuffed a ball of crumpled clothes into my backpack and hugged my sisters. As I stepped to my mother's bedside, a worn-out secret masked her face. I took her slight hand in mine, kissed her on the forehead, and silently said goodbye, hoping she heard me, knowing she didn't. And in that moment, I wanted it to be over, wanted her to die, wanted an end to the pain.

My pain.

In the marrow of the following night—long after Chicopee had wrapped itself in a dream—Cheryl awoke from a light sleep on my parents' couch to the sound and smell of vomit. Next to her, on the portable bed, Mom writhed in agony. To prevent our mother from choking, my sister needed to turn her onto her side. She worked her hands under the diminishing woman's shoulders and back, careful not to vex her brittle body. Then Cheryl lowered the bed rail and said, "Okay, Mom, I'm going to move you now."

No answer was expected. None was given.

Before pushing, Cheryl braced for leverage and counted out a warning.

One.

Two.

Three.

At that, our mother's exhausted soul broke free. Her eyes flew open, and she sat up with a jolt. Then with a final gasp, Cindy Gagne exclaimed, "Hi, Mom! Remember me?" And she collapsed into Cheryl's arms, like she was made of flowers.

In the morning, I left Maplewood again to be with my family back in Chicopee. During the trip, I recalled the two nights I spent with my mother, thought of what she said and what I didn't say—how neither of us understood what the other wanted, or needed, as our time together ended. Without her, I'd lost my bearings, felt like part of me was missing. My lighthouse beacon had burned out before sunrise; I'd wait in the dark until dawn.

The river alongside the highway welcomed my arrival home. Considering the road traveled, what Mom gave and what she took, I estimated the cost of wasted time. I never really knew her, and I never knew me, only knew who I needed to be *for* her. She was my reason. She was all of my reasons. Now, I was nobody. But for my father, I had to be somebody still.

We held her memorial service the following Saturday. Behind the pulpit at the altar of my boyhood church, I stood in a black Hugo Boss suit—same one I wore at my wedding, the only suit I owned—ready to deliver Mom's eulogy.

Friends and relatives from the span of my life packed the sanctuary. Scattered among them were members of the Fairview Gang, steps away from the parking lot where they took me in, initiated me, and ushered me from my childhood. I saw Craig first, sitting up straight, solemn and strong. I hadn't spoken to him in a decade, but he was there, as always, an example for me to follow.

A contingent of coworkers from NBAE filed into the church and filled two rows of pews. The sight weakened my knees, and I blinked my eyes dry. I locked in on John Marion. He stared into me and understood. I felt his steady hand on my back once more, propping me up, helping me be brave. Next to John, my buddy Nooch gave me a reassuring nod, speaking with the same unspoken language we used when we played the outfield together. Back then, that nod told me if I dove for a ball and missed, he'd have my back. Same situation here. Comforted by the outpouring of love and support, I took a deep breath and scanned the whole crowd. They were there for my mom, but they were there for me too.

At the same time, back in Jersey, George Land excused himself from his graduate school classroom in Florham Park and sat in the hallway with a printed copy of the eulogy. He'd asked me to email him my speech because he couldn't skip class that morning. He regretted not being in Chicopee, but he wanted, somehow, to be with me and my mom. The two of them had shared a special connection. She always knew he was the one watching out for her little boy. And he regarded her as the source of the kindness and companionship he'd found in me. When we both left home, George and I needed each other to take the place of the families we left behind. And we carried one another for years, like brothers. So in that vacant hallway, George silently read the words I'd written for the woman we both loved.

At the pulpit, tears slid down my face and I struggled to speak. My heart slammed against my rib cage, and I sniffled between sentences while attempting to paint a picture of how Mom gave everyone the benefit of the doubt. How she lived with a quiet grace, hoping to make only a sliver of difference. How she walked the world with stature and poise, knowing she was never alone, knowing that those who loved her—and *love* her—accompanied her along the way. How she saw God in us all.

With hollow eyes, my father watched me at the altar that morning, too empty to feel proud. Did his wife ever see God in *him*? How could she have? Their forty-four-year marriage had withered like a poisoned rose bush, producing many more thorns than flowers. But it didn't have to be that way. What did he take from the eulogy? That he'd never get back what he wanted over all else: more time.

I blabbered some final words and staggered to my seat while my mother's best friend, the Reverend Ann Geer, invited the grandkids to join her on the altar steps. Twelve-year-old Jason sat with his arms wrapped around three-year-old Lucy. Next to them, Caleb cuddled with Jason's little sister, Brooke. On the other side of the pastor, Linda's kids—Makenzie, Quinn, and Aidan—nestled in a row.

Ann held a stuffed bunny in one hand and a children's book in the other. "Have you kids ever heard of *The Velveteen Rabbit*?" she asked.

The sad children shook their heads.

"Well, it's the story about a toy rabbit who wishes he was real." Ann handed the raggedy stuffed animal to Lucy, who accepted it with suspicious arms, then smiled and squeezed her fuzzy new friend as Ann read: "Real isn't how you are made. It's a thing that happens to you. When a child loves you for a long, long time, not just to play with, but *really* loves you, then you become real."

Ann wanted to ensure the kids remembered their grandmother, how much she loved them, what she taught them. And she wanted them to understand why their Grammy looked the way she did when they last saw her, with her thinning hair and frail body and withdrawn face.

A well of tears distorting my vision, I watched Caleb and Lucy, trying to guess what they were feeling.

Ann continued reading: "Generally, by the time you are real, most of your hair has been loved off, and your eyes drop out and you get loose in your joints and very shabby. But these things don't matter at all, except to people who don't understand."

The grandkids were convinced.

"Once you are real you can't become unreal again. It lasts for always."

ELEVEN

"Hey! We Don't Say That Word in Our House"

Summer, 1999

IN AN EMPTY tin can of a bedroom, I stared at seven cardboard boxes stacked in the corner like giant Jenga blocks.

Two weeks earlier, Jackie and I had moved into this 1931 colonial in Maplewood and, other than these boxes, had finished unpacking. Neither of us had owned a house before, and we had all kinds of plans. We decided this spare room would be a future nursery for whenever our first child decided to join us. I had an idea to paint a colorful kids' mural on the side wall—maybe a zany menagerie of cartoon farm animals, maybe a funny, fishy underwater scene.

After two years in a cramped Little Falls condo, we were overjoyed to live in Maplewood, a diverse and accepting town evenly split between Black and white. As an interracial couple, we had good vibes about the place and sensed we'd find companionship and comfort in our new community.

Stillness filled the house that Saturday morning. We hadn't laid down any rugs and owned only a few pieces of furniture. Each breath I took reverberated in the walls, bandied down the halls. As I stepped around the room, the ripened hardwood flooring held a creaky conversation with me. Jackie was out for her daily run, discovering new routes in the hilly, well-manicured neighborhoods near and around Kendal Avenue. Before she left, I'd promised to tackle these old boxes, exhumed from my past, the contents of which hadn't seen daylight since the last time Crockett and Tubbs busted a drug smuggler.

My parents had visited a week earlier, hauling with them these packed-up remnants from my childhood, forgotten relics I'd stashed in their Chicopee basement. "Now that you have your own house, you can take all your junk back," I remember Dad joking. "Get this stuff outta my life."

I scraped off the packing tape on the first five boxes, each containing hundreds of issues of *Sports Illustrated* magazines. My sisters had gifted me the *SI* subscription for Christmas when I was thirteen, and I'd saved every weekly issue for eleven years. When I moved to Jersey, I left my folks with four thousand wrinkled witnesses to nearly half my life, four thousand steps on the staircase from kid to adult, four thousand musty dreams of becoming a pro athlete.

The sixth box contained a few of my old drawing pads and several spiral notebooks. In one of the pads, I found a caricature I'd sketched of NBA star "Clyde the Glide" Drexler and a silly illustration of my Chicopee Comp varsity basketball team featuring Patla, Robbo, Droopy, and Nads. The notebooks were from my college courses in Latin American History, Leadership in Sport, and Intro to Logic. I remembered nothing about those subjects, but if asked when and where I drew the picture of Drexler, I could recite every detail: how my mind wandered that Friday in Mr. Fleury's physics class senior year at Comp; how I relied on my freckle-faced pal Lisa Dowd to catch me up on the lecture about inertia; how I drew Clyde, his eyes even with the hoop, soaring through the air, right knee bent toward his chest; how I took extra care manicuring his Clark Gable mustache and the aerodynamic Afro flowing behind his head.

The final unopened box was smaller than the others. Its top four flaps overlapped, locking the lid in place. I pulled it open and discovered long-lost artifacts of my youth: a faux wood-grain plastic clock radio; a floppy red and white bucket hat from Disney World, with *Kenny* embroidered on the brim; my high school and college diplomas; a Smurf-colored shoe box overfed with audio cassette tapes; the model car Jimmy Uzsynski's father helped me build for my Cub Scout troop's Pinewood Derby; my first-grade lunch box displaying the kids from British TV's *The Double Deckers*; and a dusty, stained, black and silver Bradford tape recorder, with a squiggly cord attached to a stick microphone.

I opened the shoebox of cassette tapes, including the likes of Luther Vandross, Public Enemy, the Stylistics, and the Beastie Boys. Added to the anthology were a few mixtapes I'd labeled: *Gags Trail Mix*, *Love Tunes Mix*, and *Inspiration/Desperation*. Continuing my dig, I uncovered a rare cassette from the pre-eminent rappers of the mid-'80s, the sublime and genre-altering princes of hip-hop: The Vicious III (also known as, the high school rap group I formed with Mike Kijak and Mark Nadeau).

Between '84 and '86, Droopy and I wrote fifteen original raps and recorded them on the retro Bradford tape recorder with the stick mic. Though he and I did all of the writing and rapping, we still included Nadeau in the group, touting him as our mix master "Mad Nads." I took the moniker "G-Force," and Mike donned the alias "Droop-L."

I popped the tape into the recorder and listened to the first few tunes: "Rap Reigns Supreme" and "The Girls Go Crazy" and "The V-III Takeover," which boasted the seminal stanza:

Our rhymes are better than the best of them,
rougher than the rest of them.

When suckers disagree, we apathetically suggest to them,

To never mess around with Droop-L or the Force,

Cuz in the classroom of rap the suckers failed the course.

I recalled sitting with Droopy on his basement floor, passing the microphone back and forth, imitating the trade-off style of our heroes, Run-DMC. Whenever we messed up a line, we'd break into laughter, rewind the tape, and take it again from the top. While our high school friends picked up girls at the mall and got loaded at keggers in the woods behind Shop Rite, we were in that basement recording raps, watching sports, chugging Cherry Cokes, and demolishing family-sized bags of Ruffles.

The Bradford recorder had been my grandfather's. When I was a kid, Pop-Pop was a toast master in Western Mass, delivering speeches at senior centers and awards ceremonies and annual gatherings for the East Hampton Grange. Tom Colthart practiced those speeches on that tape recorder, and when he upgraded to a newer model, he gave the Bradford to me. "You're a creative lad," I remember him saying. "You might find this fun." He was right.

Alone in my bedroom, when I was ten or eleven, I'd clutch the stick mic and pretend I was calling Yankee games on the radio. When puberty hit, I'd sing my favorite love songs into the recorder and then laugh at my cracking voice on the playback. Later on in high school, I'd channel Freud and tape psychological self-analysis experiments, spouting long stretches of stream-of-consciousness babble, pure drivel, whatever came to mind. The following day, I'd listen to the recording (with no memory of what I'd said) and determine the meaning behind my words, trying to figure out who I was, what I was all about.

One of the tapes from the shoebox, a flimsy Philips, had no case and nothing on the label. I slid the cassette into the Bradford, pressed Play, and waited. Nothing at first, then static and crackling, then the faint hush of breath. Probably the prelude to one of my nonsensical mumbo-jumbo sessions, I thought. But I was wrong.

Dueling on the rolling cassette ribbon, drowned-out adult voices engaged in a muffled conversation from what sounded like another room. The voices belonged to my parents, for sure, but they weren't having a conversation; they were ensnarled in an argument. I never realized how thin the walls were in our house.

Tuned into the crackles and muffles, I rubbed the top of my prickly head, trying to extract a memory with my fingertips. I closed my eyes, picked the lock on a secret door to my boyhood, and remembered what else was on that tape. It was 1979, early June, the day of my brother David's funeral.

I was in the sixth grade and had stayed home from school that Friday, my first absence since kindergarten, killing my perfect attendance streak. Staying home also meant missing our end-of-the-year class trip to Quabbin Reservoir and "Field Day," a mini-Olympics with games and contests. Teams for this battle of skill and grit had already been chosen, and mine was stacked. We would've dominated with me and Craig Patla leading the charge (alongside my cute and athletic neighbor, Dani "Frog Legs" Fortin). No doubt we'd win a bunch of ribbons, maybe even a trophy, and we'd have bragging rights all summer long. But my brother died, and I missed the best day of the year.

In that spare room on Kendal Avenue, I tried to remember David's memorial service. Who was at the church? What was said? How did we get to the cemetery? The faulty camera in my mind could focus only on one image: his casket. It was longer than it should've been for a kid, made of mahogany, with golden rails running along the sides. And a wreath of flowers—roses, I think—resting on top, like what they put around a horse's neck after winning a race.

I remembered a group of relatives (more Coltharts than Gagnes) gathered at our house later that afternoon. Clad in black, the mute mourners offered awkward hugs and sweaty handshakes, ate ham sandwiches and macaroni salad and brownies, clumped in clusters of four or five in the living room and basement and breezeway. A half dozen bottles of wine, copious cans of beer, and a galactic silver coffee maker—scuffed and dented and hot to the touch, like a percolating space shuttle—crowded our kitchen counter. Bambi roamed the rooms, meandering around a forest of legs, scoffing up crumbs, licking up spills.

After everyone left, the house smelled like it always did after one of my parents' parties: a hodge-podge funk of stale alcohol and cigarette smoke and body odor. It was early evening. Legs crossed on the living room couch, with a Bud in his grip and a toothpick on his lip, my dad half looked out the picture window, half watched *One Day at a Time*. In the kitchen, my weary mother, looking and feeling every bit of her forty-three years, filled two Hefty bags with trash (dirty tins, plastic platters and utensils, paper plates and cups, ashtrays, and beer cans). She squeezed leftover sandwiches and salads and desserts into Tupperware bowls and, by some minor miracle, found room for it all in the fridge. I watched her work from my seat at the kitchen table, where an untouched slice of strawberry-rhubarb pie challenged me to a staring contest.

"Empty the garbage for your mother," I remember my father ordering.

"I will," I replied with zero concern.

"Ah-Tu!"

"I said I will."

"Now."

"Yep, okay." I stabbed at my pie. My snide tone grabbed Mom's attention. I caught her eye, saw nothing worth moving for.

"I'm going to count to three." My father's voice was angrier than before. I couldn't stand when he bullied me, treated me like a child. Normally he saved those power play tactics for my sisters and mother. I slammed my fork on the table and instantly regretted putting my mom through the melodrama. But my mind was made up. I slid my chair back, overplaying the scraping sound, leaving skid marks on the linoleum. I remained seated.

Dad barked, "One... two..."

"I'm doing it." I ripped off a chunk of pie crust and popped it into my mouth.

"Three. Go to your room. Now."

"I said I'm doing it!"

"Your room. Go!"

"Are you kidding me?"

"You want the plastic spoon or the belt?"

"I'm gonna empty the trash. Calm down."

He rose from the couch. I got up from my chair. He stormed around the cinder-block planter and into the kitchen, stopped directly in front of me. I stood my ground, skinny arms folded across my chest. I craned my neck to lock in on his eyes hiding high above his double chin. Looming, snarling, he snatched the toothpick out of his mouth and his body tensed. It was the first time I'd been in direct conflict with anyone, but I had no plan to scrap with him, didn't even know how to throw a punch, wouldn't last two seconds if I tried to fight.

"You heard me," Dad thundered.

The day David died, I vowed to sacrifice myself for my parents and do whatever it took to give them joy. Now, just one week later, my father faced me, breathing smoke, like a dragon to slay instead of a villager to save. My secret promise to make him happy hadn't lasted long. So much for willpower.

Fed up and running on empty, Mom intervened from behind the counter. "Bob, stop. He's going to do it."

He ignored her, clenched his fists, and slugged me right in the nose with an airborne assault of nicotine and booze. "I said go!"

He waited for my reaction, but I held back, just stared for what seemed like a lifetime. Then I turned, walked slowly down the hall, entered my hole in the wall, and closed the door without a squeak. I pulled the Bradford tape recorder off my bookshelf and slid in a fresh Philips cassette. Clear-eyed and unfazed, I composed a mental manifesto while my parents argued in the kitchen, debating my fate, sealing their own.

Bob & Cyn

If my parents had told me how they got together, if I had actual, legitimate details instead of Dad's unsubstantiated claims that Mom proposed to him the first night they met, then I'd be clear of their love's foundation. If only I'd asked about their engagement, I'd know the truth and wouldn't have to settle for this fantasy.

It's 1960…

On a balmy October evening, bursts of yellow and red from heating machines in paper mill factory windows twinkle like supernovas below the Willimansett Bridge.

Bob Gagne, comfy in his Cadillac convertible, cruises from Holyoke to Chicopee. Cindy Colthart glows in the passenger seat. A frisky swatch of hair obstructs her eyes as she steals a glance at her man. He's twenty-nine, basking in the warm hollowness of bachelorhood. She's five years younger, nursing fresh burns from the fires of recent breakups.

Minutes from their destination, they simultaneously crush cigarettes in the ashtray. Their hands touch, blending in the night breeze. The Halloween bash at the American Legion won't kick off for two more hours, but Bob always pops his corks early.

He sports a fake nose and mustache attached to plastic glasses—a la Groucho Marx—and wears a plaid suit jacket, complete with polka-dotted bow tie. Bob's costume hits the mark, especially since he shares the comedian's receding hairline. As the Caddy rumbles over the bridge, a rubber chicken, like the prop on Groucho's radio game show, *You Bet Your Life*, bounces in the back.

Cindy is an angel. Flowing white robe? Borrowed from the choir room closet at her church. Halo and wings? Fashioned by her little sister, Heather, for last year's school Christmas pageant. Peaceful and radiant spirit? A gift from God.

Bob fiddles with the knob on the car radio, scanning for a boxing match: the professional debut of an exciting, young fighter, a real up-and-comer. As the fuzzy static scrapes the autumn airwaves, Cindy suggests they listen to some music, but her date shrugs off the request. "This kid Cassius Clay's only eighteen, won gold in Rome this summer," Bob says. "Maybe the boys at the Legion can get the fight on the tube."

"Hope so," replies Cindy. Her glittery halo sparkles in the moonlight like a ring of gemstones.

Bob reaches beneath his seat, pulls out a flask and gives it a shake. It's empty. He drops it onto the floor. "My dad loved boxing," he says. "All the greats. Dempsey, Robinson, Louis. He would've loved this kid too."

The conversation doesn't completely bore Cindy, but it's getting close.

"It's hard to be humble when you're as great as I am. That's what Clay said in the paper the other day. Boy, I sure can relate to that." He winks at the angel in the passenger seat.

Cindy has never participated in sports, never had time for athletics. Or fools.

Bob stretches his arm, drapes it over his date's shoulder. "Yeah, I boxed as an amateur in the New England Golden Gloves tourney when I was nineteen," he lies. "Sparred a little with Rocky Marciano's brother, Lou, in '51. Trained some more in the army. Probably could've gone pro if I didn't hurt my back."

With the sass of a diner waitress, Cindy taps the braggart's plastic schnoz. "But if you kept boxing, your nose might *really* be this big."

In the Legion parking lot, Bob pulls into his reserved space by the back entrance. A man dressed as Bozo the Clown unloads deejay equipment from his car and throws the couple a knowing salute.

"This party should be really fun," Cindy says, rubbing Bob's knee. His eyes swap out starlight for stone. A cloud shrouds the moon.

Bob turns off the car engine, removes his fake glasses, and pushes his date's hand off his leg. "You know, Cyn, I've been thinking." His voice is hesitant and serious, out-of-the-ordinary. "This is hard for me to say cuz you're really great. Really, you are. But I think maybe we should take a break, split up for a while, give each other a little space."

Cindy freezes. Her head spins. She's bedeviled, furious, dumbfounded. Words escape her, so she lets the silence have its say. The last six months, the best of her life, rewind in her brain like high-speed film. She juggles the concepts of *now* and *then*.

They met at the Legion on a dull spring night, May eleventh. She remembers the date because ever since, on the eleventh of each month, he's given her eleven roses. He was tanked that Wednesday, barely standing, hitting the hard stuff, whiskey straight from the bottle. She sidled next to him at the bar, ordered wine for herself and a girlfriend. He took one whiff of her Chanel No. 5 and offered to buy her drinks, on the condition that she marry him. The boor's liquid-enhanced confidence charmed her, but she turned down his wedding proposal, agreed only to a date.

Her family approved of Bob. He made them laugh, dressed nicely, and flaunted a spirit they admired (in the way zoo visitors esteem a frolicsome chimp). Bob was good to Cindy—and good *for* her in a way—but no one predicted he'd stick around.

"She'll get her heart broken again," some alleged.

"That guy will never settle down," others said. "Not the self-proclaimed 'Playboy of Chicopee.'"

But the prognosticators were wrong, and soon the couple dropped a bomb, announcing they were serious. The blast reso-nated on both sides of the bridge, blowing away Cindy's circle of square friends and leaving Bob's drinking buddies shell-shocked. Other men in her life fell away, their strings of hope snipped. Bob was the one for her. His zest for life, his spontaneity, infected her. And in time, her love spread to him.

They took romantic drives around the Pioneer Valley; attended parties at the Legion; listened to Sam Cooke records; danced slow to no music; enjoyed scenic dinners at the Mountain View in Easthampton; hiked the Seven Sisters range; and snug-gled at Friday night picture shows, where she clamped his arm during *Psycho* and nuzzled his neck during *The Grass Is Greener*. Then there were the times—her favorite times—when they'd borrow his cousin's boat and voyage the Connecticut River, cares adrift under the weekend sun. Filled, in those days, with infinite potential and tingly expectations, Cindy reveled in the exposure of an inaccessible life, floating on a river of songs, dancing each dance as if it were her last.

As the Earth orbited around the impervious lovers, they ignored world-changing events careening against their protec-tive force field. That fall, the Nixon-Kennedy debates proved that preparation and style mattered. Earlier in the summer, the United States rolled a grenade into Pandora's box and sent troops to Vietnam. And that spring, Harper Lee's acclaimed *To Kill a Mockingbird*—with its themes of morality and racial justice and loss of innocence—astounded avid bookworms like Cindy. She especially sympathized with the plucky main character, Scout.

Now, in a hot mess and a cold sweat, stewing in a lidless Caddy, Cindy wishes for a smidge of Scout's courage. She'd use it to tell Bob exactly what she thought of him, right that instant. How he'd let her down, deceived her, used her heart as a bath mat. How weak he was. How—

"I just don't think this is going to work," Bob continues. "It's not you, it's *me*. I mean, I love you, Cyn, but I'm not *in* love with you." He stares dead-eyed at the steering wheel, detached as a lobotomized toll booth operator.

Cindy's baffled. Like reading a book written in reverse, she understands less as the pages turn. Love had tossed her high, and she flew free for a time, only to land here now, in the American Legion parking lot of all places. *Thud!*

As Bozo unpacks the last of his deejay equipment, Cindy prepares to lay into the joker sitting beside her. She lowers her temperature, bringing the boil to a simmer. Boy, is she going to let him have it. "Bob Gagne," she says, "you are the cruelest—"

"What's happening, kiddos?" A scruffy buddy of Bob's, masquerading as Tinkerbell, prances in front of the convertible and flings pixie dust confetti onto the windshield. The elastic waistband on his emerald tutu winces as he sings, "Let's go, lovebirds. The beer's gettin' warm."

Cindy, congenial even in distress, laughs and waves. But when Tink flitters into the banquet hall, and the pixie dust settles, the woman scorned returns. "You coward. How dare you—"

"Oh, hey, wait a minute," Bob interrupts, reaching into his suit coat pocket.

Cindy fumes, wonders how the buffoon could possibly make

this insufferable situation worse? A goodbye letter? A hanky to dab her tears?

"Before we take our break," Bob says, removing his hand from his jacket, "I want you to have this." He presents a black velvet jewelry box.

She shoots him a conflicted look. "Oh my goodness, Bob," she says, quivering, sidestepping colliding emotions. "Is this what I think it is?"

"You'll never know if you don't open it."

"I can't believe it," she says.

"Believe what?"

"Everything. Us. Now. Here. This."

The ring fits as if she'd been born with it. Might be the only thing about them that doesn't clash or appear disjointed, the only thing that truly "fits."

Their hometowns, Holyoke and Chicopee—Siamese twins connected by riveted steel—wriggle to get out from each other's shadow. Their countries of origin, Scotland and Canada—cultural and topographical opposites—jibe as well as a kilt on a hockey goalie. Their religions, Protestant and Catholic—foes since Luther first nailed paper to door—vie like Cain and Abel for the love of the Father. And this newly engaged couple, Cindy and Bob—inverses in personality and approach—compare to one another like apples to forklifts.

But their search for love is over.

From under the rubble of loneliness, Bob unearths the converse of his mother, someone sweet and positive and loving, someone who might save him from himself. He wants to be like his father, charismatic and adored and drunk, moderately successful in business. His goals are plain and attainable. But his priority, for now, is Cindy. He won't let her slip away. She's his chance at happiness, a promise for an alternate ending. His chance to live.

From under the ruin of dead-end relationships, Cindy unearths the converse of her father, someone gregarious and instinctive and a little wild. She loves her dad, of course, but her home life has been strict, burdened with responsibility. Her opportunities for pure joy have been limited. Now she'll let loose, cut the cuffs of innocence. Bob is her chance to be free. Her chance to dance.

᪥

In Maplewood, I sat on a bloated box of magazines and listened to the cassette roll in the recorder, waiting for what was next. And it all came back to me: the funeral, the argument, the punishment, the rage.

As the tape unspooled, I tapped into the soul of my twelve-year-old self, trying to communicate with him. He wanted to tell me something, wanted to share the pain he felt that day. I envisioned that boy—as someone other than me—slumped against the sky blue wall in his tiny bedroom. A poster of deceased Yankee catcher Thurman Munson watched from above like a guardian angel as the kid plotted and planned. Ticked off at his father, for so much more than being sent to his room, the boy wouldn't yell or scream or overreact. He'd remain calm and slay the man with quiet, cutting words.

I remembered how the kid slid the blank Philips cassette into the old tape recorder, closed the deck softly, and raised the stick mic up to his dry mouth. I remembered how, with sociopathic deliberation, he pressed the Record button. And how he threatened to detonate a relationship that should've lasted forever.

Then I remembered how the boy's mood flatlined as the tape rolled. How he methodically gathered wild inclinations and frayed emotions. Measured and precise, devoid of empathy, he delivered a clear and cruel message to his father. A message no one would receive for twenty years. A message beginning with—

"I hate you..."

I stopped the tape. Jackie would be back from her run any minute. I glided a finger over the Bradford's dusty buttons, debating whether to press Play again. Did I really want to hear the vile message I recorded for my father? I'd never been one to revisit my mistakes or punish myself for choices I made as a kid, always let myself off the hook. But I wasn't that same kid anymore.

Over Kendal Avenue, a 707 leaving Newark Airport split the sky in two, and a jet-fueled timpani rattled the bones of our old house. The empty rooms amplified the rumble, slung its echo up and down the stairs. The roar of aircraft consumed our neighborhood on an hourly basis, but the sound typically eluded me. For Jackie, not so much. The noise bothered her enough that she'd called the airport to question flight patterns. The stress of purchasing a home had put my wife on edge, and she was hypersensitive to every imperfection. I convinced her to wait a few weeks before reselling the house. She'd already gotten used to the most glaring imperfection in her life, I argued. Like with me, she needed to give this new situation a little time.

When the house stopped shaking, I settled and played the recording again. How bad could it be?

Crackle. Breath. Crackle.

And then.

"...I hate you, Dad. I hate the way you treat us and the way you think you know everything."

Breath. Crackle.

"I hate how you make fun of everyone, especially Mom."

Crackle. Breath.

"And I hate that she hates you."

Crackle. Breath. Crackle.

"And it's just that—"

Click.

I remembered how the boy stopped the tape when he heard footsteps in the hall. How he watched the bedroom door handle twist, listened to the hinges sigh. How he saw his mother's eyes, devastation personified. How he unclenched his jaw and separated his lips as a speechless devil ran from his mouth. I remembered the kid's mom entering the room and closing the door.

I'd told Jackie all my childhood stories, the fairy tales and the fiascos. She knew the roots beneath my soil. We'd dumped the details of our lives onto each other's laps and didn't judge. We shared and learned. But I hadn't told her this story. She didn't know about this tape recording, this secret. But I didn't hide it from her on purpose. I never told her because I'd hid it from myself.

When my dad sent me to my room that day, I shut the door on the memory. David's funeral—and all that happened after-ward—existed only as a box of blurred images from the past. They were faded snapshots, underdeveloped and overexposed, distressed naturally with time. Hearing my voice on that tape, and the growls of my hatred, restored those images in my mind and colorized the truth. I hung my head and relived the scene.

In my childhood bedroom, the clock radio had flipped to 4:11 p.m. The tape recording had stopped. Standing in front of me, my mother appeared confused, unsure of who I was. She used to know me as a boy who never did anything wrong, never said anything cross. But I wasn't that good boy anymore. And I saw her there, dressed in black, eyes caved and vacant, looking like she'd lost another son.

"I heard you talking," Mom said, firm but fatigued, her face drawn and blank.

I stiffened.

Another minute flipped on the clock. Never before had my mother and I experienced such collective intensity. Did she want to hold me or hit me? Thrown off by the moment, I gave up trying to read her and focused on the floor. The anger I felt for my father mutated into disgrace for myself. How could I have been so selfish? How could I have trashed the private vow I'd made to keep her happy? She took a small step forward. Her eyes were alive now. And fierce.

"Kenneth John," she said, "don't you ever say anything like that about your father again." She trembled as she spoke, her voice the color of fury.

I turned away and pulled my knees up to my chest, aching for her to leave. But she had more to say.

"You will never disrespect him. Do you hear me?" The weight of her precisely enunciated words crushed me like anvils off a balcony, and the warning tremors of a breakdown rocked my shoulders.

My mother swallowed her convulsions. "You will stay in this room for the rest of the night. I do not want to see you or hear from you until tomorrow." She walked out and closed the door. And I cried harder and more violently than I ever had before— or would again.

She'd stuck up for my dad, chose him over me. No matter how much I wished she hated him that day, she didn't have the desire or the ability. Of course she didn't; that word wasn't physically allowed in our house, and neither was the emotion. And Mom wouldn't allow it in her life. I didn't hate my father either, never did, but had no idea how to tell him otherwise.

Jackie popped into the house. "Hey, I'm back. How's it going up there?"

I ejected the tape, placed it back in the box, and transitioned from past to present while ghosts of long-ago words circled the room. "Just about done," I called down to her.

Outside the walls of our new home, life on Kendal Avenue chirped and bounced. Preteens ran from yard to yard, laughing and shouting in the throes of a made-up game. Sleep-deprived fathers balanced preschoolers on sparkly bikes, plastic training wheels clickety-clacking down the street. Neighbors drank coffee and chatted on the sidewalk. Sparrows sang.

Someday, Jackie and I would weave ourselves into the fabric of this neighborhood, sync with the heartbeat of this town. Our *own* children would laugh in the yard. The training wheels on *their* bicycles would clickety-clack on the pavement. We'd chat with *our* neighbors on *our* sidewalk. The sparrows would sing to *us*.

Our future family would create vivid and lasting memories in Maplewood. And we'd fill our house with loving words, not hateful ones. We'd preserve crystal-clear images of our days, remembrances of growth and discovery and connection. We'd amass moments of joy. And we'd pack up those moments and put them in storage and open them some other day. Like my dad said when he dropped off my boxes, "We are what we don't throw away."

TWELVE

"That's the Way Life Goes"

Summary, 1984

*P*RACTICE WOULD BE over in ten minutes.

Through the gap in my front teeth, I rocketed a stream of spit—like a frozen rope—into my Spalding mitt. Before the saliva pooled, I rubbed it into the worn leather as the alluring fragrance of glove oil seduced my nostrils. From my prime spot in center, I checked the position of the late morning sun strung above Rivers Park and pulled my cap down low. The #6 charm on my gold chain stuck to my sweaty chest like a branding iron.

Reclining on the bench, the seniors had called it quits for the day, taking off their cleats and planning that night's keg party. We underclassmen stayed in the field, getting our reps, earning our stripes. One player still hadn't taken BP.

Marek "Mud" Drabinski was a sophomore, a grade below me, and one of the best hitters at Comp. He was a husky catcher with a canon for an arm, a six-foot-four frame, and a fun-loving personality. Of us wannabe pros, Mud was the only one with the requisite talent, work ethic, and physique to make it to "The Show." All he needed was a chance.

I'd spent my middling high school baseball career as an infielder but loved roaming the outfield during practice. As a personal challenge, I worked hard to get a jump on every fly ball. The strength of the batter determined how deep or shallow I played. His stance, open or closed, informed me what direction the ball would travel. The location of the pitch, inside or out, high or low, told me which way to start leaning. My coach, Dan Dulchinos, a legendary figure in Massachusetts coaching circles (reverently referred to as "Mr. D.") always told me, "Don't be afraid to make a great play, Kenny. Expect the ball to be hit your way. See it before it happens. The first step is key, but to make a great catch, the biggest thing is *wanting* to make it."

Mud was a line-drive hitter who made a living lacing lasers into the gaps. He rarely hit long fly balls, so I played him shallower than most outfielders would. As Mr. D. fed the pitching machine, pumping seventy-five-mile-per-hour meatballs straight down the middle, I bounced on my toes. Mud took his rips. After he pulled the first three pitches down the third baseline, I sidestepped a few feet to my right. The outfield grass glistened, still slick from an evening storm. Staying focused on Mud's bat, I pounded my mitt and dug my spikes into the soft ground, testing my footing. Mr. D. dropped another ball into the machine. Mud turned his hips. I shifted my weight. He swung.

Pinnng!

The ball exploded off his aluminum Easton, a scorching line drive over shortstop. I broke in hard with four quick steps and springboarded into the weightless Willimansett morning. Hanging horizontal, I stretched out my arm beyond plausibility, fraying my tendons, and willed the ball into the webbing of my glove. Using my ribs as landing gear, I touched down and skidded, prone on the wet grass, like a greased penguin on a runway of ice. My heart jumped, thumping in exaltation. Whoops and shouts of "Atta boy!" and "Way to go, Six!" rang through the air.

The force of my landing had knocked the ball loose, and it rested next to my elbow. Before anyone noticed, I smothered it with my mitt, sprang to my feet, and flipped it back to the infield. A brownish-green smear covered the front of my T-shirt like a superhero's insignia. I didn't wipe it off.

When practice was over, I called "shotgun" and jumped into the front of Steve Geoffrion's stallion-black pickup. My slow-on-the-draw buddies, Mike Kijak and Mark Nadeau, shoveled into the cab's tiny back seat amid a clutter of stinky baseball gear. At the intersection of Memorial Drive and Pendleton Avenue, we stopped at a traffic light. Mike and Mark bickered about when and where our upcoming American Legion tryouts were scheduled, while I tried to convince Geoffrion to go out for the team.

"Hey, isn't that Patla's car?" someone said.

In his beat-up cobalt Nova, accelerating to outpace the light, my BFF Craig Patla sped through the intersection, and as I caught a glimpse of his passenger, my world flipped. A tangle of squirrels tussled in my belly; the taste of liverwurst struck the back of my throat; embarrassment and confusion and rage ran afoul, playing duck-duck-goose around my brain.

That was my girlfriend with him, wasn't it?

Sure was.

I saw Kimmy first—in that eyeblink of time—sliding down fast in the passenger seat, like she'd fallen through a trap door. Her baby blues apologized as she vanished; a trail of feathered hair waved "buh-bye" in the wake. Her disappearance exposed concern on Craig's once-friendly face, a face I'd always turned to for quiet guidance, a face now unable to forge its signature, toothy grin.

That split second dragged on like a bad date. While Kimmy and Craig's expressions super-glued themselves onto my skull, Mr. Awkwardness squeezed into the truck. He was an obese hitchhiker with horrible hygiene, stinky pits and unbrushed teeth. And his flatulence? Silent but deadly.

With caring but clunky bluntness, my buddies offered their support. "Damn. Sorry, KG. That sucks," Geoffrion said.

"I heard a couple days ago that they might've been seeing each other," Nadeau added. "But I didn't know if it was true."

"Forget about her," Kijak said.

Their words couldn't mellow the humiliation and betrayal churning in my gut. I'd been duped, and man oh man did it hurt.

Kimmy and I had been "going out" since that beautiful day, that dreamy day, in October when Robbo pulled me aside in gym class with news that she liked me. She and I had been the quintessential high school couple. I was the jocular junior jock with charming, albeit unworldly, charisma. She was the sophomore stunner with a wicked wit and personality to boot.

We spent our time at the movies or the mall with Kijak, Nadeau, and their girlfriends, the six of us piling into Droopy's raspberry Honda like a heap of hormonal circus clowns. Though I was seventeen, I hadn't yet applied for my driver's license. Eschewing four wheels for two, I'd pedal my ten-speed across town with the fortitude of a mail carrier to hold clandestine make-out sessions with Kimmy at her babysitting jobs. Nothing could keep me from her.

The image of my girl dipping out of sight in Craig's Nova took up permanent residence in my head. What was it my physics teacher said? "The brightness of a nova star is blinding at first then slowly burns out after a few million years of fusion." (I never liked physics.)

Steve dropped me at my house, and I shuffled in to find my father shaking salt into a frosty glass of Coors at the kitchen counter. Without breaking concentration, he asked, "How was practice, KG?"

"Fine." I sniffled and wiped my eyes to make sure no tears got outta Dodge.

"Allergies bothering you again?"

"Uh-huh, really bad today," I fibbed.

"Well, your lawn needs mowing, so take a Sudafed and get out there."

Mowing the lawn was the last thing I wanted to do. Actually, it didn't even make the list. What I *really* wanted was a little sympathy. For a nanosecond, I dreamed I could talk to my father about my problems. But how would telling him what happened with Kimmy and Craig lift my spirits? The man never wanted to hear anyone complain about anything. There were no Ward Cleaver words of wisdom rolling around under that comb-over. If I opened up, I had a hunch how the conversation would unfold:

Me: Dad, can I talk to you?

Him: Free country.

Me: Today after practice I caught Kimmy cheating on me with Craig.

Him: That's the way life goes.

Me: But he was one of my best friends.

Him: What is he now?

Me: I dunno. *Not* one of my best friends?

Him: Takes all kinds to make a world.

Me: See, this is why I never tell you anything.

Him: Okay. If you're done, then get outside and mow your lawn.

Kimmy called later that night. I used the phone in my sisters' room for privacy. Sprawled on their bed, I listened to my ex claim I'd been spending too much time with Mike and Mark. She felt unimportant, she said, like she was playing third fiddle. Her complaint struck a chord because it was the truth. Kijak and Nadeau had become extensions of me, like extra appendages, always by my side, helping me reach higher than I thought possible.

Our connection was rooted in sports and music and teasing and trust, pretty simple stuff. Uncorrupted, and proud of it, we didn't drink or smoke, and our straitlaced personas tied us together in double knots. We complemented each other in baseball, basketball, and soccer like we were tethered by athletic tape. As top-billing performers, we lip-synched to New Edition songs in the limelight of Friday night school dances. Our bond fastened during annual summer vacations with Nadeau's family in Cape Cod, where we rocked killer tans and wished for big enough gonads to hit on every girl in West Dennis. And while Chicopee teens banged their heads to rock and metal, we formed a fictitious hip-hop group, The Vicious III, and tossed our figurative Kangols into the ring of rap.

With Mike and Mark's unconditional loyalty and unspoken endorsement, I resisted forces prodding me to be "typical" and "ordinary." My buddies liked the wholesome kid I'd been trying to be for my parents. To them, my saintly veneer wasn't a tired act or a disguise, and they stayed close, staving off the mob of peer pressure, while I fought the instinct to become a creature of societal expectations, a high school cliché. And under the full moon of their friendship, I transformed into *an original*. If not quite a "Thriller."

On the phone with Kimmy, ensnared in a twisted paradox, I sought both exoneration from being the reason why she cheated and release from the mandate to break up with her. I didn't have it in me to be spiteful or vengeful. *She* was the one who cheated. *She* should marinate in shame (at least a little), not me. I shouldn't have to be the bad guy. How could I live with that blot on my resume? With my squeaky-clean reputation on life support—and our relationship in a vegetative state—I waited for Kimmy to pull the plug. After a lengthy silence, she tapped into her inner-Kevorkian and did the deed. "So, I guess it's over."

"Yeah, I guess so." (Sweet emancipation!)

I'd been wronged but still emerged the victor. Blameless and vindicated, morally intact, I hung up the phone while Cyndi

Lauper's "Time After Time" played on the radio. The next day I wrote Kimmy a gushy letter crammed with passive-aggressive subtext, implying her guilt and asserting my innocence, a letter I'd never mail:

Kimmy—I had to write this to you because I can't keep my feelings about what's happened to us inside forever. When I told you I understood how you felt, I was making a mistake because I really don't understand. I guess I said that because it's hard for me to accept that I did something to hurt someone else and I wanted you to know that if I had hurt you in any way, I didn't to it intentionally. I think, by now, you know that about me.

But Kimmy, what you did was totally unlike you. It's hard for me to believe that the girl I asked out would ever do anything like that. I suppose I misunderstood you from the beginning. But you were never like that before. I used to think that you were the kind of girl I would like to spend my life with, that the woman I marry would be exactly like you.

It would be wrong of me to remember you solely from this incident because the good times that we had together are far more important to me. Your feelings are the most important thing to me now though. And knowing each other's feelings is the secret to our relationship. We have to be honest with each other if we want this new, but different, friendship to last.

You can change the way you feel for me a thousand times, but you can never change the way I feel for you. I care about you very much. I always will.

Robert & Cynthia

If Mom and Dad had told me about the day they were married, if I knew more than what their wedding album had to say, then I'd appreciate the friction between their religions and the biases their love overcame. If only I'd asked about their controversial union, I'd know the real story and wouldn't need to conjure this one.

It's 1961…

The last Tuesday in May. Trails of smoke from charred hot dogs and fizzled fireworks, Memorial Day weekend leftovers, climb a bell tower that sits like a tiara atop Holyoke's First United Church of Christ.

Thirty-year-old Robert waits at the altar, cocky in his tux— white jacket, black pants. He adjusts his bow tie as the organ moans the first notes to "Here Comes the Bride." Stately double doors at the rear of the sanctuary open like the pearly gates, ushering in a mix of shadow and light; the congregants stand. Cynthia grips her father's arm, takes one step forward, then another. A vision of perfection in her lacy gown, she lassos every male breath in God's house.

Shoehorned into cramped pews, eager guests on the bride's side swivel well-coiffed heads, squirming for a glimpse of Cynthia's aura like the multitudes angling for a crust of bread. Across the aisle, on the groom's side, a smattering of attendants scan the wedding program. Slowing his pace, Tom Colthart leans in close to his daughter and whispers, "You're more breathtaking than Liz Taylor when she married Conrad Hilton." Then adds, "Bob's no Conrad Hilton, but he does have his forehead."

"Shhhh, Daddy."

Modestly prepped for the occasion, the Presbyterian house of worship hums along with the honking organ. The presiding Reverend Norman Farnum, a former air force pilot from

Lowell, familiar with the indomitable spirit of a dying mill town, stands beside the groom and surveys the half-filled sanctuary. Robert's older brother Rheo Jr., the best man, whips a comb from his pocket and slicks back his oily pompadour. Opposite him, Cynthia's older sister Jane, the maid of honor, squiggles in asphyxiating heels.

The tuckered organ staggers to the finish line as father and daughter reach the aisle's end. Their last steps together finish in rhyme. This is goodbye. Tom lifts his little girl's veil and kisses her softly on the cheek. "I've never been prouder of anyone," he says. "Now, go shine." He addresses the groom with eyes that both warn and approve, a crooked look that'd make Mona Lisa crack an actual smile.

Robert cradles Cynthia's hands in his, caresses them with the gentleness of a lumberjack. "You look pretty good for a Presbyterian."

Cynthia smirks, peeks at the congregation, and mouths, "I can't believe your mother isn't here."

"At least you showed up," Bob says, loud enough to make the minister's eyebrows jump.

To no one's surprise, Annette Gagne disapproves of her son's marriage, and she's convinced her daughters they do too. In protest, all three women blow off the ceremony. Even if they accepted Cynthia, they wouldn't be caught dead in a Protestant church.

Like lots of French-Canadian Catholics in Chicopee, Annette believes interfaith marriage degrades the sacraments and character of matrimony, a subject on which she somehow considers herself an expert. "The Admiral," as she's known, has abandoned ship because—God forbid—her son marries the woman he loves. For now, Cynthia has bested her future mother-in-law, wresting control over Robert's heart, if not his religion.

Staring into his bride's veiled face, Robert knows his father would've approved. If Rheo Gagne Sr. were still alive, instead of backslapping at some speakeasy in the sky, would he be here? *Definitely*. Would he bless this union regardless of an ages-old culture clash between Canada and Scotland? *Certainly*. Why should a political power struggle in Quebec, a century back, between Anglo-Scottish bourgeois and the francophone middle class, matter at all now? *It shouldn't*. And why should anyone care in the least that boozy Catholics in Canada have always blamed teetotaling Protestants for the rise of Prohibition? *Well, actually…*

Sure, Canadians and Scots make for rumpled bedfellows, but shouldn't "love" be able to tidy up the mess. *Of course.*

The kind reverend recites the vows. "Do you, Robert, take Cynthia to be your lawful wedded wife?"

"I do."

But what if love's not enough?

"And do you, Cynthia, take Robert to be your lawful wedded husband?"

"I do."

What if life's surprises are too much?

"Then by the power vested in me by the state of Massachusetts…"

What then?

"I now pronounce you man and wife."

Despite the religious feud and familial conflict, seemingly all of Chicopee attends the reception at the Legion. The open bar is a powerful draw, and the disc jockey plays everyone's favorites. Tipsy guests swing to Chubby Checker's "The Twist" and Del Shannon's "Runaway." The bride and groom brush cheeks to Etta James's "At Last." Bob clams up when the Shirelles read Cynthia's mind and, in four-part harmony, ask her husband, "Will You Still Love Me Tomorrow?"

He tosses back another Tom Collins, slips the deejay an extra

Jackson, tells him to play Ernie K-Doe's "Mother-in-Law," then pulls Cynthia's mom onto the dance floor. Fran Colthart loses her composure, after a quick twirl and a dip, and bursts out laughing as Bob, in an excess of high spirits, belts the song in a blaring baritone.

The lights go down. The newlyweds envelop one another and sway to *their* song, "Let It Be Me" by the Everly Brothers. From the corners of the beer-soaked hall, cutting comments slice lengthwise through the music. Catholics chugging Manhattans make harsh predictions about how long the marriage will last, chasing down those shots with bitter hopes for an inevitable annulment.

"It contradicts the Holy Scripture," a hidden whisper proclaims.

"Their poor children will have no faith in God," a guarded voice groans.

"It's so selfish." The concealed claims fly, rising above the crowd.

Bob hasn't heard any of the insults. Or if he has, he's ignored them. Either way, he lends his dissenters no credence, refuses to dignify snipes with an argument. Maybe after a few more drinks.

He's been conditioned by the karmic burden of past experience. His parents' union—unstable and unloving—taught him nothing of marriage, or its alliterative tenets of commitment, cooperation, and communication. He'd have to figure all that out on his own. But not to worry; after seven intolerable years living alone with his mother, Bob has the will and motivation to figure out *anything*.

After honeymooning in Miami, the couple takes another step over the threshold of adulthood when they purchase a three-bedroom ranch house in Chicopee's wide-open Fairview section. In Bob's blustery opinion, the pastoral backyard view, overlooking the Connecticut River, is tops in the city. He's certain his tolerant, pure-hearted, and submissive wife will add to the scenery.

Cynthia opens up to the world after twenty-five years of giving her family (and everyone else) more love than she can afford. In her hushed opinion, she's owed a handsome return on her investment. But she'd never ask. She's positive her decisive, fun-loving, and understanding husband will help her discover the awaiting wonders of an untapped life. She hopes the sameness of their love will release him to be what he *can* be, unaware that the goodness in him is compromised by ancient notions telling him what he *should* be.

They expect much from each other, believing in the fallacy that a ring on a finger can change a person. But people, like opinions, are hard to change.

⋐

My girlfriend had cheated on me; one of my best friends had betrayed me; no one in my family noticed. They had matters of their own to deal with, and we paid attention to each other with equal amounts of apathy.

My sisters had careers to worry about and had taken initial steps into the workplace. Cheryl had graduated from Baypath and measured up well as an office manager for an architect. Linda had bowed out of community college but was tailored perfectly to run a local women's clothing store. *Congrats, you two! Good luck with that whole adulthood thing.*

Dad was neck-deep in the quicksand of selling his business to pay for my college and his retirement, and things were getting messy. But that was *his* headache. *Contaminated soil under the gas tanks? Whatever. A potential lawsuit? Tough break. How many times is that lawyer going to call anyway? Geez.*

My parents' relationship was on the rocks, just as my father had ordered. They enjoyed each other's company with the frequency of a Halley's Comet sighting, and the tension in our hothouse tightened. Stuck in the worn grooves of habit, Dad nit-picked Mom's every word and disregarded her opinions like they were lint on his bathrobe. He got a kick from upsetting my mother, and that kick caught her right in the teeth every time.

They sleepwalked through marriage counseling and tolerated a religious couples therapy program called Cursillo, a weekend retreat at the Springfield Sheraton, where well-meaning clergymen lent God's help to spatting spouses for about the price of a romantic steak dinner for two. My father came home from that encounter on a Sunday night, slapped a *De Colores* sticker on the French door in our breezeway, and considered his marriage "redeemed."

The day after Kimmy quit me, I came home from church, belly-flopped into a pit of malaise on the couch and watched a recap of the NBA draft on SportsCenter. The draft had been five days earlier, but anchors Chris Berman and Tom Mees continued the hot debate: Should the Portland Trail Blazers have chosen Sam Bowie over Michael Jordan? After Akeem Olajuwon went first overall, followed by Bowie, Chicago selected Jordan. Mees said history would prove the Bulls got the best player. Time would tell.

The kitchen phone rang, and my dad answered it the way he always did. "Goodbye."

Ugh. Same stale routine, the usual schtick.

"Yep, Kenny's in the shower. Hold on a sec, I'll get him."

Get a new act while you're at it.

I rolled my eyes; not in the mood for his shenanigans. I didn't want to talk to anyone, not even Kijak or Nadeau. Still, I peeled myself off the couch and snatched the phone.

Dad hoisted a brow and said, "It's Craig."

I pressed the receiver to my hip and bit my lip. I waited for my father to leave the kitchen and lifted the phone to my ear, like it was a plastic explosive, to hear what my "frenemy" had to say.

"Hey, KG, wanna go to the park and shoot around?"

"Sure."

With the urgency of a funeral procession, I dribbled down Langevin to the Fairview Elementary School playground. A blistering air bubble on my balding Spalding gave it a lop-sided effect. The disloyal ball, its bounce untrue, tried to distract me from my showdown with Craig. Keeping my dribble alive, I played out the scene in my head, repeatedly, again and again, putting the ball around my back and through my legs.

Again. *There was only...*

Again. *One way to handle...*

Again. *Our confrontation.*

I got to the court first, surprised to find the parks department had repainted the backboards and strung new chain nets onto the rims. It had rained earlier that morning. I spun the ball on my finger and paced, stepping over puddles on the cracked asphalt. In the distance, across the baseball field, Craig strolled toward me, his ball wedged under his arm. I acted like I didn't see him, and he got closer. I snuck a quick peek, noticed two Cokes in his hands. With his first move, my opponent had spent fifty cents on a peace offering: a bold gambit. I took note.

We slugged swigs of soda in silence, placed the bottles on the sideline. Then we shot around, make-it-take-it, without so much as a grunt. Sticking to my sweet spot—fifteen-foot jumpers from the left wing—I trained my eyes on the hoop, intent on hitting every shot, denying Craig a chance. I swished five straight and basked in the chain's glorious chimes. But then—

Clank. Done in by doggone double rims.

Craig grabbed the rebound and, as I knifed to the hoop, he fed a perfect bounce pass that found my hands with the feathery intention of a homing pigeon. I flicked in a lefty finger roll, and after letting the ball bounce to a stop under the basket, I picked it up and fired a one-handed rocket into his chest.

He took a couple of uninspired dribbles and said, "Hey, I really dicked ya, huh?"

"Yeah."

I don't remember much of our conversation after that, but Craig said he'd understand if I never spoke to him again. I told him that no girl was worth more than our friendship. I'd been humiliated but didn't want to make "a thing" of the whole thing. We'd been buddies since meeting on this playground twelve years earlier; Kimmy and I had dated for only seven months. It was obvious which relationship I needed to salvage.

Craig's apology was curt and sincere and appreciated. I forgave him and, eventually, forgave Kimmy. The lingering pain didn't bother me; it was more a dull, somewhat satisfying soreness, like how an aging athlete's knees ache when remembering past accomplishments. The competitor in me chalked up another moral victory, and though the high road's altitude had given me a nosebleed, the breakup didn't cause any real harm. Being without Kimmy hurt at first, like a baby tooth falling out, and the empty space felt weird for a while. But she was a part of me I only *thought* I needed. If I wanted to keep growing, I had to lose her.

No one blamed the Trail Blazers for selecting Sam Bowie instead of Michael Jordan. And no one blamed Kimmy for choosing Craig over me. He was a great guy with a car and some money and a job at Cumberland Farms. He was funny and good-looking, had an edgy confidence. On top of that, he was seven inches taller than me, and as the old hoops adage goes, "You can't teach height."

The scouting report on me had all the flair of a *Farmers' Almanac*: solid, all-around nice guy, three-sport athlete, respectful, funny, decent-looking, and drama-free. But I had no job, no money, no car of my own, and no edge. Plus, I barely stood eye-level with Craig's broad shoulders.

At the University of Kentucky, before he got to the pros, Sam Bowie had an allure about him. A seven-footer who shot from range, handled the ball, and defended, he had talent like nobody else. Michael Jordan developed into a special player for the North Carolina Tarheels, but no one predicted his *absolute* potential in the NBA— except him. Only he saw the greatness within because only he knew the size of his heart.

The Chicago Bulls didn't win the NBA lottery in 1984, but an all-time great still fell into their laps. Fate, I thought, would bless a lucky girl (waiting for me somewhere) with a similar fortune. I'd been dumped, but my loss would be that girl's gain.

I walked home from the playground that day and compared myself, for the first and last time, to MJ. No one knew the size of *my* heart either. Maybe getting passed over would work out for *me* too. Maybe everyone overlooked *my* greatness. A draft snub had put a chip on Air Jordan's shoulder, would lift him to unreachable heights. I saw no reason why I couldn't fly just as high.

THIRTEEN

"All You Have to Do Is Look"

Summary, 1973

THE ATLANTIC GRUMBLED.

Tourists peppered the beach; locals gave them the evil eye. Icy breakers boomed like M-80s, their explosions showering me with salty sprays. I backed away from the water, squatted, and dug my nubby hand into the beach. I scooped up a pile of burning sand and let it run through my fingers till all that remained was an empty palm. My sisters giggled nearby while poking at a dead horseshoe crab with a piece of driftwood. I grabbed my yellow plastic bucket and looked out at the waves.

Dad came from behind and threw an arm around my slender six-year-old shoulders. "You know, there are more stars in the sky than grains of sand on every beach in the world," he said.

"No, sir, really?"

"Yes, sir, really." My father loved tossing random facts and figures at us kids, and we thought he was a genius, back when we didn't know any better.

"Have Cheryl and Linda found anything yet?" I asked.

"Nope. I predict you'll be first."

Our family was on a week's vacation at Misquamicut Beach in Rhode Island. Dad had taken me and my sisters for a walk to find sea glass for Mom's birthday. The night before, Cheryl and Linda had cut a pizza box into the shape of a heart. We planned to color the cardboard red and tape our sea glass onto the home-made heart in the form of a "37." She'd love it, we thought. Best. Gift. Ever!

Daredevil seagulls swooped like kamikazes as we hunted our treasure. Cold waves rolled in, numbing my roasted ankles. Above the horizon, a prop plane dragged a banner displaying two lobsters in chef hats. A nearby radio played a song about a man "meaner than a junkyard dog." A feisty foursome of girls fussed over a blow-up raft while a windblown Frisbee wobbled past me like a lost hubcap. A circle of adults in nylon folding chairs smoked cigarettes and argued about "a water gate"—sounded to me like a fancy entrance to the beach.

A wave receded and a shiny object tumbled in front of me. "Hey! I think I see one," I yelled. The crash of another wave devoured my exclamation.

I rushed toward a shimmering light buried under a stew of seaweed and crab legs. Picking through the shelly slime, I spied the most glorious shard of sea glass King Neptune ever coughed up. But as I reached for it, the ocean washed in again and stole my mother's gift. Like a crazed pirate, I pursued my fortune but stopped short of the water. Mommy always said, "Never go into the ocean alone."

Another wave broke and chased me back. When it retreated—and the foam soaked into the silt—the glistening glass sat on the sand and called to me. I hustled over and snatched it.

"Yahoo!" I screamed and thumped my chest as a jungle of hyper sandpipers, startled by my aping of Tarzan, deserted their smorgasbord of tiny mussels.

The size of a clam shell and the color of a lime popsicle, the radiant glass glowed, translucent when held to the sun, smoothed from years of churning in salt and sand. My jewel of the sea had surely come from a shipwreck, I thought, sunk during a violent storm; the glass was probably from a shattered bottle of rum—could've been Blackbeard's.

Yes! Had to be.

I turned to flaunt my booty for my father and sisters, but they were gone. I fussed with the drawstring of my scarlet bathing suit and plunked the sea glass into my bucket. My heartbeat synced with the manic rhythm of "Rockin' Robin" hoppin-and-a-boppin out of a phantom transistor. I stumbled in one direction, then the other. Which way to our blanket? Which way were we walking?

Cheryl? Linda? Dad?

My spot in our family had always been right at the top, propped up and supported by everyone else. I was the prince, the golden child, the boy who did no wrong. My parents and sisters watched out for me, always took care of me. Now I was alone, in foreign territory, left to fend for myself. In a dizzying spin, I scanned the beach again.

Laughter. A football. A wave.

A crash.

Singing. A kite. A wave.

A crash.

The crush of beachgoers multiplied and coagulated into one amoebic mass, like a glom of psychedelic colors in a tin kaleidoscope. Isolated among them, I was a microscopic grain of sand in a galaxy of stars.

Mom?

That previous school year, I spent four hours a day in kindergarten and the rest of the time with my mother, running errands or "stopping by" to visit her army of friends and relatives. While she shopped at Perrault's, I'd sit facing her in the cart like a backward race car driver, feet dangling, probing for an invisible gas pedal. When Auntie Lorraine invited Mom over for coffee, I'd toss tennis balls in the yard to her dog, a dim Dalmatian with different-colored eyes who never fully understood our game of fetch. On special days—with no shopping or visiting on the docket—Mom took me to McCray's Animal Farm in South Hadley, where she'd hand me two quarters to buy a cupful of pellets from the dispenser then watch me sprinkle feed onto the sticky, icky pumice tongues of eager goats, sheep, and spitting alpacas.

Then there were those mornings, every other Monday, when we went to Markie's house on Ingham Street. Save for those tagalong visits, I didn't know this strange boy or his family. In his backyard, I'd play with Matchbox cars while Markie squirmed and groaned on a raised gurney, our mothers manipulating his arms and legs like they were pumping water from a well, steering his spindly limbs in directions they were unwilling to travel. On those peculiar days, I saw "love" and "faith" and "grit" written all over Mom's face; saw how she looked at that woman, like she could read her mind; how she reassured her, spoke to her with confidence; how she eased the troubled heart of another suffering mother, helped to heal the severed soul of another broken boy.

Once a month, before Mom drove to Palmer to visit my brothers, she'd drop me off at Memere's house. My father's childhood home was a symphony of mothballs and meat pie, with crescendos of gossip and scandal. On those equally boring and entertaining afternoons, I'd bang on the electric organ in the living room and watch *The Price Is Right* while Memere knitted a shabby sweater—or a pair of booties, or a scarf—for anyone who walked in the door.

Her telephone rang off the hook the whole time, and I'd overhear sordid conversations with her "friends" about who wasn't speaking to whom, or who wrote a letter of complaint to LaCroix's Market, or who showed up to church with cognac on her breath again.

At a rickety card table in the kitchen, I'd snack on stale shortbread cookies or homemade pecan pie that gave me sugar shock. Whenever my grandmother opened the fridge, I'd cringe, praying she wouldn't take out the weird plastic cylinder packed with celery and carrot sticks. These painted containers, lovingly made from drained vodka bottles, littered her house. Memere would guzzle a liter per week, saw off the empty vessel's neck with a steak knife, then decorate the carcass with green and red nail polish. Kept her busy, I suppose.

Normally, my mother would visit my brothers alone; now and then, my sisters went along. A few weeks before our Misquamicut vacation, I met Robert and David for the first time. I guess Mom thought I was ready.

She held my hand as we followed a cheery nurse in a white dress down a long hallway decked with framed crayon scribbles. The place reeked of dead flowers. As we walked, I peeked into bedrooms smaller than mine, where wool blankets and striped pillowcases made up modest cots. In some of those rooms, on some of those cots, twiggy arms and legs hung limp off the side. In front of me and behind, I heard what sounded like laughter, but I couldn't be sure. The nurse led us into a sunlit room where my brothers occupied two short beds on opposite walls. Mom's steps lightened when she saw their faces; I turned away. To me, the twins were abnormal and unreal, looked like grievous characters from a Brothers Grimm fairy tale.

"Well here they are, the two most popular residents in Hoskins Hall." The woman in white spread her arms wide, as if presenting a perfectly cooked ham. "I'm not supposed to say this, but Robby and Dave are my favorites. Such darlings."

In a familiar singsong voice, Mom greeted her eldest sons as they writhed and grunted. "Well, hello. How are my sweet boys?"

She leaned over Robert's bed, caressed his arms and tidied his mussed hair. She pressed her cheek against his, and he wriggled with glee, thrilled by the warmth of her skin and the sweetness of her breath. Then she moved to David's bedside. He squealed when she took his hand in hers, his head bobbing in approval.

My brothers were lanky and frail, knees knobby, elbows pointed. They were eleven now, five years older than I was, but it was hard to tell the age difference between us. My mother moved around the confines of that room with a selfless joy. And as she covered her twin boys in unreciprocated love, I was amazed by her dedication to them. Like a shady cedar unaware of its sprawl, she attended to their unspoken needs with benevolence and care. Did they know her? Did they know each other? Did she have enough love for all three of us?

I glued myself to a metal chair in the corner, but my mother urged me to get closer. "Come and say hi to your brothers, Kenny," she suggested. "Let's go. Quick-quick like a bunny."

I hesitated.

She smiled and led me to Robert's bedside. She placed my palm on his forearm, gentle and deliberate, and together we stroked his skin. Then she brought his hands up to my face and put them on my cheeks. His palms felt like sheets of damp sandpaper. I shuttered my eyes as she navigated his fingers over my nose and mouth, down to my chin, back up to my ears, to the top of my head. He tapped his jagged nails on my scalp and twisted my hair. When I lifted my lids, his nose was an inch away from mine, and his vacant blue eyes shined with unwieldy pleasure. I pulled away, shaking, and hurried back to my chair. Robert spasmed. A frantic seal bark pulsed from his throat.

Across the room, David thrashed on his cot, as if sensing

the commotion. Mom alternated from bed to bed, calming her startled sons. I slouched in the corner and eyed a stack of musty magazines and pamphlets in a bookcase next to me. I picked up a thin, leaf green storybook titled *The Giving Tree*, by someone named Shel, and flipped through its worn pages. To further avoid Robert and David—their strangeness, their otherness—I disappeared into this book. Unable to read well, I zeroed in on the opening sentence and mouthed the words: "Once there was a tree... And she loved a little boy..."

The Twins

If Mom had told me how helpless she felt while advocating for my brothers, if I knew more about her doctor's apathy than what she'd scribbled in her old appointment book, then I'd understand her suffering. If only we could talk to each other again, maybe I'd assure her she did all she could, and maybe she'd know it was true.

It's 1962...

On a steamy Wednesday in August, Lorraine Gaffney pays a birthday visit to her best friend, Cindy. It's midmorning. They drink coffee and smoke cigarettes and chat at the kitchen table. Ray Charles's smash hit "I Can't Stop Loving You" dances out of a radio on the windowsill. Down the hall, Cindy's two-month-old twin sons, Robert and David, nap in their cribs while the music and conversation build.

"So, how are the boys doing?" Lorraine says into the cluttered air.

"They're really no trouble at all," replies Cindy.

"Should we turn the music down so they can sleep?"

"It's okay. Loud noises don't seem to bother them." Cindy's tone reveals a hint of surprise. "I think they've gotten used to all the racket around here, especially when Bob's home." The friends laugh hard, like they did when they were clerks together at National Blank Book.

Cindy and Lorraine slip into the bedroom and find the boys awake. They lift the twins out of their cribs, enamored of the creamy skin and powdery scent of these perfect children.

"Golly, Cyn, they are so adorable. But how on Earth can you tell the difference between them? I don't even know who I'm holding," says Lorraine.

"It's easy," says Cindy. "You've got Robert. See how his eyes are a darker shade of gray? And David's got a tiny beauty mark on his neck right here." She tickles the mole and runs her hand over the boy's gauzy hair.

Lorraine taps Robert's cheek. "Oh, is that a smile I see?"

"It sure looks like one. Let's see if they can nap for another hour."

The women place the silent babies into their cribs and head back to the kitchen. Cindy's voice bounces with typical cheer; her movements are light and precise. But in recent weeks, her eyes have become like Robert's, a shade darker, like a gathering of weather. The sparkle she once had is gone, dulled by an alien sadness.

Lorraine refills her friend's coffee cup. "You know, Cyn, you don't turn twenty-six every day, and *The Miracle Worker* is playing down at the Willow Theatre. Any interest? My treat."

Cindy unveils a grin and moans, "I'm sorry, Lorraine, but I don't want to see a picture about a blind, deaf, and mute girl on my birthday. It's probably really sad. And it'd be an *actual* miracle if Bob came home in time for us to make the show."

Lorraine laughs. "Well, how about we see *The Music Man*? Everyone says it's swell. There can't be anything depressing about a charming con artist, can there?"

"Hey, enough about Bob." Again, uncontrollable giggles knot their bellies.

"C'mon, it'll be fun," says Lorraine. "We already know that song everyone's got stuck in their heads." And the giddy women break out singing "Ya Got Trouble."

Yep, right here in River City.

For Cindy, life in Chicopee appears trouble-free. She has two beautiful baby boys and lots of trusted friends. Her sons are easy to care for, her marriage is fine. Her husband is "unique," juvenile one minute, pragmatic the next.

Before the twins, she and Bob had enjoyed each other's company, going out to dinner, attending parties, taking spontaneous trips on the weekends. But in the two months since Robert and David arrived, the relationship has changed. Bob's out a lot now, either working or golfing or bowling or drinking at the Legion. He has it all, it seems: a gorgeous wife, two angelic kids, and a successful business. What he doesn't have: the knowledge that each of these successes contains the seeds of a subsequent failure.

Staring past Lorraine, Cindy answers an unasked question. "Sure, it'd be nice if Bob were more involved with the boys. But he works hard at the garage, and this is such a big adjustment for him. Plus, he's president at the Legion now. He's got a new family, a new house. I think he's just a little overwhelmed, but he'll come around."

Her husband had fainted on the first of June, when the second of his two boys wriggled into the world. As far as anyone remembers, it's the only time Bob Gagne ever blacked out without leaving an open bar tab. Fortunately, Cindy's well-equipped to carry the load. Motherhood suits her, and she wears it well. She makes it look easy, has a magic touch with children, an unfair advantage (according to some). She's built for this, has prepared for it. By bringing up four younger siblings, she's developed the requisite skills, and temperament, to raise a family of her own. *On* her own.

From the start, she's handled the challenges twin boys

present with nuanced tenacity. Through osmosis, Robert and David have absorbed their mother's demeanor, have taken on her characteristics: sedate, quiet, and "no bother at all." In a corner of the nursery, she rocks them in a chair, one in each arm, cradles them close. As the hours drift, she hums a honey-hushed ballad born on the banks of a Scottish loch, a melody that floats in the room like fog until sleep takes her sons away.

I mind where we parted on yon shady glen

Hmmm, hmmm, hmmm, hmmm

Hmmm, hmmm, hmmm, hmmm

And the moon shinin' out from the gloamin'

Only then does Cindy shut her eyes and imagine their lives together in the years ahead. The twins mirror each other in appearance, but she knows, as they grow, their personalities will split, and they'll become separate, distinctive individuals. She smiles and lets her mind decorate the future.

Robert, she dreams, will be like his father: funny, stubborn, and mischievous. David will be the quieter sort, a gentler soul, thinking before acting, deferring to his slightly older twin. She envisions both boys will develop into thoughtful, caring, respectful gentlemen. It's a perfect picture, this dream she paints.

But her eyelids unlock to a palette of troubled colors.

As summer turns to fall, her sons miss milestones other children their age have already hit. They don't react to her when she walks into their bedroom. They don't respond to her voice. A foreign fear seeps into her mind. In late October, she takes the boys to their physician, Dr. Pechman, for scheduled vaccination shots.

"We'll be giving these tykes their smallpox, diphtheria, tetanus, and polio boosters today," the doctor says as he fumbles through a drawer of syringes. "That sound okay to you, Mom?"

"Of course, it's fine. But I need to talk to you about the boys' development. There's something wrong. Remember when we were here last month, and I said they weren't able to sit up yet? They should be able to do that now, shouldn't they?"

The practitioner sighs, plops onto a swivel stool, removes his wire rim glasses, and looks down his nose at Cindy. Her sons squirm atop the crinkly paper on the examining table; the irritating crackle is a cherub's hymn compared to the grating lecture Dr. Pechman regurgitates.

"You know, Cynthia, I see all kinds of kids every single day. And I see all kinds of mothers too." His plodding, patronizing pitch drips with condescension. "Every child develops at his own rate. Some are fast, some are slow. This is really nothing to worry about."

They've engaged in this circular conversation before, but Cindy musters the gumption to address the issue again.

"I don't mean to be rude, but please listen to me." Her voice quivers. "My boys are almost five months old, and they can hardly lift their heads. That should've happened months ago. And look, none of their teeth have come in yet." Gently, Cindy opens David's mouth and runs a finger over his gums. He balks at her touch.

"It's all natural. No need to overreact, Cyn," the doctor says, brushing a smudge of baby powder from his bony hand. "You know, if I had a nickel for every new mother who thought her little boy should be running around like Bob Cousy right out of the womb, I'd double my salary." He tugs at the stethoscope hanging around his Slim Jim neck and forces a cockeyed smile. "Maybe it's time we rule out the chance of your sons joining the Celtics someday."

"My sons don't even know who I am!" Cindy's words come from an unfamiliar place, one she's rarely visited. Her legs go weak. The doctor recoils. She finds her balance, gathers up the twins, and storms out of the office. Defeat and defiance commingle in her heart. All her life, she's listened to the voices of male authority. Now—for the first time—she hears her own.

Fueled by frustration, concern, and exhaustion, she hurries through the parking lot, whips open the rear door of her vehicle, and places Robert and David into their car seats. The boys shoot blank stares at her and slump as she meddles with their coat zippers. She props her sons up and secures them behind the metal safety bars on their seats. Their heads sag. She slams the door, jumps behind the wheel, closes her eyes, lifts her chin, and exhales, her life a perfect graveyard of buried hopes.

While Cindy navigates the streets of Chicopee in a daze, a herd of fighter jets rumbles across the clear autumn sky. Her steering wheel shakes as the plane engines roar, demolishing the air. She's oblivious to the din and to an emergency newscast on the radio: "We interrupt this program to bring you the following announcement. The United States has discovered Russian military bases being constructed in Cuba with missiles reaching up to one thousand miles and aircraft able to carry nuclear warheads twice that far."

Cindy drives unconsciously, the shocking broadcast affecting no one in the car as they cruise past Westover Air Force Base.

At the same time, across the river in South Hadley, beneath a section of Bare Mountain called the "Notch," near the old Gagne farmhouse, leaders of the U.S. Strategic Air Command (SAC) meet in a secret underground bunker. This part of the mountain had been owned by Aristide Gagne and passed down to his son, Rheo, Cindy's father-in-law. Before his cirrhosis purchased its own property, Rheo sold the land to the Pentagon to hollow out their lair. Now, SAC has given Westover Air Force Base its orders: ready seventeen B-52 bombers for a counterattack should Russia drop a nuke on the United States.

Expressed through heavy static—and a heavier Massachusetts

accent—President Kennedy's declaration over the radio is measured and assertive: "This urgent transformation of Cuba into an important strategic base, by the presence of these large, long-range and clearly offensive weapons of sudden mass destruction, constitutes an explicit threat to the peace and security of all Americans. Our policy has been one of patience and restraint, but now further action is required, and it is under way. And these actions may only be the beginning."

Chicopee is at the epicenter of a potential nuclear war, but Cindy is deaf and blind to the threat of world annihilation, and to the world itself. She's dedicated solely to the advocacy of her sons. Like JFK has explained, the time for patience and restraint is over. She needs to act.

⁖

I'd been walking on that beach for years, it seemed, in who knows which direction.

The noises of Misquamicut had quieted, and the thumping in my heart had slowed. There was no sign of my family's blanket, but I kept calm, resigned to my plight. Certainly, my father and sisters were looking for me, feverish and panicked, no shell unturned. My eyes were bleary from the strain of my search and spots dotted my pupils. My legs ached, but I kept moving. If I stood still, I'd surely sink into the sand, lost and gone forever.

Then my bravery gave way, and a tidal wave of dread nearly capsized my flimsy raft of hope. I held on tight and shoved back my tears. *Everything will work out.* Isn't that what Mom always told me? But what of my mother now? Was she hopeful? Was she scared? Was she blaming my father for another forgotten son?

With two older sisters who spent the bulk of their days at school or with friends, I was used to being by myself. My world in Chicopee was compact, digestible, and easy to navigate. I'd spent a hefty chunk of my six years alone in the hills behind our house, with freedom to roam. But no matter how far I wandered, I knew how to get back home, back to my mother, my ever-present comfort.

Even as she cuddled on the couch with Johnny Carson, she kept her eyes peeled for me and my nightly routine: sleepwalking. Careful not to disrupt my trance, she'd intercept me in the hall, guide me to my room, and with satiny words, talk me into going back to bed. The following morning, she'd tell me about my evening adventures: that I'd opened the refrigerator and announced, "I'm going to the bathroom"; that I'd carried my pillow into the living room and said, "It's sleepy time," before curling up in the corner behind the television; that I'd stood in the breezeway and stated, "Gotta do my jumping jacks."

She liked to tease me about the sleepwalking, and we laughed at those funny stories, but she'd get quiet whenever I blamed it on my "shadow dream."

On the beach, I tried to remain unnoticed and didn't tell anyone I was lost, didn't ask for help, didn't want to impose on strangers, thought it'd be rude. Mostly, I was afraid what they'd think of me: What kind of kid just wanders off? Is he dumb or something? How could he disobey his parents like that? Assuming the next woman on the next blanket would be my mother, I kept walking, kept seeking. The crowd, and the commotion, grew. I was no taller than an award-winning sandcastle and couldn't see through the lather of Hawaiian Tropic hardbodies. To find my family, I'd need a bird's eye view. I wished for a tree to climb, like the one in our front yard, the one I could scale to heaven—with all its rings of memory.

The rugged bark on that ginormous oak was perfect for my little fingers and toes to grip. The trunk, too thick to wrap my arms around, leaned at an angle, allowing me to shimmy to the first limb. Once I grabbed hold, I could pull myself up to branches galore. Each day, I set a goal to climb a little higher, a cinch for a monkey like me. That tree was my haven, my citadel, my throne. And depending on the season, it offered something different. In the center of summer, the oak flush with leaves, I could hide in the branches for hours, but the growth obstructed my view. In late autumn, the branches stripped naked, I was left unprotected, open for discovery, but I could see forever.

It was difficult to figure how long I'd been lost, or how far away I was from our blanket. I'd turned around and changed course a few times, had combed the entire beach, and everything looked the same. The sun scorched my shoulders; sand singed the soles of my feet.

I thought if I found our car, I could hunker down and wait for my family in the parking lot. I walked off the beach toward a row of automobiles that stretched on for miles, assuming I'd pick out our car in a jiffy. But Dad drove a rotating gaggle of rag-tag clunkers, and I forgot which bucket-of-bolts we'd taken on vacation.

After walking alongside the lot for ages, I dropped my pail in the sand and sat on a splintered, tar-stained wooden bulkhead. I'd done all I could to find my way back, but it wasn't enough, and I was ready to let someone else do the work. I checked on the sea glass in my bucket. It had lost its shine.

A golden teen, who must've beamed down from the starship *Enterprise*, appeared out of nowhere. He wore bright orange swim trunks and mirrored shades, and his sculpted physique blocked out the sun. Except for the white gunk on his nose, he looked like a god.

"Hey, kid. What's your name?"

"Kenny."

"How old are you, Kenny?"

"Six."

"You lost?"

"Uh-huh."

He called someone on his walkie-talkie. "Yeah, blondish hair, little guy, says he's six." The whistle around his neck swayed in slow circles like a woozy pendulum. "Hold on, lemme check." He squatted down and examined my face.

"What are you looking at?" I asked.

"That thing on your face. Is that a scar from a wart?"

"Yeah. Why?" I put a finger over the bump near the corner of my mouth.

The previous summer, our family physician, Dr. Pechman, had scraped off the wart. All I remembered of the experience was a Charleston Chew–length needle puncturing my cheek; a frozen scalpel lopping off a chunk of my skin; and, later, Dad telling me he'd heard my screams from the waiting room. The wart removal left an ugly mark, one that embarrassed me. Now that scar would bring me back home.

The golden beach god communicated with his fellow life-guards to determine the location of my family. He held my hand and walked with me to the far end of the beach. Fifteen minutes later, we approached our blanket. I saw my mother. She ran to me, a river of joy flowing down her face. "Oh my God, Kenny! Oh my God!" She hugged me tight, and the heat emanating off our skin soldered us together. "I knew you wouldn't go into the water alone. I knew you wouldn't," she cried.

"I'm sorry, Mommy. I'm sorry," I said through blistered lips, my head against her stomach. "I didn't mean to make you sad."

She took my face in her hands. "Oh, you didn't do anything wrong. Not one thing."

Her son was with her once more, and she pledged to never lose him again. Constricted in her arms, blanketed by her smile, I'd made it back to the place I belonged. Her breathing slowed, and relief crashed over her body. I'm not sure which of us was happier.

"Oh! Mommy," I yelped, recalling my life before that

moment, "I found a piece of sea glass for your birthday, but I put my bucket down in the parking lot and forgot it there."

"That's okay. I'm sure it was very pretty. Maybe later we can go for a walk and find your bucket. It might still be there; you never know." She squeezed me harder and kissed my salty head.

Even if she owned all the sea glass in the world, it'd mean nothing to my mother. Loving her children was all that mattered, all she needed. With Robert and David, she'd found that love—and lost it. After learning to live with the trauma, she got a second chance at motherhood, and life explained itself. She understood then how people, more than objects, needed to be wanted and fixed and saved. And she never gave up on anyone.

I stared at the sea that stretched on forever; somewhere out there was hope. I thought of how I felt earlier, lost on the beach, knowing my mother was nearby but unable to find her. Was that how my brothers always felt? Missed and sensed and remembered? Searched for, and yearned for, relentlessly?

FOURTEEN

"You're Gonna Miss Me Someday"

Spring, 2007

I MET CHERYL OUTSIDE Room 323 at Baystate Medical Center in Springfield, my fingers throbbing from squeezing the string to a balloon monkey I'd bought at the hospital gift shop. The inflatable primate holding a half-peeled banana was a birthday surprise for my father, who'd be seventy-six the following day.

A plump nurse pushing a dinner cart rattled past us, humming a tune to herself. Linda sat by Dad's bedside as Cheryl and I spoke in low tones about the "do not resuscitate" papers she'd signed a half hour before, a formality she ran by me to confirm (when the end came) that I wouldn't want to keep my father alive unnaturally. She needed to know I'd be on board with letting him die.

"Cool with me. You're the boss," I said. The balloon monkey dropped his banana, covered his ears, and heard no evil.

It was late March. Dad had bounced between the hospital and rehab center for weeks. He wasn't doing well, and I needed to visit.

I was run-down and road weary, having left Jersey that morning at dawn for a four-hour drive to the Boston Celtics practice facility in Waltham, Mass. I'd gone to interview star player Paul Pierce and head coach Doc Rivers for a feature about the team's snake bitten season and how they'd stayed positive through adversity. Five months earlier, Celtics team president and Hall of Famer, the iconic Red Auerbach, had passed. After that, Boston suffered through a franchise record eighteen-game losing streak, during which the indestructible Pierce missed seven weeks with a stress fracture. In forty-two games, from mid-December to Valentine's Day, "The Green" had only three wins. Then in late February, Celtic legend Dennis Johnson died from a heart attack at fifty-two. Somehow, the exalted Boston Celtics, the winningest team in NBA history—whose logo boasts a leprechaun and four-leaf clover—had run out of luck.

During our interview, I asked Coach Rivers about Auerbach's impact on the organization and the legacy he left. Doc paused before saying, "It's amazing how Red would make you feel. He created a family atmosphere around here. He wanted you to know you were special, that you were better than everyone else, because you were part of the Celtics family."

I couldn't keep my mind off my father.

I asked Pierce how difficult it'd been to lead an inexperienced team and what they might learn from losing. With his signature rasp, he said, "Champions aren't built overnight. I understand it's going to take time, and we have to grow with one another. These young pups are taking their lumps, but they're proving they belong." Then he smiled and looked into the future. "When I hold up that championship trophy, I'm going to think about these tough times and say, hey, you gotta go through the valleys to reach the peaks."

Sounded familiar.

A month earlier, a jaundiced prophet had leaked out of Dad's skin, crying for help, while scaly plaques of psoriasis littered the bloody battlefields of the old man's arms and legs. My sisters demanded he see a physician, but he just bragged that he hadn't been to a doctor in his life. "I got a million friends who work out every day," he gloated, "and they're always getting sick. But not me."

He must've known this situation was no joke though because, for once, he put his pride aside and listened to my sisters. Linda booked his appointment and drove him there herself. The doctor took one look at the guy and sent him to the hospital. He'd never go back home.

Before then, my father had been hitting the sauce with a vengeance. His liver took a brutal beating, but his heart and mind didn't fare much better. On the average day, he'd wake from his afternoon nap, sink into his dent on the couch, and smoke a pack of cigs. Encased in a carcinogenic haze, he'd drink his weight in Bud while clawing at the festers on his skin and scratching his cable news itch.

The noise oozing out of the TV filled his empty soul, distracted him from reality. The anchors pumped him full of gloom and doubt, confirming life was scary and unfair. They told him who to blame, who to suspect, who to revile. The constant discord riled him up, stirred something inside his belly, kept him alive while killing him at the same time. A barrage of spin and propaganda whip-shut the door to reason—too thick and heavy to budge—until my father's close-mindedness imprisoned him so totally, he didn't even know he was locked up.

He'd spent the '90s in bankruptcy, not a cent to show for thirty-five years in the family business. After Mom's cancer diagnosis at the turn of the millennium, everything started to crumble. The shaky structure of my father's life weakened further when the Twin Towers fell and the whole world shook. The following year, his brother Rheo died, then his mother the year after that. At Memere's wake, I stood next to Dad over her open casket. Adorned in a floral pantsuit and her customary costume jewelry, she lay there, hair dyed the color of beef gravy, gaudy makeup masking ninety-nine years of hard living. I remember my father's delight as he pinched her powdered nose and gave it a wiggle, a harmless and silly gesture considering the torment she'd put him through.

"See ya later, Annette," he said for my benefit, typical of the levity he brought to serious moments. It was a fitting goodbye, and behind his eyes, I could see he forgave his mother. But he'd never forget.

Like a frozen explosion, my brother Robert's death in 2004—twenty-five years after David passed—unearthed the guilt Dad had buried in his bones. The loss razed his emotional state and drudged up memories of his greatest mistake: neglecting his wife when she needed him most, after they sent the twins to Monson. Now my father was dazed, rocked to the core. And the year to come threatened to finish him off.

In the spring, his younger sister Jacqueline died. Then, that summer, his loyal friend Jerry Gaffney passed. After Mom departed in the fall, Dad reeled, hiding his pain and his readiness to give up. He kept busy a few hours each day running routine errands: the cleaners, the gas station, the package store, maybe a visit to see my sisters and their kids. Then each night, he lost himself in a bottle, and as the hollow bottles piled up, the nights grew deeper and darker.

In the mornings, he assumed his position on the couch, sipped tomato juice with vodka, and watched the sunrise. The glow on the other side of the picture window proved the outside world was still alive, while the yellowing of his eyes and the toxic waste bubbling to the surface of his skin indicated that, inside, he was already dead.

Alcohol was powerless to fend off the growing shadow of disappointment that had trailed my dad through the years. The collateral damage of his binge drinking: faltering internal organs, the latest failure in a magnificent line of failures.

Over the entirety of his life, the people closest to him—those who were supposed to love him dearest—let him down. His siblings neglected him. His mother abused him. His father abandoned him. His twin boys shamed him. His brother betrayed him. Linda dropped out of college. I moved away. Cheryl got divorced. That all hurt my father, took an unaccountable toll, and when cancer stole his wife, a parade of death trampled the pointless years to follow. The final brick toppled when his closest companion, the Reverend John Geer, died in 2006. In a heartbreaking and gracious farewell note to my dad, John wrote about valuing the final season of his life and appreciating his friend:

> *No matter how you glorify the coming winter, something*
> *tries to hold you to the past. You have given me a treasured*
> *autumn. You have been a strength to me. You have softened*
> *my steps among you. Help me now; help me with your prayers*
> *to move to a future season. I have a heart filled with thanks.*
> *I thank you for making our seasons so special. I thank you for*
> *being you and for loving me.*

Ann and John Geer were the strongest link to the best part of my parents' marriage. The couples had a blast together, with the Geers putting Dad in his place and filling my mother with the love and self-esteem she couldn't get from her husband. Ann and John's generosity allowed the four friends to travel and laugh through two decades of my father's financial struggles. Those were happy times for my parents, perhaps the happiest of times.

John's death was a forceful whisper that convinced my dad he had nothing, and no one, left to live for. The demolition complete, Bob Gagne lay in ruins.

Bracketing him on either side of the hospital bed, my sisters wished Dad a happy birthday, kissed him goodbye, and vowed to come back the following afternoon. I gave them both hugs and watched them leave while my father stayed quiet for only the second time in his life. As he sang his song of silence, I sat beside him and shook a strainer of memories; the bitter ones fell through and the sweet ones remained.

"It's gonna be okay," I said. We both knew it wouldn't.

A sour awkwardness overpowered the smack of urine and Lysol, while the beep from my dad's heart monitor did its best to entertain. I struggled to say something impactful as my hand ran out of bounds, trespassed onto his papery fingers. I'd never touched him like that before. I wanted to tell him I loved him, but we weren't comfortable expressing our emotions to one another, didn't operate that way, and it'd be out of character to do so now. If I opened up to him while he hobbled down the homestretch, it'd smell like surrender. And I wasn't about to let either of us give up, at least not outwardly.

"C'mon, Dad, let's go for a walk," I said. "Just down the hall and back. You could show off your sexy body to everyone. It might make you feel better."

"What difference does it make?" His tone told me he'd reconciled with the end, the dying written all over him.

Painful bedsores and a fractured bone in his back limited his movement. Even if he had the will, he'd be unable to stand. The man who never complained—and never gave in, and never admitted his failings—was done. The sands of time flowed fast, and he had no desire to turn over the hourglass. He pulled his hand from under mine and turned away. Losing helium, the balloon monkey sank like a flag lowered to half-mast.

An exhausted and bloodied boxer, my father begged me to throw in the towel. His stubborn and overly competitive corner-man, I barked at him to keep swinging, foolishly hoping he'd land a miracle punch on the chin of the undefeated champ. I didn't want him to die, knew if he did, I'd never be the same. I still needed him. And I wanted to believe he still needed me.

I'd tried to be good, tried to make my parents proud and be for them what my brothers never could. But my dad didn't need me to be that perfect little boy anymore. He needed me to be a man and a husband and a father, needed me to be better than him, needed me to tell the frightened boy he used to be—the child hiding deep inside—that everything was okay, that none of this was his fault. But I said nothing.

And I thought that might be enough.

Hope

If Dad had told me how it killed him to give up his twin boys, if I had his side of the story and not just the entries in Mom's diary, then I would've forgiven him for pulling away from her. If only we had another chance to share our feelings, maybe I'd understand my father, and he'd understand me too.

It's 1963...

January is joyless, the days cold and dark.

If Robert and David could see, they'd look out the living room window at winter's white wonders, while lying with their mother on a patchwork quilt. They'd watch feathery flakes float in for snowy landings. They'd delight at the sight of their yellow pup bounding in backyard drifts. Far behind the house, at the base of a powdered mountain, a frozen river would grin. The baby boys would lie content on that soft quilt, follow their mother's gaze, mimic her expressions. And like prolific alchemists, they'd turn the joy on her face into enough love to fill both their hearts ten times over.

But they can't see.

Not any of it. Not the flakes, not the river, not their mother. They can't see her cry, but they can smell the salt in her tears. The drops fall off her cheeks and sting the boys' skin. Every day in darkness, Robert and David feel their mother's stares, sense her searching for signs of life in their empty eyes. And each night, she writes in her journal, tracking her sons' lack of progress and her husband's lack of understanding. Like a marooned castaway's lonely days etched in stone, her words are a constant and painful reminder of how they're all hopelessly stranded.

1/1 — New Year's Day, stayed home, Boys 7 months old, still don't react when I enter their room. I lie to everyone and say they're doing fine...

1/5 — Saturday at home, cards with Lorraine & Jerry, Elaine & Frank. Hard pretending to be happy...

1/6 — Sunday, Mother, Father, and Heather over for ham dinner. Bob and I had another fight...

1/26 — Hairdresser 2pm, Shopping with Lorraine. Bob with boys all day. French Night at Legion...

2/1 — Boys 8 months old, Home, they still have not smiled or rolled over...

2/6 — Home, Bob bowling and Legion. I can't sleep. Feel he might leave us...

2/9 — Boys first tooth, should have happened months ago...

2/20 — Home, Alone. Bob bowling and Legion...

3/1 — Home, Boys 9 months old, they still can't grip anything. How long can I do this...

3/3 — Sunday church, Home, car ride with boys...

3/22 — Appointment with Dr. Pechman again, what's going on? Why doesn't anyone know what's happening...

If Robert and David could hear, they'd wake at dawn in adjacent cribs to the melancholy coo of mourning doves. They'd tune in to the plip-plop of spring rainwater, residue from a late-night storm, dripping from a gutter into a puddle below their bedroom window. Each boy alert to the hush of his brother's breathing, they'd resynchronize their body rhythms. Their ears would perk up and, in unison, their excited heartbeats would quicken, detecting their mother's soft steps in the hall. Then they'd hear the sound they lived for, the only sound that mattered. After the subtle grind of the twisting door handle, and the low creak of hinges, Robert and David would hear their mother's soothing voice, the voice of pure love, a melodic embrace welcoming them to the promise of another day.

But they can't hear.

Not any of it. Not the doves, not the rain, not their mother. And though nightly screams of frustration fill the house, drowning out the angriest thunderstorm, Robert and David can't hear the arguments or the storms. But they shake inside from the loud nothing all around.

4/1 — Boys 10 months old, still don't seem to recognize my voice, Home, Bob bowling...

4/2 — Took boys to specialist at Springfield Medical Center...

4/7 — Church, Home, Bob Legion and golfing. We haven't spoken in days...

4/30 — Robert finally rolls over. Bob thinks it's great news. He doesn't understand...

5/1 — Boys 11 months old, still don't respond to their names. Home...

5/3 — Friday, took boys to Boston Hospital for appointment with another specialist, need more tests...

5/6 — Monday, took boys back to Boston Hospital, admitted for tests all week...

5/10 — Picked up boys from Boston. Confirmed they can't see or hear...

5/12 — Mother's Day, David had three slight fits. I couldn't calm him...

5/13 — David has a seizure, put in request to send boys to Monson Developmental Center, doctor says they should go if we want more kids...

5/30 — Wedding anniversary, stayed home. Tough day today...

6/1 — Boys first birthday, stayed home, No party...

6/14 — Friday till Sunday, to Truro Cape Cod with Roland, Dottie, Jerry, Lorraine. Elaine watches Robert, Connie watches David...

If Robert and David could walk, they'd wobble barefoot across the chilly kitchen floor, one unsteady step at a time, toward their mother's waiting arms. As the neophyte travelers zeroed in on their destination, their father would cheer. The toddlers would lose their balance on the sleek linoleum, stumble and fall, then pull themselves up in a gritty attempt to keep moving. Brave together, the brothers would venture into the outside world, conquering three steps in the front of the house while keeping a viselike grip on their mother's fingers. Once at the bottom of the stairs, Robert and David would let go of her hands and stagger onto the lawn with the sturdiness of tipsy high-wire performers. Prickly blades of grass would tickle the soles of their feet, and the boys would giggle on their journey, side by side, under the summer sun, before finding the way back into their mother's embrace.

But they can't walk.

Not anywhere. Not on the floor, not down the stairs, not to their mother. Underdeveloped muscles limit Robert and David's movements but don't limit their parents from moving on with their own lives. As the days extend—and the sun dawdles in a horizonless sky—mother and father make the impossible decision to start over, without their sons, casting away an endless season of torment into the doleful past.

7/1 — Ethan's birthday, Boys thirteen months old, shopping, Heather babysat boys, they still cannot sit up…

7/16 — Tuesday, Cards at Mother's with Dotty, Elaine, Joan, Gail. Bob stayed home. I think he's trying…

7/28 — Nauseous, Bob golf tournament, Connie's for visit, Bob and I to Legion…

8/1 — Boys fourteen months old, Home. Bob out all day…

8/8 — My birthday, stayed home, Bob golfing again. I can't do this by myself anymore…

8/19 — I'm Pregnant! Need Tay-Sachs test? I know I can be a good mother. Weight 125...

9/1 — Boys fifteen months old, Home, still no letter from Monson...

9/2 — Labor Day, Bob hole-in-one golfing, Legion all night. Home for me, babysat Elaine's kids. Worried another child will be too much for Bob...

9/7 — Bar Harbor Maine & Nova Scotia with Lorraine and Jerry, Connie has Robert, Elaine has David...

9/13 — Home, David rolled over for first time. Starting to tell people the truth. Don't care what they think...

9/14 — Robert has measles, Bob gone to stag party. I can do this...

9/15 — Sunday, Bomb in Birmingham church kills four little girls. Told Elaine that I'm pregnant...

9/16 — Monday, received acceptance letter from Monson, saw Dr. Pechman to discuss. Bob's unsure. Will decide with or without him. Weight 131...

9/17 — Tuesday, Elaine's to talk about what to do, agree to put boys in Monson at end of month. Bob is supportive...

If Robert and David could talk, they'd babble an endless stream of senselessness. They'd squeak and squawk, prattle and natter in ways only they understand. They'd string together jingly chains of half-formed words—eager to communicate with their mother—falling into fits of laughter before they finish. She'd laugh with them and learn to decipher every silly sentence.

"Wobber an Dabie wuv Mama."

"And Mama loves you too."

She'd hold nonstop conversations with her fledgling orators, and they'd hang on each word from her mouth. In cheerful tones, she'd quiz them.

"Can you say ball?"

" Ball."

"Good job, Robert. What does a doggy say?"

"Woof."

"That's right, David. Where's Daddy?"

"There he is!"

But they can't talk.

Not a word. Not to themselves, not to each other, not to their mother. Robert and David never find their voices, so they can't tell their parents they love them. Can't say they don't want to leave. Can't ask why they have to go away. Summer is over. Soon, the trees will let go of their own leafy children. The decision's been made to send the boys to Monson Developmental Center, to live in the care of the state. The Gagne family, fragmented and misshapen, will take another form. There will be hope for happiness, deserved or not.

9/23 — Registered for swing dance class with Dottie and Lucy B. Trying to make things normal. Boys leave for Monson next week...

9/24 — Home, Bob bowling, Legion. Had a difficult day with Robert & David...

9/25 — Home, Bob Legion. Boys fussy all day...

9/29 — Sunday, Moved boys into Monson. Everyone there is so nice. Can't believe this. Log Cabin for dinner and Legion with Dottie and Roland Bessette...

9/30 — Went to Daddy's for his birthday, Donald didn't speak to me. He doesn't understand. Elaine's house after...

10/1 — Home alone. Boys sixteen months old...

10/5 — Saturday, Went to visit boys at Monson, then Italian Night at Legion with Lorraine and Jerry...

10/6 — Bob golfing. Church by myself, Feeling better. It will be okay...

10/7 — Doctor appointment, weight 135 lbs. Swing dance class with girls...

10/13 — Sunday, Annette visited boys at Monson, told Bob she'd bring them back home if she was him. She needs to stay out of this...

10/25 — Church, Bob Legion, visit with Elaine to put custody request in writing in case something happens to me, want boys to stay at Monson...

11/1 — Boys seventeen months old. I miss them, don't know if I did the right thing...

11/9 — Saturday, Visit Monson alone, Bob bowling and Legion again...

11/14 — Doctor appointment, weight 141 lbs. Today was a good day. I have to have faith...

11/22 — JFK shot in Dallas, everyone in shock. Lunch with Lorraine. Told her I'm having a girl. We both like the name Cheryl...

∽

I set my eyes on the doorway; Dad stared stone-faced at his IV bag, its tubes and wires dangling like Medusa's snaky curls. If the walls of his hospital room could talk, they'd be the only ones with anything to say.

My gut predicted that when I left my father that day, it'd be for the last time. Conjuring my nerve, I moved my eyes from the door to his withering face. If I were ever going to tell him I loved him, the moment had come. My declaration should have been resounding, my tone unwavering. The occasion—and my dad—deserved so much more than I could give.

"You know, I love you. You're a great dad." The sentiment fell flat, like it was tossed out of a bar.

My father adjusted his pillow. I didn't bank on him to counter, but with a puff of stale breath he said, "I love you too, Ken."

His words, a foreign language I never quite understood, didn't hit me hard. Rather, his first *love* came as an expectant relief, a late-arriving train crawling into the station. I'd waited patiently, certain that stubborn iron horse would show up, and when it finally did, I was more pleased than annoyed. "I know you do," I said.

I wanted to leave but stalled. A cute nurse came in to check Dad's vitals, and he flirted with her as if he were a bachelor on the prowl (which I suppose he was). I always got a kick watching him in action with the ladies and didn't waste the chance to bust his chops.

I caught the nurse's eye and joked, "Hey, don't let Romeo here give you a hard time, okay?"

"Oh, he's no problem at all. I wish all my patients had his attitude and sense of humor," she said, her dimpled cheeks blushed.

My father smiled, revealing a mouthful of jagged teeth protruding from his bleeding gums like corroded kernels of corn. The nurse surveyed his medical chart and moved around the bed carrying a blood pressure band.

"I hope you're not measuring me for a casket," my father said, "Cuz I'm going in an urn. Shake 'n bake, baby."

The playful, and morbid, banter cut the emotional gravity and gave me an easy out. "Okay, Dad, I'm gonna take off." I leaned over and kissed him on the forehead; flakes of dried skin stuck to my lips.

At the foot of the bed, the nurse made a final note on his chart and hung the clipboard on the rail. "Sorry, Bob, but that smooch from your son's the only one you're getting today." She grabbed his swollen foot and gave it a wiggle.

"You'll be back," he swooned. "You can't resist me. Everyone says I look like Robert Redford."

She blew him a kiss and left the room. Dad watched her go and then turned to me, a twinkle in his bloodshot eyes. "See, Kenny, that's what it's all about. You gotta make an impression on people."

I laughed to keep from crying, said I loved him again, and told him I'd come back to visit the following weekend. "Hopefully soon you'll feel well enough to go back to the rehab center. I'll bring Caleb and Lucy to see you there. When you get better, maybe we can all take a drive out to Quabbin."

As I made my half-baked suggestion, I imagined Father Time rolling in the aisles, possibly peeing his pants. I grabbed my coat from the rack, pulled out a crinkled envelope from the pocket, and placed it on Dad's nightstand, using an unopened cup of cherry Jell-O as a paperweight.

"Hey, this is for you. Don't forget to read it. See you soon."

I leaned over to peck his cheek, and before I could straighten up, he threw his arms around me. For just a moment—one that lasted the forty years we had together—we held on tight. And by doing so, we let each other go.

"Don't get any nurses fired while I'm gone." I turned from him then and walked away.

Dad—There are so many things I want to tell you. That I admire you. That I'm proud of you. That I love you. That I understand you. I hope none of that comes as a surprise. I hope you knew, or felt, it all before.

I don't know what childhood memories you have of your father, but I can tell you a few of mine. I remember looking forward to the drive home after church every Sunday, because you'd let me sit next to you and steer the car down the street. I remember wrapping my arms around your neck and holding my breath as you dived underwater into the deep end of our pool. That was always more fun for me than any ride at Mountain Park. I remember playing catch with you in the front yard and wondering if you ever played catch with your dad. I remember you were always the pitcher at our end-of-the-season father/son baseball games for St. Anne's—and you were the one who made those games so much fun for everyone.

I remember going to Abdow's for breakfast together on Saturdays and ordering strawberry pancakes and hot chocolate almost every time. And I remember one autumn day when I had gone for a walk with you around the block. I was probably seven or eight. As we passed the Stewart's house, I realized just how fast I had to walk to keep up with you. And I remember telling you that for every step you took, I had to take two. I remember a little boy trying so hard to be like his dad that day.

So many people have a hand in shaping our lives and molding us into who we ultimately become. Our parents do most of that work. I've always been proud of who I am, of who I've become. All my life I feel I've been aware of the person I wanted to be. It's the same person you and Mom wanted me to be—respectful, caring, forgiving, and understanding. You

instilled those values in me and showed me their importance.
By watching you two, I learned a lifetime of lessons. Jackie
and I will pass those lessons on to Caleb and Lucy. And they
will be better people because of you.

Thank you for doing that for them. And for all you've done for
me. I love you.

The following night, back in Maplewood, I lay in bed, half-conscious, when Cheryl called. We spoke for only a minute or two before I hung up and told Jackie my father died, news I compared to yet another delayed train chugging into the station. I tried to sleep, but a sensation of "being lost" overtook me, and I became disoriented, felt abandoned and orphaned, left wandering. I wasn't anyone's son anymore. That identity, the one I thought I'd perfected, dissolved with a phone call in the dark, and I lay there, my wife's hand cupped in mine.

Who was I now?

My whole life, I'd tried to be who Mom and Dad needed me to be; I was their replacement son, a good son. I was someone they could be proud of together, someone who'd never disappoint, someone who'd help others like they did. Over and over, day after day, I gave my parents hope. Little by little, drop by drop, I topped off their empty hearts.

I reflected on my work in the world, what I'd always seen as a purely philanthropic mission. I'd been a caring person, had kept my name clean, but the stainless reputation I'd built came with a price: the feeling that it wasn't enough, and that it was all for me. In bed that night, I stared down the darkness, questioning my honesty, motives, and true character, all the while second-guessing my lifelong endeavor.

Had I done *anything* to make my parents happy? After all the hoops I dove through, had I failed them? I couldn't get them to love one another like they once did; that was impossible. But maybe I saved their marriage, kept them together somehow. Wasn't that more important than love? I followed every rule, upheld my end of the bargain, sacrificed for Mom and Dad, tried the best I could. But did I have to be that perfect little boy so my parents wouldn't leave *each other*? Or so they wouldn't leave *me*?

Like they left my brothers.

I fell asleep probing for reason, for understanding, for release. I'd journeyed so long in this myth of myself I'd forgotten I was its author, and I'd forgotten the truth. The search for who I really was, and why, would continue. To find what I was looking for, I'd travel a new path and follow a new light. My parents gone, I'd need to hold onto my wife and kids in their place. For Jackie, I'd trust she understood me because, at that moment, I was a stranger to myself. For Caleb and Lucy, I'd pray to always be someone they believed in, someone they'd count on, someone they'd keep forever. And for all of them, I'd hope to be the man Mom and Dad expected me to be.

There I was again, one week later, standing behind the pulpit in the sanctuary of Faith Church, delivering a eulogy. Only yesterday, it seemed, I was in the same place doing the same thing: saying goodbye.

I was comfortable on that stage, under that familiar spotlight where I'd hammed it up as a boy during church plays, starring as the ardent Noah and the vulnerable Samson. Where I sang, unashamed, front and center in the junior choir, regaled in a powder blue robe and a puberty-wracked falsetto. Where, as a teenager, I assisted the Reverend Ann Geer in teaching the parable of the mustard seed to a dozen impressionable Sunday schoolers, fidgety in their pleated dresses and pressed shirts. I remembered them sitting on the altar steps, looking up at me, eager for their hero to tell them a story.

"You know, the tiniest seed in the whole world, the mustard seed, can grow into a giant tree," I explained to the children. "All it needs is some sun and some water and some time."

I gestured wildly with my hands to keep the kids' attention, changed the inflection of my voice to spice up the tale. In her second-row pew, Mom smiled.

"It's just like all of you will grow up to be as big, or probably even bigger, than me someday." I emphasized the statement with gusto, the kids beaming with delight at the insane prospect. "Because, you know what? I was small like you once, and I remember sitting on these same steps not too long ago and looking up at all the adults. To be honest, back then, I thought I'd never be big. But with lots of fruits and vegetables and love from my family and friends, I grew up. Just like that giant tree grew from a tiny mustard seed. You know, the same thing happened with Jesus. He started with only twelve disciples, but they followed him for a long time, shared his stories and his beliefs. And guess what? Pretty soon he had followers all over the Earth."

I could've gone on to say how big things can come from small beginnings, could've explained to those kids how my father was the perfect example. But I didn't know the topic well enough (the Bible lesson or the man) and figured my audience would detect the ambivalence.

I'd never been a devout believer, doubted Dad was either. But my mother had faith in the Father *and* the Son, and that was enough for us all. In my search for a higher power, I'd only found God in "good" and stuck with that as my true religion; my dad almost found Him in "home," where he was most at peace, most himself—in that house, on that couch, with that drink—staring out that picture window at what might've been. And what always was.

The funeral sputtered. Shaky behind the pulpit, I tried to compose myself while the congregants waited for me to read my father's eulogy. I finally began by telling the crowd that "Big Bad Bob" wanted to get a reaction out of the world, wanted to be noticed, wanted to make sure that once you met him, you'd never forget him. "But mostly," I said, "When he was gone, he wanted to be missed." I ended my tribute by assuring everyone in that swollen church I was at peace because, I claimed, my parents and I had bared our hearts to each other. "I'm lucky," I said, "I have no regrets."

And since that day, I've lived with that lie. I wish I'd appreciated my parents more. I wish we'd known each other better. I wish we'd shared our stories. I wish.

CONCLUSION

Summer, 2016

How about you, Cheryl? Is there anyone you'd like to connect with?"

My sister flinched, surprised by the psychic's query. This was *not* Cheryl's thing. She'd attended the spirit-channeling session to comfort a friend who was hoping to communicate with her deceased husband. The clairvoyant, Nina, had given no sign of a bonus offering.

Cheryl hesitated before throwing out an option. "I don't know. Maybe my mom, I guess."

On the kitchen windowsill, crystals of quartz and amethyst and bloodstone observed Nina as she shuffled a deck of tarot cards. Cheryl sat across from her, helpless to suppress an internal eyeroll.

The medium placed the cards face up on the table. "Now, Cheryl, I want you to take three deep breaths and imagine your mother's face," said Nina. "Then ask what she wants to say."

The two women sat silent until a stillness stirred the space between them. "Your mom is coming through." Nina's eyeballs twitched under their lids. "She's saying something's not finished. You need to take care of it. Just get it done. Something about flowers. Lilies, maybe."

Quivering now, Cheryl ran a finger across her lip and stared, glassy and glazed, at the magical cards that brought her mother back from the dead.

"There's something else," Nina continued. "She wants you to talk to her more often. She's saying you can look for her in the clouds. You can find her there."

Cheryl didn't need a conversation with the clouds to understand what had to be done. We needed to bury the ashes: Mom's, Dad's, and Robert's.

But since our parents died, my sisters and I had procrastinated to take care of business, and like lazy college kids on a term paper deadline, we'd lost track of time. And the urns.

Each of us double-checked our basements and attics and storage closets, fishing around for anything resembling a decorative box or vase. It'd been ten years since we thought about the ashes, and our hunt quickly devolved into a Lucille Ball skit, performed for two weeks in two different states.

"Linda, don't you have them?"

"No, I thought you did, Cheryl."

"Really?"

"Kenny, did you take them?"

"Me? Why would I take them?"

Finally, Cheryl found all three urns stashed in a corner of her cellar among a hoard of our parents' belongings. We chose a day to meet at David's gravesite in Chicopee, where we'd carry out our plan. Fairview Cemetery was a short relay throw from Szot Park, home of the quaint baseball stadium where, for a decade, I played American Legion and semipro ball. I must've driven past the graveyard a hundred times, never remembering that it was David's eternal napping spot. We'd found the ashes but had a bigger problem: none of us were sure exactly where in the cemetery David's headstone was located. I couldn't speak for Cheryl or Linda, but I'd been to his grave only once, seemed like a thousand years ago. It was the day of his funeral—and *Welcome Back, Kotter* was still on the air.

On our arranged date, I arrived at the cemetery before my sisters and set out to search for my brother's gravesite. It was early evening, but the soft summer sun still hung above the treetops. I drove around brooding over the breadth of buried bodies, thousands of Chicopee's finest, mothers and fathers and sons and daughters, all gone forever, loved beyond comprehension, missed daily and dearly. What was that famous Napoleon quote? "Every graveyard's filled with irreplaceable men." If only my brothers had been irreplaceable.

The grounds were more expansive than I expected. I parked my car and strolled alongside a lumpy row of graves closest to the gate. My steps sank into the grass, agitating the residents below. Behind me, a murder of crows cawed and flapped on a statue of Mary the Virgin, their poop dripping like tahini sauce down her concrete headscarf. Out of nowhere, a casket of clouds entombed the sun; I walked among the shadows.

For twenty minutes, I scanned the headstones but couldn't find David's. The odds of success weren't in my favor, but I didn't fret. My "training" guaranteed that things always, somehow, worked out. *Leave a problem alone and, most of the time, it resolves itself.* That's what my father taught me. What he didn't say was if a problem isn't dealt with, and doesn't work itself out, it could steamroll everyone in its path.

Wouldn't there be a groundskeeper who'd point me to the plot? Wouldn't there be an office building somewhere? Or a gate-house with a guard handing out maps to visitors? Or a box with brochures listing the names of the interred, and markers to guide me to their respective graves? Alas, there was no office or gate or guard or map or brochure. Only me and my naivete, left by ourselves to find David, like finding a pulse on a cadaver. It'll be fine, I told myself for the trillionth time.

I jumped back into my car, drove to a different section of the cemetery, and searched for another fruitless twenty minutes. Darkness was an hour away. Needing to reconsider my game plan, I pulled behind a Ford Explorer parked under a stereotypically creepy oak near the middle of the grounds. My Outback's AC provided little relief as I collected my overheated thoughts. In a moment of clarity, I reached for my iPhone and interrogated the Internet, tapping out the keywords: "david gagne chicopee fairview cemetery."

Like a gift from the gods, Google Images delivered a photo of my brother's headstone: a stubby marble block, the color of smoke and the size of a carry-on suitcase.

Engraved at the top: *GAGNE*. Underneath: an etched outline of an open book bearing the names, *David G. and Robert A.* No dates of death, only the date of birth: *June 1, 1962 —*

The riddle of why my parents cremated Robert, instead of burying him with his brother, took a back seat to the question of where David's grave was located. (When my folks died they left me with more mysteries than memories, but I could only handle one mystery at a time.) My sisters hadn't arrived yet, and I needed help. So why not proposition the stranger in the Explorer to join my ghoulish wild goose chase?

I walked up to the truck. The window on the driver's side was open. "Excuse me," I said in my best *trust-me-I'm-not-an-axe-murderer* voice. "Hi. Sorry to bug you, but any chance you could help me find a headstone?"

A woman near my age, I gauged, picked her chin up from a meditative state and smiled. "Of course." She pinned her hair behind her ears and wrinkled her freckled nose. "My name's Kathy." Or maybe it was Janice. I'd always been lousy at remembering names and forgot hers as soon as it scooted off her lips.

Either way, Kathy-Janice wore large-framed glasses and a short, brown, bobbed haircut; she resembled Velma from

Scooby-Doo, minus the orange turtleneck sweater and mini-skirt. She told me she sometimes goes to the cemetery to think, normally with her dog—whose name I also forgot. In a bizarre stroke of luck, she explained how she'd helped a friend map the graveyard a couple of years back and had taken photos of all the headstones.

Sure she did. Just as I suspected.

I pulled my phone out and showed her the picture I'd found. She recognized the name but didn't know the location.

Jinkies!

"It might be in the back corner, near the Greeks," she said, and we started off on our expedition, chatting like old chums.

I texted Cheryl and Linda to check on their ETAs and tell them where they could find me and my sleuthing compadre. When my sisters finally arrived, I jogged over to their cars for quick hugs. Linda made fast friends with Kathy-Janice and the four of us continued to canvass the Greek section.

Dusk snuck up on us like a killer. Thirty more minutes had passed when Linda noticed an angel figurine with a broken wing lying on the clumpy grass. From two burial plots away, I watched my sister take a knee and carefully examine the fractured icon. She was remembering, I guessed, how our mother used to collect Willow Tree angel statuettes, how she placed them on shelves all over the house. I sensed the exercise of burying these ashes meant more to Linda than to me or Cheryl.

Linda had been deeply—perhaps irreparably—affected by our mother's death and missed her in a way that can't be described. Maybe simply because, of us three children, Linda was most like our mom. Unabashedly vulnerable, our middle sister filtered her sadness through a cotton candy smile. That was her poker face, but it was an easy tell. She had no desire to hide her cards, no need to swallow her sorrow. Every day for a month after Mom passed, Linda saw a bluebird outside her kitchen window, an obvious omen from above, she claimed. I never dared disagree.

While Linda dusted off the fallen angel—as if she were caring for a wounded bluebird—I noticed a dragonfly tattoo fluttering on her shoulder, left bare by her sleeveless shirt. The inky insect, with wings dotted purple and red, entwined in a pink cancer awareness ribbon, flew frozen against the backdrop of my sister's tanned skin. Linda had gone under an artist's needle a few years back, vicariously fulfilling Mom's long-ago wish of getting a tattoo. Our mother wished for a lot of things.

Linda propped up the angel atop its rightful grave, lifted her eyes, and locked onto an adjacent headstone. The name *GAGNE* faced her; she found David. And all she had to do was look.

My sisters and I retrieved three potted lilies, a garden spade, and three urns from Cheryl's Jeep. Robert's cremated remains were in a charcoal box; Dad's were in a black glass sphere with an off-gold top; and Mom's were in a classic white-and-gray-speckled marble urn.

I dug three holes, from left to right, in front of David's headstone. I poured Mom's ashes into the one on the left, Robert's in the middle, and Dad's on the right. I had the sense to keep my parents separate; Mom would've wanted it that way. She'd had only seventeen short months of heavenly peace before our father showed up to harass her for all eternity—assuming he was invited to the same club.

The sun sank behind a sea of trees. Dismissing the sweat droplets congregating on my bald head, I placed the lilies into their ashy dugouts and filled in the holes with dirt, kicking up clouds of dust. I covered my mouth and stymied a cough. The already-wilting flowers glowered and swayed, as if asking how they'd ever survive in such spoiled soil. I had no answer and figured they'd die soon. I regripped the spade and patted down the earth.

The following morning, I took a detour before heading home to Jersey. Referring to a crinkled map of memories, I turned down a one-way street called atonement and found my way back to Monson Developmental Center.

The defunct asylum had been padlocked for years, but I wanted a belated mulligan for how I'd disregarded Robert and David's lives. Including our introduction when I was six, I could count the number of times I visited Monson on one finger. After that infamous meeting, whenever Mom asked me to go with her, I trumped up an excuse, ignoring my brothers' existence to bolster my own, leaving a woman worthy of so much alone with sons who gave her so little. That guilt should've eaten away at me, but my life breezed onward, unaffected. I'd erased the idea of Robert and David. In my mind, they weren't real. And though Mom never questioned my brothers' existence, she doubted her own every day.

When I crossed the Palmer line, it was lunchtime. During my trip, I'd gobbled the remainder of a two-week-old bag of Trader Joe's trail mix. For dessert, I'd spaced out and chewed off the tip of my thumbnail, plus its cuticle and a flap of adjoining skin. Blood dripped to my knuckle, and I tended to the injury, lapping the salty goop with the thirst of a masochistic vampire. As I drove through the town, darkening cumulous clouds threw unwelcome shade, and a chill coated my arms. I cruised over shaggy hillsides, along lonely rivers, and beside rolling farmlands, passing dozens of dwellings, simple and unaware. In front of every other house was a *Trump/2016* lawn sign. My toes curled up in my Sketchers.

A drizzle misted the windshield. I flipped on my wipers as the comforting voice of Barry Manilow—forever my guilty pleasure—floated out of the car speakers and brightened my mood.

The saccharin sentimentality was the ingredient I'd always used as relief from true emotional responsibility. Like so many times before, Barry spoke to me and "I Made It Through the Rain."

Noticing a *Trump/Pence* bumper sticker on a tan sedan in front of me, I was reminded of what President Barack Obama had said in a recent speech: "History doesn't always move in a straight line. And without vigilance, we can go backward as well as forward." I imagined my father trying to pass off that quote as his own. I was glad Dad wasn't around for this election cycle but was sorry he'd died before our country had elected its first Black president. Something told me he would've liked Obama, his way with language, his character, his thoughtfulness.

And what of "The Donald"? What would "Big Bad Bob" have thought of *him*? A former used-car salesman, well-versed in *The Art of the Heel*, Dad no doubt would've sensed a conniving kinship. I imagined him, sunken into the couch, beer in hand, nodding along with a fawning blonde and the latest Trumpian conspiracy theory.

My father was a socially inclusive small businessman who voted against his beliefs and best interests every four years. But I understood his party allegiance and sympathized. He was an easy mark, susceptible to the dictates of charismatic strongmen, a grown-up boy left longing for the attention of his father, the man he admired most. My grandfather's withheld love—and early death—convinced Dad that life had rigged a perverted plot against him, a lie that left him damaged and sullen, languishing for something, anything, to believe in.

I corkscrewed around State Street's curves, rising into the mountains. Bits of orange and yellow shot through the lattice of roadside pines and exploded off my windshield. Signposts telling of *Deaf Children Playing* followed by claims of *Blind Person Ahead* tipped me off that I was getting close. Ignoring the entrance's *No Trespassing* notice, I pulled into the developmental center and parked near an office building, in a deserted lot overgrown with weeds. The office, a three-story brick structure with skull-white pillars, had been consumed by crawling ivy. Its wood awning sheltered five concrete steps leading to a faded red door with a warning: *Danger: Hazardous Area Keep Out.* Behind the building, a sprawling six-hundred-acre campus spilled down the hillside. The weight of the place was halting.

I recalled online assertions of Monson's disturbing history. Legend of the developmental center had grown like scrub brush since budget cuts slammed the doors for good in 2012, displacing one hundred fifty disabled residents and four hundred staffers. Originally built in the mid-1800s, the State Almshouse of Monson thrived as a charitable refuge for poor immigrants and neglected children. Then after fifty years of goodwill, the place was repurposed and renamed Monson State Hospital for Epileptics, a seamy sanitorium with (allegedly) questionable methods of treatment. In 1963, when my brothers arrived at the rechristened and reputable Monson Developmental Center, they were two of a thousand occupants with special needs cared for by the state.

Now, in the four years since its closing, assorted websites insinuated the grounds were haunted. Shaky YouTube videos of the abandoned buildings, shot by delinquent teens scurrying through narrow hallways and dank rooms, gave flesh to the creepy rumors. The footage was prankish but unsettling: doors pulled off hinges, radiators ripped from floors, upended tables and broken chairs, mangled cots, vulgar graffiti on moldy sheetrock, bulging tiles, and blistered paint peeling from ceilings like the dying skin of leprosy.

Not intent on staying long or straying far, I swallowed hard, stepped over a braided steel barricade strung across the roadway, and walked back in time, down a passage lined with past indifference, into a sprawling maze of seventy brick cottages, each with an engraved name above the doorway: *Infirmary. Laboratory. Women's House. School.* Etcetera. As I continued down a pebbled path, the crunch of my footsteps chipped away at the crumbly walls of residential halls. Scanning the names above the cottage doors, I recognized only one: *Hoskins.*

Like all the buildings, the windows on the first floor of Hoskins House were boarded up, while those on higher floors were broken and black. I kicked at clusters of thistle creeping out of fissures in the asphalt and remembered Mom telling me, on the day of our visit here, that Robert and David lived in the best cottage, because it was named after a famous doctor: Bernard Q. Hoskins. That day, as she and I walked this path hand in hand, I wondered about that man, more curious about why his middle name was only a single letter than about his accomplishments. I recalled Mom saying that—before she was even born—Dr. Hoskins discovered lots of ways to help kids with problems like my brothers had. I remembered she told me he was a good man.

Now, the soul of the building whispered secret clues about the past, as if pulled from the pages of a Poe short story, and I tried to recollect what else my mother said about my brothers' hidden lives here. As the medium suggested to Cheryl, I listened for Mom in the wind and looked for her in the clouds but heard only lonesome creaks of iron chains on a decaying swing set, spied only the faint pumpkin-glow of the sun pressing through the cottony sky.

Then something cut my legs out from under me, and I buckled. Cradling my face in my hands, I collapsed into a crouch, ambushed by guilt. Amid the waiting silence of days gone by, I gave way to a surge of words. "I'm sorry, Mom. I don't know if I helped. I tried to do what I thought you wanted." Sobbing my apology, I begged that—somewhere in the clouds—my mother heard me and understood. "I hope it was enough. I really did try. I promise I did."

In the shadow of that place, I let it all out, till there was nothing left inside. Warm tears slid halfway down my cheeks and soaked into my skin. Then I stood and steadied, overcome by a profound ache, a sense that whatever I hoped to accomplish on this visit was much too little, much too late.

I trudged up the hill toward the main building. Ahead in the parking lot, a security guard idled in a white pickup next to my car. When I reached him, he lowered his window. "Hey, you ain't supposed to be here."

Rebel hairs on his straggly stache dripped in front of his lip like dead dandelions drooping over a curb. His voice, a mix of pubescence and authority. A straw Stetson sat on his haystack of hair, and his arm dangled out the window like a broken stick. An inconceivable combination of Ichabod Crane and Boss Hogg, barely drinking age, the kid puffed out his bony chest under an official *Security* windbreaker and said, "Yer gonna hafta get going."

"Yeah, I'm leaving."

Tilting his head, the rural rent-a-cop shook me down. "Whatcha doing here anyway?"

"I was just driving by, wondered what this place was." I tugged down on the brim of my Celts cap and turned toward my car.

"Oh, that's the old retard center. Used to pen 'em all up here to get 'em away from society."

I froze for a second, whiplashed by the guy's ignorance, then swung around to face him. My disgust was easy to read, even at his remedial level. "Really?"

"Yup. My grandpa worked here as a cook back during one of them world wars or somethin'. Said the docs used to experiment on those 'tards with radiation and all kinda shit."

I prayed the stickman would stop talking, but God had checked out for the day, and the excrement spewed. "Said them mental patients would get tortured so bad that a bunch committed suicide, and one of 'em even murdered a nurse." His eyes bugged out. "Yeah, my buddies say that dumb motherfucker's ghost still hangs out in this hell hole looking for revenge. Say they seen it."

"That sounds crazy." I pinched my lip and walked away.

"It do sound crazy," he yelled, "but I believe that shit."

It takes all kinds to make a world.

I left the lot, drove down the hill, and pulled off the road near a shallow stream. I walked onto a short bridge and stood for a minute, my forearms baking on the wooden rail, my head full of voices. Above me, the barely visible rooftops of the developmental center took cover in the hills. The stream babbled below, its slow current twisting around glossy stepping-stones that dotted a passage between sides, like the people in the course of my life who led me to this place, who provided solid footing as I traveled an unsteady pathway.

My parents raised me. My sisters nurtured me. My best friends, Craig Patla and Mike Kijak and Mark Nadeau, supported me. They all helped design and construct my identity. And there were others, without whom the river of my life may have meandered. Dave Uszynski and Mike Beck served as idols I could reach up and touch. The Fairview Gang forced me to spread my wings. My high school coaches encouraged me to attend UMass to study sport management. First loves, Elise and Kiki, opened my heart. At college, Mike Zdrojewski reintroduced me to myself. Out in the real world, my brother-in-law Mike Labrie set me up with the Hall of Fame job. Then my coworker, Wayne Patterson, pushed me to interview with the NBA. My future sailed after I moved to New Jersey. George Land—and my NBA Entertainment family—showered me with confidence and comfort away from home. Then George and Lisa introduced me to Jackie, who gave me a life made of dreams, and molded me into a man.

I looked toward the buildings in the hills and conjured my parents, who protected me from (and exposed me to) life's realities. To them, I was a redemption project, a third son after they lost two, their chance to forget the pain of the past, and a way to move forward. They struggled as husband and wife but succeeded wildly as parents. Wrapping my sisters and me in lessons of sacrifice, patience, and grit, they taught us how to confront life's non-negotiable guarantees: unforeseen circumstances and impossible decisions.

The musk of marsh marigolds acted like smelling salts. I shook off the nostalgia and let go of the bridge's rail. My eyes moistened, and I squeezed them tight to stop the burning. It was time to leave. If I lounged any longer, lost in the past, I wouldn't make it back to Maplewood for my softball game. Patrolling the outfield for the Aging Bulls—a ragtag crew of over-the-hill athletes, all dear friends—turned the clock back forty years every Sunday night. *That* was important. Ribbing each other like brothers (while downing a cooler of frosty brews in the post-game parking lot) cemented our affections. *That* was invaluable.

I walked off the bridge and got back into the car. Scouring my face in the rearview mirror, I noticed a pesky gray hair protruding from my eyebrow like a bent paperclip. I yanked it out, for the hundredth time, and smiled through the sting. With that smile, as with all the others, the laugh lines chuckling down my cheeks and crow's feet perched in the corners of my eyes dug in deeper. I shifted the car into drive, rolled off the gravel and onto the road. Soft light shimmered through the rolling pines, and a tingle radiated up my spine. I glanced in the mirror again, at all that was behind. The clouds grew small above the hills. The signpost warning of *Deaf Children Playing* faded in the distance.

And disappeared.

EPILOGUE

IMAGINE TWO DIFFERENT realities. I imagine them so often they feel like memories.

In the first, dedicated newlyweds from Chicopee, Massachusetts, welcome twin sons into the world. The baby boys are beautiful and healthy. The parents, Bob and Cindy Gagne, are overjoyed. But as months pass, something's wrong. The twins, Robert and David, aren't developing as they should. Cindy's concerned. Her pediatrician tries to ease her mind. Everything's fine, he says; her husband echoes the sentiment. But she knows in her bones things are not "fine."

More months go by, and the boys still can't lift their heads or turn onto their stomachs, nor have they ever responded to their mother's voice. Cindy takes them to a specialist, who confirms her fears: something *is* terribly wrong. Robert and David are afflicted with a mysterious condition affecting their muscular and neurological development, stealing their hearing and eyesight. The specialist tells the shaken parents the twins will never be normal and won't, in all likelihood, live more than a few distressed years.

Bob and Cindy are destroyed. They need to make a choice: give up their imperfect sons to the care of the state or take on the challenge at home. The first option would allow the young couple the opportunity to have more children, and a way to *fix* things. The second option would snuff out any hope of having a conventional family.

The guilt and self-blame are too much. The overwrought parents can't give up the boys, can't send them away, can't let go. They keep them at home and brace for the unknown. Cindy faces the task head-on, offering her children an endless supply of love and attention. She spends nearly every waking hour with Robert and David, nurtures them, caresses them, feeds and bathes them. She sings to them and dances with them in her arms. Their body rhythms become her own, day after day after month after year.

Medications are prescribed. Wheelchairs are purchased. Ramps are installed. Seizures are survived. Once a week, a physical therapist visits the yellow ranch house on Langevin Street to help the boys make the best of their thrashing, twisted bodies. Cindy's friends—those who've remained—help occasionally. Her sister, Elaine, provides constant support. The work is consuming and exhausting. To Cindy, it's a labor of love. Her trademark patience and optimism are tested each day. Somehow, through it all, she keeps her smile. Her heart is broken in half, but both halves are full. Her tears are too tired to fall.

Bob throws himself into his job, selling used cars, working longer hours than ever. Each night, he returns home after the twins are asleep. Often, his wife is asleep too. He spends more time with his friends at the American Legion than with his family. He lends Cindy a limited hand, watching the boys on Sundays while she's at church. In the sanctuary, she recovers from the toil of the previous week and recharges for the one ahead. She follows her faith's credo to the letter: Love. Forgive. Repeat. No exceptions.

Her husband isn't emotionally equipped for this. He continues his late nights and his drinking binges and his Friday afternoon golf outings that bleed into Saturday. He justifies his actions, convinced his sons are better off without him. It's an easy out, the kind he's always been able to find.

I imagine the years grinding along and the couple aging rapidly. I imagine the arguments, the silences, the doubt, the helplessness, the alcohol.

I imagine dark shadows moving into the house on a gray afternoon in May, menacing shadows that engulf the family when a seizure kills David days before he turns seventeen.

As Bob and Cindy drown in medical expenses and grief, the shadows grow bigger and darker. In an attempt to get out from under, Bob tries to sell his business, but he's blindsided by a river of toxic soil beneath the property. The EPA files an undying lawsuit that leaves him bankrupt. Bob laments the tainted well of despair poisoning his life.

Time ticks away. The destitute couple can no longer afford to care for Robert, now twenty-two. Out of options, they send him to Monson Developmental Center in nearby Palmer, handing over guardianship to the state two decades later than many thought they should.

Without her children, Cindy is empty. They were all she knew, her purpose and her meaning. She pulls away from Bob, while he mines a nugget of love buried somewhere between them. But as far as Cindy is concerned, his withdrawal years earlier sealed their fate. Now, they're two blades on a pair of scissors, working in tandem to shred what's left of their tattered marriage. Connected by a bond of bitterness, they blame each other. They barely speak. The house is cold.

In this reality, one misty Monday morning, a tired middle-aged woman finds a hand-written note from her husband on the kitchen counter. His nearly indecipherable penmanship spells out what she'd been anticipating, at times praying for: Bob is leaving. His note contains a whiff of an apology, a hint of regret, and an abundance of hope for Cindy's future without him. At the bottom of the page, he's scratched out an account number and the name of a life insurance company. He writes that it isn't much, that he wishes he had more to give. For once, Cindy agrees with him. But it was never money she wanted.

Bob vanishes.

Cindy looks and sounds happier alone. Her energy returns. She's new again. Her longtime friend Susan Cassidy helps her find a full-time job. Her days become pleasantly routine. Her weeks are dotted with regular visits to Elaine's house, and to Robert's bedside, and to David's grave. She enjoys each stop equally, sharing laughter and tears with all.

Years later, Cindy receives a phone message from Bob's sister, Connie, unloading gruff news of his death. Something about organ failure and Vermont. The details are sketchy. Cindy says a silent prayer for him, for the husband and father she wishes he'd been. She rummages through the junk drawer in the kitchen and pulls out the wrinkled note he wrote the day he left.

As promised, the life insurance money isn't much, but it helps. It pays for Cindy and Susan's weekly lunch date at Mel's restaurant. It pays for a weekend trip to Niagara Falls with friend and former minister Ann Geer. It pays for swing dance lessons with an old flame from Holyoke High School (Cindy still loves a night on the town, still loves to dance). The money also pays for her son Robert's funeral when, at age forty-two, *fate* beckons, finally and completely. And the money pays for Cindy's cancer treatments.

I imagine Cindy Gagne holds on tightly to her life, like she held onto her sons, like she couldn't hold onto her marriage. I imagine she tolerates the disease with a quiet ferocity. She tells only a few friends, doesn't want to be a bother or a burden, wants pity from no one. Her smile's more ubiquitous than ever.

But, like the shadows that took up residence in her house all those years ago, cancer makes itself at home and overstays its welcome. The hospice nurse tells Elaine the morphine drip will let her sister slip away peacefully. In a final restless dream state, Cindy greets acquaintances and relatives from beyond. She searches for—and finds—her parents and her sons and her husband. I imagine Elaine holding her big sister's hand as Cindy takes her last gasp.

I imagine her gone.

❦

In the second reality, in an alternate universe, our family sits around a dinner table. The main course, as usual, is laughter.

My twin brothers, RJ and Dave, share the same infectious giggle as they make fun of our father's tyrannical household rules. My sisters, Cheryl and Linda, take a back seat to the antics, wearing broad smiles as they soak up the hijinks. Between sips of wine, our mother snickers, enjoying the mockery her teenaged sons make of their father. She places a sarcastic, yet comforting, hand on her husband's shoulder. He turns to his wife and grins. The wisecracks render Bob Gagne uncharacteristically speechless, and he loves every second. Affection and wit fill the air. During the excitement, I slide my brussels sprouts to the side of my plate and sit tall in my chair. Then I wait for an opening to mimic my big brothers and get a zinger in on Dad.

I imagine our family is close. Our parents love and respect one another. My siblings are encouraging and supportive but tease mercilessly. I get picked on the most and welcome the attention. I imagine RJ and Dave are popular high school athletes. They're smart, funny, and caring. They're my heroes and the glue to our family.

Our household is hectic; we thrive in the chaos. We children work hard and do our best without taking life too seriously. Our father reminds us, in his unique way, that the world has challenges in store for everyone. He says things won't always be easy.

"That's the way life goes." But daily, he and our mother reiterate how we're endlessly lucky. We have each other. "Our wealth is our family."

My childhood is idyllic. My thirst for life cannot be quenched. The wonder of the world seizes me. I drink in every moment, every book, every song, every movie, every sporting event. For me, it all represents the potential of my existence. And in those moments, I am infinite.

I try to hold on to my youth, but it slips away.

Weeks and months blow by, whisking us all up in the gust. Chicopee isn't big enough for RJ, who studies medicine in Boston and settles there after graduating. He specializes in a field I can't wrap my head around, something about genetic coding. He's passionate about his job, but not as much as he is for his wife and two daughters.

Dave stays closer to home, becomes a social worker in Holyoke. He has a temperate soul. His work with disabled children is tireless and rewarding. He and his partner adopt an infant boy with Down syndrome. They name him Aristide, after his great-great-grandfather. My sisters marry good men and raise families of their own. I follow my own path and move to New Jersey.

Time goes by. Life is full.

I imagine my mother and father dying gracefully. Her from cancer, him from a broken heart. At least that's the joke he tells the night before his liver finally fails.

I imagine a warm Sunday afternoon in July. My siblings and I congregate at our childhood home on Langevin Street. Our parents gone, Dave and his family now live in the spruced-up yellow ranch house. We walk with our spouses and kids into the backyard, past the point where the grass of the lawn meets the hay of the field. In the distance, the smug waters of the

Connecticut River roll under an endless bridge stretching into the future. The picture window behind us doesn't miss too much.

The cousins sprint off to pick blueberries and search for arrowheads. Cheryl carries a black metallic box with our father's cremated remains. Linda has a white marble urn with our mother's. We gather the rambunctious kids and place ten Tupperware bowls into twenty tiny hands. My sisters move down the line, doling out ashes into each container with cereal spoons. I imagine the children skipping through the hay, giggling and flinging and scattering, fulfilling Mom and Dad's final communal wish.

I imagine Dave's son, Aristide, apart from the others, his bowl still full. He smiles and waits until his cousins stop running and laughing, waits until all eyes are upon him. I imagine little Ari full of spirit and calm, standing proud on the mossy ground, lifting the container above his head and spinning in wobbly circles. Faster and faster, he spins. Ash swirls out of the bowl, forming a protective gray mist around the twirling boy, wrapping him in a shroud of a million microscopic angels. Jubilance is everywhere. Gratitude. Peace.

I imagine saying goodbye to my mother and father in summer's lasting, loving light. But still, they remain. I look at my sisters and brothers, the sun on their faces, reflections of the man and the woman who gave us each other. The kids are running and laughing once again.

I imagine a gentle wind, soft and warm and unforgetting, sweeping in and carrying away my parents' ashes, which rise and billow like smoke signals high in the Chicopee sky.

"You are a story worthy of being told, a person made to be loved, with a life meant to be lived."

—Nazia Hassan

ACKNOWLEDGEMENTS

I'd like to thank the following people for making this book possible: My wife, Jackie, for understanding what this project meant to me and for cheering me on. Our children, Caleb and Lucy, for inspiring me every day. Venerable pro Dan Barry, who told me at the onset, "The good is the bad and the bad is the good; you have the ability to write your book, so now you have to write it." Will Allison, for graciously offering his professional editing expertise and endless encouragement. Author and podcaster K.M. Weiland, for unknowingly leading our weekly workshops. Willow Logue, Cindy D'Altorio Sherman, Amy Alissi Donofrio, Lara Pennington, and Dave Chmiel, for helping make sense of an incoherent jumble of words. Innumerable friends and relatives, for digging deep into the past, opening windows to another lifetime. Mark Nadeau and Mike Kijak, for being by my side. The NBA, for providing me with an undying brotherhood and for giving me the time to start, and finish, this journey. Maplewood pals Lou Sartori and Dave Ethan, for believing in my story—and in me. Kiki Tobin and Craig Patla, for offering me a clear conscience and the green light to tell my truth. The city of Chicopee, for providing the seminal and unforgettable moments of my youth. My parents and sisters, for building my confidence and nurturing my imagination. My brothers Robert and David, for everything.

ONE LAST THING

I need to request a favor. If you've gotten anything out of this memoir, if you've felt any sort of nudge to open up to your family or to search for the truth about your past, please give this copy to someone else. Drop it in a friend's mailbox, wrap it up as a gift for your spouse, or offer it to a coworker. It's my wish that we all pass along our stories—the ones that make us unique—to the people we love, especially to our children, so that we might know and appreciate each other, and ourselves, just a little bit better. Thank you a thousand times over.

ABOUT THE AUTHOR:

Born in 1967, Ken Gagne grew up in Chicopee, Massachusetts, where all he did was eat, sleep, draw, and play sports. By a nose, he won the high school superlatives of "Class Athlete" and "All-American Guy," while running away with "Most Likely to Stay Home on a Saturday Night." After getting dragged out of adolescence kicking and screaming, he earned a degree in sport management from UMass Amherst and worked for twenty-nine years as a TV producer for the National Basketball Association. He's now a full-time writer (which may or may not be a legit, depending on your definitions of "full-time" and "writer"). He and his wife live with their cat, Gary, in Maplewood, New Jersey, and are the proud parents of two grown children.

Please visit theunboundopenbook.com for contact information, companion photos for this memoir, and details on upcoming projects.